A NATION ON WHEELS

THE AUTOMOBILE CULTURE IN AMERICA SINCE 1945

Mark S. Foster

University of Colorado, Denver

THOMSON
™
WADSWORTH

Australia • Canada • Mexico • Singapore • Spain
United Kingdom • United States

THOMSON

WADSWORTH

Publisher, History: Clark Baxter
Development Editor: Sue Gleason
Assistant Editor: Julie Iannacchino
Editorial Assistant: Jonathan Katz
Technology Project Manager: Jennifer Ellis
Marketing Manager: Caroline Croley
Marketing Assistant: Mary Ho
Advertising Project Manager:
  Brian Chaffee
Project Manager, Editorial Production:
  Matt Ballantyne
Print/Media Buyer: Robert King

Permissions Editor:
  Stephanie Keough-Hedges
Production Service: Shepherd, Inc.
Photo Researcher: Mary Reeg
Copy Editor: Jeanne Patterson
Cover Designer: Preston Thomas
Cover Image: Gary and Vivian S.
  Chapman, copyright © Getty Images
Compositor: Shepherd, Inc.
Text and Cover Printer: Transcontinental
  Printing

For more information about our products,
contact us at:
Thomson Learning Academic Resource Center
1-800-423-0563

For permission to use material from this text,
contact us by:
Phone: 1-800-730-2214
Fax: 1-800-730-2215
Web: http://www.thomsonrights.com

ISBN 0-15-507542-X

Wadsworth/Thomson Learning
10 Davis Drive
Belmont, CA 94002-3098
USA

Asia
Thomson Learning
5 Shenton Way, #01-01
UCI Building
Singapore 068808

Australia
Nelson Thomson Learning
102 Dodds Street
South Melbourne, Victoria 3205
Australia

Canada
Nelson Thomson Learning
1120 Birchmount Road
Toronoto, Ontario M1K 5G4
Canada

Europe/Middle East/Africa
Thomson Learning
High Holborn House
50/51 Bedford Row
London WC1R 4LR
United Kingdom

Latin America
Thomson Learning
Seneca, 53
Colonia Polanco
11560 Mexico D.F.
Mexico

Spain
Paraninfo Thomson Learning
Calle/Magallanes, 25
28015 Madrid, Spain

CONTENTS

Chapter Eight

A REMARKABLE REVIVAL   167

Chapter Nine

THE FUTURE OF THE AUTOMOBILE   192

PREFACE

Having been born in 1939, I have largely hazy childhood memories of the World War II years. My family resided in a comfortable upper-middle-class suburb of Chicago; at the time, of course, I had no understanding that a secure home environment was a distinct privilege, not a birthright. I gradually became vaguely aware that there was something very frightening happening somewhere far away. However, my immediate family members' lives were not significantly changed by the war. A married thirty-six-year-old with three children when the Japanese attacked Pearl Harbor, my father was never drafted into the armed forces; rather, he volunteered for the Civil Air Patrol. Although we younger children were shielded from the tragedy, my extended family suffered, as my Uncle Ted was lost in a plane over the English Channel in 1942. One winter, my sister and I spent several weeks at a school on the west coast of Florida. Although most of my attention focused on such boyish delights as swimming too far out into the ocean and chasing the thousands of fiddler crabs scuttling across the beach, we heard scary rumors of German submarines—possibly still lurking just off shore. There were nightly blackouts; windows were shaded and lights were turned off whenever someone entered or left buildings. I also recall being sad the night President Franklin Roosevelt died. Adults in the family were somber, hushed; all I knew was what I was told—that a great man had died. At five years old, I had no sense of death; yet, somehow I wanted to share their experience. But I also remember happier times, such as when my Uncle David returned home from the war unscathed. A few weeks after V-J Day, he showed up at our house in uniform. I tackled him around the knees; he tolerantly collapsed and allowed me to conjure up the fantastic notion that I had beaten up a soldier!

All family members made sacrifices for the war effort. While my father diligently searched the skies for enemy planes, my mother spent hundreds of hours tending her "victory garden," which produced endless bushels of produce. My older brother participated in scrap drives, and he may have honed his potential as a future soldier by active participation in neighborhood war games. My younger sister's and my contributions consisted mainly of eating without too much fuss countless servings of the tasteless, grayish green Swiss chard and other mysterious vegetables that my mother had dutifully canned.

However, some of my sharpest memories of the war years were of automobiles and rationing. Due undoubtedly to restrictions on use of fuel, the milkman delivered dairy products by horse and wagon. The appearance of his wagon highlighted my sister's day; she invariably rewarded the gentle, faithful nag with an apple or two from our apple tree. It was then and there that her love affair with horses began. Fortunately for me, there were far fewer cars on the streets than there had been before the war; and, in order to conserve precious fuel, they traveled a lot slower. My mother insisted that I was so heedless in dashing into the street from our driveway on my tricycle that, had it not been for rationing and dumb luck, I would undoubtedly have been a wartime casualty myself.

In my family, it was considered a privilege for children to be around adults, and we heard them talk a lot about cars. They stoutly disapproved of the occasional teenage "peeler" who, besides making lots of noise, "burned rubber" and wasted gas. In order to save fuel, my parents entrusted me to walk to nearby stores to pick up small orders of food on several occasions. When it came to fuel, I never thought of making a distinction between the needs of horses and cars. I had seen my sensitive and compassionate sister provide water to the hot and thirsty dairy wagon horse with offerings from a garden hose on countless sizzling summer days. Naturally, I assumed that cars needed the same type of fuel. Thus, one lovely summer morning I took the very same garden hose and filled the gasoline tank of the family car, then marched proudly into the house to announce my achievement to the family. One can only imagine the temptation they had to blister my derriere. In later years, my parents claimed they never laid a finger on me; I have little recollection of their reaction, other than expressions of horror and incredulity on their faces.

By their account of the incident, they restrained their mutual urge to make me a wartime casualty then and there. During the war, the modest sacrifices made by American civilians paled compared to those made by the British, not to mention the far more extreme sacrifices endured by Soviet citizens. However, the single "entitlement" Americans may have missed the most was easy access to their motor vehicles. Even though I was as a toddler, restrictions on automobile use created intense, vivid wartime recollections for me.

More than half a century later, I was extremely pleased and flattered when two distinguished historians, Gerald D. Nash and Richard W. Etulain, invited me to contribute a volume on the American automobile culture in the post-World War II era for their *Contemporary America* series three years ago. I was just wrapping up another project, and I happily accepted their challenge. Earlier in my career, I had written several books based largely on primary sources, and I naïvely thought that crafting a book synthesizing the insights of hundreds of other commentators, ranging from the most objective scholars to the most facile and glib industry shills, occasionally stirring in small doses of my own analysis, would, somehow, be a comparatively easy task.

As I began sifting through hundreds of varying perspectives on the automobile culture, the enormity of my task slowly settled in. I had to make many difficult choices about what to include and what to leave out. One of my first decisions concerned whether or not to include pre-World War II historical background. I am convinced that many of the most unfortunate decisions about coordinating the automobile with public policy in general and public transportation in particular have been negatively affected by lack of historical background knowledge on the part of key decision makers. Therefore, I have included considerable discussion of the pre-World War II era in several chapters. As the twentieth century closed, the automobile became a key element in increasingly contentious public policy debates. Should I attempt to include *all* voices? Doing so would have consumed chaotic babble and would have consumed far too much space; instead, I attempted to allow room for somewhat lengthier consideration of a few of the most representative.

Another challenge I faced was deciding *which* aspects of the car culture I should address. Clearly, I could not provide comprehensive coverage of every ramification of the car's impact on American society in a brief volume. Therefore, I attempted to provide much of the essential *flavor* of the automobile's impact on various facets of American life. Still, I had to leave some seasonings out. When I addressed the relationship between the automobile and American music, for example, I discussed the rhythm and lyrics of rock and roll at some length, while downplaying sentimental ballads, even blues. Any true movie buff may challenge both my selection and discussion of movies with powerful automobile themes. I covered drag racing, stock car racing, and demolition derbies, but I ignored tractor pulls, monster truck rallies, and swamp buggy events. Although motorcycling is a step-child of the automobile culture, I decided to leave it out entirely. Moving into the realm of public policy, the book addresses the issue of building the interstate highway system and boring massive freeways through built-up cities, but it pays little attention to street widening.

Readers looking forward to wallowing in specifications of 400-hp engines featuring complex performance enhancers will no doubt be disappointed with this book. There is little of that here. This book devotes almost no attention to what is *under* the hood; rather, the focus is *beyond* the windshield. The automobile has been an incredibly powerful, aggressive shaper of American culture. Few facets of American life are immune from its impact. In 2000, roughly one in seven Americans still were gainfully employed in some automobile-related enterprise. My objective is to provide not only an informed, reasonably balanced perspective on the automobile's enormously complex and varied impacts on contemporary life but a foundation of knowledge that will serve as a starting point for those interested in responding intelligently to the serious challenges the automobile presents at the dawn of the new millennium.

Mark S. Foster
Denver, Colorado

Chapter One

SETTING THE STAGE

In early August 1945, American aircraft released atomic bombs over Hiroshima and Nagasaki. The near total destruction of property and horrific loss of human life persuaded Japanese Emperor Hirohito to override the wishes of his most fanatical military advisors and seek peace with the Allies. A few weeks later, Japanese and Allied officials formalized surrender documents and World War II was finally over.

Americans were overcome with joy, and not just because wholesale killing would finally stop. Ever since the stock market collapse of October 1929, the nation had been engaged in a seemingly endless series of crises, and its citizenry—at least those who could remember the generally prosperous days of the 1920s—longed to return to "normal" conditions. Many Americans had experienced the nightmare of months—even years—of unemployment during the Great Depression in the 1930s. World War II had reversed the economic stagnation virtually overnight. Millions of Americans had worked full-time during four years of the United States' participation in the war, and their wallets and bank accounts were stuffed, often with war bonds. They dreamed of spending their newfound wealth.

The only problem for most civilians in the late summer of 1945 was that, unless they had access to black-market products, there was very little to buy. Conversion from a wartime economy to peacetime production would take time, and the process would generate a good deal of frustration for consumers and businessmen alike. Having been denied access to big-ticket items for nearly a generation, most everybody wanted them. Very few houses had been built during either the war or the Depression, and many GIs and their new wives were crammed in with relatives on farms, or they endured dank tenements in the nation's cities. They dreamed of suburban homes adorned with tidy lawns and white picket fences. Yet, almost invariably, their material fantasies included new cars. Most Americans fortunate enough to own any type of vehicle had patched them together and kept them running with baling wire, bald tires, and prayers. Although almost 26 million cars were on the nation's roads in 1945, the number had remained virtually unchanged for sixteen years, and several million wheezing jalopies were ready for the junkyard. Gasoline and tire rationing, which had severely restricted civilian driving during the war, may have been the chief reason so many wrecks survived until V-J Day.

The next five and a half decades marked an amazing transformation in Americans' automobility. By 2001, the number of automobiles in the United States had grown almost eightfold since the end of World War II. Millions of Americans owned more than one automobile. Statistically, there was one car for every American over the age of sixteen! In almost every part of the country, any adult without an automobile was effectively denied access to most of the fruits of an abundant American society. Although the nation's car culture reached full maturity after World War II, the political, economic, and social frameworks affecting it were clearly in place well before the outbreak of the conflict. Between 1945 and 2002, the car culture increased mainly in scope and size, but its foundation had been established quite firmly before the war. Thus, one cannot fully appreciate the maturation of the postwar car culture without examining its prewar roots. That is the subject of this chapter.

THE FIRST HORSELESS CARRIAGES

In hindsight, it seems clear that the United States of a century ago was an environment primed for introduction of the automobile. At first, it would be perceived as an instrument used primarily for enhancing pleasure. Any tool that would help citizens extend their horizons was bound to attract an enthusiastic following. As historian Cindy S. Aron and others have ably demonstrated, Americans had developed a culture of vacationing and tourism well before the turn of the century. Most of those seeking relief from the workaday world sought pure relaxation in largely sedentary environments, but a few pursued more active recreation. By the 1880s, traveling Americans had a choice of ships, trains, interurban trolleys, or horse and buggy. Energetic citizens rode bicycles—either high-wheelers or the new, low-slung "safeties" that came into vogue by mid-decade. Very few city and small town folk ventured over country roads for pleasure, since most of the roads were little more than rutted dirt pathways, dusty in summertime and swamplike during wet seasons. Bicycle riders longed to extend pleasure trips farther out into the countryside. Farmers, too, hoped for upgraded roads that would facilitate movement of goods into town by wagon, not to mention improve their chances for enlarging their social spheres by making it easier to visit neighbors or seek entertainment in town. Thus, even before the arrival of the automobile, very unlikely allies were pushing for improved roads. Urban bicycle enthusiasts were the primary supporters of the League of American Wheelmen, while farmers' groups and other interested citizens organized a Good Roads Movement. Savvy politicians were well aware of the growing influence of both groups and paid increasing attention to their demands.

For decades, even centuries, humans had dreamed of creating machine-powered devices that could move overland along great distances, independent from water routes and, later, rail lines. Even as early as the thirteenth century, historian Roger Bacon prophesied that "one day we shall endow chariots with incredible speed without the aid of any animal." Bacon's audacious statement earned him time in prison for "being in league with the devil." There were vague reports of two cumbersome steam-powered vehicles built by two French Jesuit missionaries in China in about 1665. A century later, a Swiss engineer, Nicholas Cugnot, was commissioned by the French government to experiment with steam devices capable of pulling heavy cannons, but a change in governments ended Cugnot's sponsored efforts. In 1805, an American, Oliver Evans, built an enormous machine called the "Orokter Amphilibos," which lumbered about the streets of Philadelphia at a top speed of about four miles per hour. Financial backing for further development failed to materialize; critics judged that it would be too slow and far too heavy to have commercial promise for moving either goods or people.

Before large numbers of people would take seriously the idea of land vehicles possessing any practical value, their potential had to be demonstrated publicly. Rapid advances in railroad technology and construction induced many inventors to experiment with devices that could operate independent from iron or steel rails. Many of the earliest demonstrations stressed the overland vehicle's potential as a sporting device. The decades before and after 1900 witnessed countless demonstrations, races, and endurance contests on both sides of the Atlantic. Without question, Europeans—particularly the French—held the early advantage in both reliability and design. By the late 1880s,

European inventors were showcasing their contraptions. The first American automobile race was held in Chicago on Thanksgiving Day, 1895. Six entries tested a fifty-five-mile course between Chicago and Evanston, but only two vehicles finished the snow-covered course, the winner averaging less than eight miles per hour. However, the *Times Herald,* which sponsored the event, reported that the race had been run under abominable conditions, ". . . through deep snow, and along ruts that would have tried horses to their utmost." After "serious" failed attempts by others at cross-country journeys in 1899 and 1901, Dr. H. Nelson Jackson and Sewell Crocker drove a vehicle from New York to San Francisco in 1903, completing a journey over atrocious roads in just over nine weeks. The famous "Glidden Tours," in which groups of genteel enthusiasts drove their favorite makes of vehicles on semi-leisurely tours of many parts of the nation in the decade before World War I, brought automobility into the consciousness of millions of Americans.

Some urban health officials saw the automobile as a welcome alternative to horse-drawn conveyances. If city dwellers converted from horses to cars, huge quantities of manure and urine would disappear from city streets. Cities would no longer be forced to remove and dispose of hundreds of rotting animal carcasses, which sometimes remained where they fell for several days before harried—or simply inefficient—cleanup crews could get to them. In the words of one historian, "In the early years of the twentieth century, the public was in the mood for progress, and a slow-footed oat-burner simply did not fit."

However, there was nowhere near universal acceptance of the noisy, rattling contraptions. Traditionalists complained that automobiles frightened horses. Others observed that drivers were often thoughtless and that the vehicles threatened pedestrians. Some municipalities passed ordinances that so restricted automobiles as to make them almost useless—if the laws were rigorously enforced. Other towns instructed police to run down speeders, using bicycles or horses. These practices generated spirited protest from many motorists, who considered such acts petty harassment. Conversely, less-affluent citizens often resented both automobiles and their drivers, and more than a few inoffensive motorists venturing off main boulevards found their vehicles being pelted with stones or themselves being struck with whips.

Class resentment could not stop increasing public acceptance of the automobile. However, by the turn of the century, there was nothing inevitable about the eventual triumph of vehicles powered by the internal combustion engine. Both steam- and electric-powered vehicles attracted considerable American interest. The famed Stanley Steamer appealed to many, and loyal owners kept a number of them on the road until after World War I. Electrics were even more popular than steamers. The former appealed particularly to women. They were odorless and virtually noiseless, and they were easy to operate since neither hand cranking nor shifting gears was required. Unfortunately, they were far more expensive to both manufacture and operate than gasoline-powered vehicles; and, as late as 1910, batteries had a range of only fifty to eighty miles before they needed recharging. Historian David Kirsch observed that, while the range of operation for electrics was adequate for most car owners, by the time manufacturers of electrics had eliminated many drawbacks, the infrastructure (gasoline stations and repair shops) to serve gas engines "made alternatives to it seem too risky to consider." Holdouts could still have electrics made to order as late as 1938, but they had largely disappeared by the mid-1920s.

THE PETROLEUM INDUSTRY: FUELING THE FLAME

The rapidly developing petroleum industry was indispensable to the emerging dominance of the internal combustion engine. The evolution of petroleum and its by-products is lengthy and complex. As long ago as 300 B.C., peasants in Mesopotamia collected a semisolid substance known as bitumen, which seeped through the rocks. The peasants used bitumen as building mortar, and it helped secure the walls of Jericho and Babylon. Bitumen was also used in road making, waterproofing certain types of containers, and to a limited extent for lighting. However, its best-known use was medicinal. At times, it was even ingested! According to the Roman naturalist Pliny, writing in the first century A.D., it "checked bleeding, healed wounds, treated cataracts, provided a liniment for gout, cured aching teeth, relieved shortness of breath, stopped diarrhea, drew together several muscles, and relieved both rheumatism and fever." It could also be used "for straightening out eyelashes which inconvenience the eyes." The Romans and Byzantines had learned how to use a closely guarded secret mixture of lime and petroleum, known as *oleum incindiarum,* or "Greek fire," as a sort of sticky incendiary device in battle. When it touched water, it burst into flames, so it was often used against enemy ships. For many centuries, it was more feared than gunpowder.

Evidently its secrets were lost, at least for Western Europeans in the Middle Ages. There were numerous accounts of oil seepage in Germany, Sicily, Italy, and elsewhere; but, outside of the Middle East, for centuries it was apparently used only for medicinal purposes.

However, after learning how to extract kerosene, which was used for lighting, Eastern Europeans in Poland, Austria, and Russia developed a small petroleum industry by the 1850s.

One major hurdle in developing the petroleum industry was figuring out how to extract the raw product in significant quantities. Fifteen hundred years earlier, the Chinese had developed boring, or drilling techniques, capable of probing 3,000 feet underground. When Europeans finally copied their techniques, the petroleum industry had a future. One remaining challenge was inventing kerosene lamps, which burned the fuel cleanly. Although they provided what was considered adequate light at the time, the kerosene lamps then available were smoky and emitted an acrid smell. However, electricity had not yet been applied to lighting, and other sources of practical illumination were clearly inferior to kerosene. At midcentury, there appeared to be a modest future for petroleum products for lighting and perhaps even a small one for medicinal purposes, but nobody had yet grasped its potential for far more widespread use. A few scientists and inventors were tinkering with internal combustion engines, but the notion of using petroleum products to power industrial or other machinery was still in the future.

By the late 1850s, a satisfactory kerosene-burning lamp with a glass "chimney" had been invented that overcame the problems of both smoke and smell. The new device created what one enthusiast christened "the light of the age." This in turn created a larger potential market for kerosene, and individuals seeking to exploit the opportunity included Americans. In the summer of 1859, "Colonel" Edwin L. Drake, an unemployed railroad conductor with a gift of gab, had insinuated himself into an effort paid for by marginally prosperous investors to try to make something of discoveries of small pools of oil in Titusville, in western Pennsylvania. With the help of a local blacksmith, "Uncle Billy" Smith, Drake and a small crew drilled sixty-nine feet into Pennsylvania dirt and rock. They were at the point of giving up when they struck oil. Drake's find on August 27, 1859, created a sensation. By the following summer, the mountains in the oil region in western Pennsylvania were stripped of vegetation and blanketed with oil wells.

Americans had discovered that they had the natural resources to support a major transformation in energy production, but they also had to develop an efficient infrastructure for collecting petroleum, refining it into usable commodities, and shipping it to markets. John D. Rockefeller, an up-and-coming young Cleveland businessman, possessed enormous powers of concentration, an exacting eye for details, a gambling spirit, and an almost inhuman capacity for work. In other words, he was ideally suited to exploit the opportunity that presented itself. Within a few years, his Standard Oil Company had wrought a transformation in extracting, refining, and marketing oil. Kerosene had a number of by-products, including gasoline. At first, gasoline was considered largely an annoyance. Some retailers felt fortunate to sell it for as much as two cents per gallon, while others simply discharged it into local streams or into the ground. However, Thomas Edison successfully developed and astutely marketed electricity for lighting beginning in the early 1880s, and this form of illumination was vastly superior to that provided by kerosene. With the slowly emerging realization that the United States possessed vast petroleum reserves, there was added incentive to speed up development of uses for petroleum products other than illumination. Thus, the three-sided marriage of gasoline, the internal combustion engine, and the automobile was timely; in retrospect, it appeared almost inevitable.

Between the late 1800s and the mid-twentieth century, the United States experienced seemingly endless cycles of discovery of petroleum reserves, rapid expansion of demand for its refined products, and temporary shortages, followed by newer and larger discoveries of crude oil. Early in 1901, producers tapped huge reserves at Spindletop, near Beaumont, Texas. Additional discoveries near Tulsa, Oklahoma, and more finds in Texas moved the center of petroleum extraction farther west. California was also the site of numerous discoveries between the 1890s and the 1920s. Between 1893 and 1903, oil production in the Sunshine State leaped from 470,000 barrels to 24 million barrels; it tripled again by 1910 to 73 million barrels. On the eve of World War I, California's output alone comprised nearly one fourth of the world's oil production. Although there was no longer any physical frontier, or open space permitting free settlement, Americans grew dangerously complacent with the notion that their land was singularly blessed with limitless natural resources. If we could not get resources at home, we would find them abroad. The commodity itself did not matter, since the story was always the same: when new needs arose, new resources would be found and efficient entrepreneurs would develop them.

Even before the turn of the century, a number of entrepreneurs, including Rockefeller, the Nobel brothers, and the Rothschilds, were developing other petroleum reserves scattered about the globe. Discoveries of important reserves in Russia, Eastern Europe, and the Middle East precipitated the rise of petroleum giants like Royal Dutch Shell and British Petroleum. Although savvy American investors made fortunes in the international petroleum market, most consumers had little awareness of or interest in the industry outside of the United States. The only things that mattered to them were that domestic producers were turning out plenty of gasoline and that the price remained cheap. At the end of World War II, the United States pumped out roughly three fourths of the world's output of crude oil; indeed, its dominance of crude oil continued into the mid-1950s, when it still controlled half of the world's output.

With seemingly limitless supplies of gasoline, its role in propelling automobiles appeared promising. Even before 1900, most interested tinkerers were convinced that motorized vehicles would be powered by internal combustion engines. Although German inventors produced the first functional gas-powered vehicles in the late 1880s, two Americans, Charles and Frank Duryea, had one puttering over the streets of Springfield, Massachusetts, in 1893. For a variety of reasons, the United States was a particularly fertile ground for new automobile ideas; by the late 1890s, dozens of ambitious mechanics were experimenting with internal combustion engines and hooking them up to wagons, carriages, bicycles, and any other wheeled contraption their minds could conjure up. That number included young Henry Ford, then residing on his parents' farm near Detroit. Ford tested his first vehicle in 1896.

A GROWING AUTOMOBILE INDUSTRY: FROM MODEL T TO MODEL A

Savvy inventors instinctively sensed that the automobile potentially had many practical uses. However, before this occurred, prices would have to drop drastically. The first recorded sales of gasoline-powered vehicles in the United States were in 1896. In the next few years, dozens of companies producing automobiles opened their doors. Most promptly ran out of money and floundered. A few were recapitalized and renamed. Automobile historian James Flink estimated that, in 1899, thirty manufacturers produced about 2,500 vehicles, an average of less than 100 units per company. All of the work was done by hand, and even the largest producers were finishing only a few units each week. Not surprisingly, with such low-volume production, the end products were very expensive, usually somewhere between $3,000 and $6,000 per copy. These prices were obviously far beyond the means of the average American worker, who earned less than $1,000 per year. Most buyers were wealthy businessmen or families blessed with comfortable fortunes. A few enterprising doctors found that automobiles greatly expanded their ability to make house calls. By 1900, approximately 8,000 motor vehicles clattered over America's streets and roads. Critics still dismissed them as playthings for the rich.

Almost from the start, the automobile industry was centered in Detroit. By 1904, even before Henry Ford became a force within the industry, almost half of all American cars were produced there. Why Detroit? Excellent hardwood forests had made the upper Midwest a natural location for production of wagons and carriages, and the same materials were used, initially, in automobile bodies. Even more than the East, the Midwest had terrible roads, and gasoline-powered vehicles were far superior to electrics and steamers in less-than-ideal conditions. Historian John B. Rae suggests, too, that Detroit just happened to possess a critical mass of businessmen with great drive and perseverance who almost simultaneously and collectively became interested in the industry and committed their resources to establishing it. Finally, by the early twentieth century, Detroit had attracted thousands of skilled workers with experience producing carts, bicycles, and other machines. Ambitious manufacturers would not have to deal seriously with labor unions for another three decades.

Although a number of other producers introduced excellent designs (including Ransom Olds, who produced the highly successful curved-dash car bearing his name), Henry Ford's famous Model T made Detroit. For fully two decades, it dominated the automobile industry. There were many reasons. Although his production system took several years to perfect, Ford established a revolutionary assembly-line system for turning out cars. Once the chassis was hooked up to a constantly moving belt, workers at various points along the line attached the body, engine, fenders, and other parts. In addition, the Model T, introduced in 1908, was exceedingly functional in design. Ford's engineers designed a vehicle whose lowest-slung parts were several inches higher off the road than competitors' models, which gave it a huge advantage on deeply rutted country roads and during inclement weather. The design was exceedingly simple, and any individual with average mechanical skills could learn to do repairs and basic maintenance. Model Ts developed a richly deserved reputation for reliability. The rugged, if homely, "Tin Lizzie" was extremely durable, able to withstand abuse from all but the most careless owners. Finally, because Model Ts were turned out in enormous volume, Ford was able to produce them inexpensively.

Henry Ford held a somewhat unique attitude toward marketing. Early on, he decided to produce an automobile for average Americans; unlike most of his peers in the industry, who generally emphasized luxury cars for the elite, Ford would build utilitarian motorized wagons for the masses. While other manufacturers thought in terms of hundreds, or perhaps a few thousand units per year, Ford envisioned selling cars to millions of Americans. Increasingly efficient mass production allowed Ford to lower prices of his cars relentlessly. Although the cost of living in the nation more than doubled between 1910 and 1920, Ford kept dropping prices of his Model T. By the mid-1920s, Ford had lowered the base price of a Model T to under $300! By then, of course, other manufacturers were also producing sensibly priced vehicles in volume.

No wonder automobile sales skyrocketed during the early twentieth century. From 8,000 in 1900, automobile registrations mushroomed to 458,000 in 1910 and then leaped again to 8.1 million in 1920. By the time of the stock market crash in October 1929, almost 24 million cars were registered—enough cars to seat every living American! The automobile age had clearly arrived.

In the mid-1920s, Henry Ford still dominated the emerging automobile industry. Roughly half of all cars on the road were Model Ts, which were virtually unchanged in basic design since their introduction. However, time was beginning to catch up to Ford, who was obsessed with the idea that simple, durable, and economical vehicles would always sell. Other manufacturers, keenly aware that the national automobile market was nearly saturated (meaning that there were very few first-time buyers of new vehicles), were developing new marketing strategies. To attract new customers, they helped provide easier financing. In 1910, Morris Plan banks became the first in the country to finance car purchases. General Securities followed in 1915, and General Motors Acceptance Corporation (GMAC) entered the field a year later. By 1925, three out of four new cars were purchased through installments. Henry Ford thought that such "high living" was foolish, if not downright immoral: "It has always seemed to me that putting off the day of payment for anything but permanent improvements was a fundamental mistake." Ford held off providing company financing for consumer products until 1928.

By the mid-1920s, however, rival producers were finally challenging Ford's long domination of the industry. At General Motors, top-level executives determined that many buyers wanted something more than basic, reliable transportation. Perhaps they could be sold on comfort, exciting styling, and aesthetically pleasing choices of colors for both exteriors and interior fabrics. In stark contrast to Henry Ford, they introduced the revolutionary concept of planned obsolescence, deliberately inculcating in consumers the idea that last year's cars were out-of-date. General Motors and other manufacturers sensed that female buyers constituted a significant market themselves and that their preferences were critically important when families bought new cars. Automobile manufacturer Edward S. Jordan bluntly stated, "Men buy automobiles, but it is the women who choose them." But

Henry Ford was not yet convinced. His initial response to such challenges was highly revealing. When asked why he did not offer color choices for his cars, he allegedly replied that his customers could have any color they chose, as long as it was black. However, as rival brands steadily chipped away at Ford Motor Company's once impregnable position, the reluctant industrialist finally abandoned his beloved Model T in 1927. Ford shut down its production lines for several months, then unfurled the much-anticipated Model A in 1928. Bowing reluctantly to changing public tastes, Ford offered buyers several color choices, along with other options.

Automotive engineering advances in the first half of the century were dazzling. Starting a hand-cranked, gasoline-powered car was an irritating, dirty, and sometimes dangerous chore, which often frustrated novices and challenged the strength of many drivers. Although self-starters of various types had been available for several years, Charles F. Kettering's introduction of the truly reliable Delco electric starter in 1911 was a critically important technological breakthrough. Four-wheel hydraulic brakes were introduced in 1920, followed by balloon tires in 1922. The automatic transmission was invented in 1937, the same year that the gearshift on many manual models was moved from the floor to the steering wheel. From the awkward, stiff, upright, and bouncy vehicles of the early years of the century, the more modern cars of the 1930s became sleek and more rounded and were built lower to the ground, potentially offering a far more comfortable ride.

THE HIGHWAY INFRASTRUCTURE

There were now millions of cars, but where could they go? As early as 1900, the League of American Wheelmen, farmers, and a few other interest groups had begun to agitate for better roads. However, little progress had been made. Almost everyone agreed that new and improved roads were highly desirable, but whose interests should they serve? Affluent Americans imagined smooth highways traversing several states, where they could run powerful cars at full throttle between large cities and major tourist attractions. Farmers, by contrast, demanded improved local roads that would allow them to convey much larger loads of produce to collection points, cut time and effort needed to get into town, and help ease the physical and social isolation they experienced, in part because of transportation difficulties.

Another nettlesome issue was who would pay for road improvements. Town, city, county, state, and federal officials all hoped others would assume the initiative. Whose taxes should be raised? Could equitable methods of calculating who benefited the most from improved roads and assessing equitable "users' fees" be devised? France, England, and Germany had made progress in developing adequate roads, but these countries were far smaller and more densely settled than most parts of the United States. For American decision makers, there were few precedents.

Before World War I, road-building efforts in the United States were uncoordinated and, in the eyes of frustrated motorists, largely ineffective. Impatient with the lack of progress, Indiana entrepreneur Carl G. Fisher and several prominent Detroit automobile men had formed the Lincoln Highway Association amidst great fanfare in 1913. Fisher and his associates originally envisioned a magnificent privately financed transcontinental highway from New York to San Francisco that would be finished just in time to convey thousands of tourists to the West Coast city's Pan Pacific Exposition, scheduled for 1915. The concept generated great initial enthusiasm. A route was duly laid out, but only a few miles of concrete had actually been poured by the eve of the nation's entry into World War I. Farmers dismissed long-distance highways as "peacock alleys," which primarily served wealthy Americans with too much leisure time on their hands. In 1904, the first year the nation's roads were systematically evaluated by census workers, only 7 percent of total mileage was listed under the category of "improved," which usually meant that it was covered only with gravel. As late as 1921, of 3.16 million miles of roadway in the country, only 447,000 miles were improved. Progress had been excruciatingly slow. In many cities and towns, roads and streets ended at municipal boundaries, where motorists encountered twisted, rutted, and, in rainy weather, impassable roads. Clearly, these efforts were not enough. With vastly increased numbers of automobiles on the road, far more aggressive steps were needed to improve roads, or one of the nation's most promising new industries might stagnate.

By the second decade of the twentieth century, many interests were pushing lawmakers at all levels and clamoring for road improvements. Following formation of the American Association of State Highway Officials (AASHO) in 1914, which became both a clearinghouse for innovative road-building concepts and a potent lobbying force, progress was more encouraging. In 1916, Congress passed the Federal Aid Road Act, appropriating $75 million, which was to be spent improving rural roads. Federal funds had to be spent through state highway departments, and states were required to supply half of the money for any project approved.

That was a start. However, as with the privately sponsored Lincoln Highway, little actual construction occurred before the nation entered World War I in April 1917. Wartime preparations graphically revealed the inadequate state of the nation's roads. By mid-decade, the federal government was shipping millions of tons of food and other supplies, primarily to the Allies. Once the United States entered the war, the volume of materiel sent to Europe increased even more. Although the country possessed a magnificent railroad system, responsible public officials could not move vast quantities of goods efficiently. Boxcars full of produce, some of it perishable, stacked up along tracks and freight yards, often fifty or sixty miles from major seaports. A major reason for shipping delays was that roads were totally inadequate. With decent service roads near seaports, goods could have been unloaded from boxcars and conveyed to ship loading docks by trucks, of which there were already 325,000 in the United States. Had there been functional interstate roads, some of the pressure on railroads could have been eased by long-haul truck delivery of goods. After the primary danger was past, military officials publicly expressed relief that the actual combat occurred overseas. If the war had been fought in the United States, the nation's ability to defend itself would have been severely crippled by its inadequate highway system. Generals simply would have had insufficient time to move men and supplies into proper position quickly and efficiently.

The logistical lessons of World War I convinced federal officials that they needed to do more than partially fund disconnected rural roadways; a comprehensive national highway system was essential. Congress responded with the Federal Highway Act of 1921, which provided that "such projects will expedite the completion of an adequate and connected system of highways, interstate in character." Reversing the earlier emphasis on building local, rural roads, each state was required to designate 7 percent of its road mileage as primary, and only these roads were eligible for federal funds, once again to be matched by states. The act appropriated another $75 million to be spent in fiscal 1922 alone. This was a significant increase from the 1916 initiative, in which the identical total financial commitment was spread over five years.

Seven percent of state roads eligible for federal funds amounted to 200,000 miles of potential improved highway, but aggressive highway builders had far more ambitious goals. As highway historians Mark H. Rose and Bruce Seely have ably revealed, by 1923, the Bureau of Public Roads, under the direction of Thomas H. MacDonald, had planned a tentative network of arterial highways serving every American city with 50,000 or more inhabitants. From that point forward, progress in road building was rapid. From 447,000 miles of improved road in 1921, the figure increased to 854,000 miles in 1930. By 1945, just over half of the nation's roads entered the improved category, as 1.721 million miles were surfaced in some manner, while 1.598 million miles remained unimproved.

The major strides in road building during the Great Depression of the 1930s merit closer inspection. In desperate economic times, when millions of Americans wallowed in poverty, some at starvation levels, why did public officials continue to finance roads and highways? On the surface at least, such responses appear callous, if not wantonly cruel. For starters, they did so because, thanks to the gas tax, the money was there. Taxes on gasoline were first imposed at the state level in Oregon, New Mexico, and Colorado in 1919. Other states quickly followed suit. From a modest total of $5.3 million in 1920, gas tax revenues multiplied 100-fold in eleven years, to $526 million by 1931. Most motorists accepted gas taxes with equanimity, largely because they seemed to be eminently fair "user's taxes"; and, with the simultaneous rise of powerful automobile, construction, and petroleum industry lobbies, it was increasingly difficult politically for public officials to divert such revenues into nonautomotive expenditures.

When Franklin D. Roosevelt was elected president in 1932, he offered a New Deal to the American people. The Roosevelt administration helped establish the federal government as the rock bottom source of "safety net" social welfare programs for Americans when their best efforts and private charities failed. This meant billions of dollars for direct relief, plus additional billions to be spent providing jobs for unemployed Americans, who comprised at least one fourth of the nation's workers by 1933. Road building became one of the cornerstones of the New Deal work programs during the 1930s. It was popular with politicians because its benefits could easily be spread between many congressional districts. Representatives who successfully backed such projects in their districts could claim highly visible "concrete" achievements. Equally attractive, road building was also highly labor-intensive, which meant that, in terms of jobs provided, there was a lot of bang for the taxpayer's buck. In fact, President Roosevelt's New Deal greatly enhanced "automobility" at the expense of mass transit. By 1939, relief and recovery projects accounted for 80 percent of all federal expenditures for roads. In the decade following 1933, the federal government poured $4 billion into construction of streets and roads.

In following this strategy, Roosevelt and his advisors demonstrated that they had their fingers on the public's pulse. Sociologists Robert and Helen Lynd, whose classic study *Middletown* was published in the late 1920s, conducted a follow-up study in the mid-1930s and discovered that families in Muncie, Indiana, would skimp on food, go without new clothes and entertainment, and would even mortgage their homes and deplete savings in order to keep their cars running. When asked by a federal official why her family had bought a car rather than install indoor plumbing, one farm woman replied, "Why, you can't go to town in a bathtub!" With the onset of the Depression, even the poorest Americans clung to their aging jalopies with startling tenacity. Historian Joseph Interrante perceived automobile ownership as a significant class issue in the 1930s. "Indeed, the business classes regard it as a scandal that some people on relief still manage to operate their cars." Foreign observers were struck by the fact that in the movie adaptation of John Steinbeck's classic novel of the Dust Bowl, *The Grapes of Wrath,* the Joads fled from Oklahoma to California in their rickety overloaded vehicle. Even the most desperate Americans, it seemed, had automobiles.

Between the two world wars, not many miles of highway were added to the nation's infrastructure, but there were impressive advances in highway design. With the explosion in automobile production, there almost had to be. In many cities and towns, traffic congestion had become a monumental headache. Colleges and universities trained thousands of traffic engineers, who quickly gained employment in burgeoning city planning agencies and traffic and highway departments. Through the 1920s and 1930s, engineers placed enormous faith in technological fixes for mounting traffic challenges. They straightened and widened streets, introduced traffic signals, and synchronized lights. They also experimented with elevated roads and "limited-access" highways. In clear anticipation of the future, by the late 1930s they were building the first freeways in the nation's largest cities. During that decade, Robert Moses, New York's Commissioner of Parkways, masterminded construction of a regional network of limited-access parkways that extended into Connecticut and far out onto Long Island. In 1937, the Southern California Automobile Club proposed the Arroyo-Seco Freeway, linking downtown Los Angeles to Pasadena; the roadway opened amidst great fanfare in 1940.

THE CAR CULTURE'S IMPACT ON MASS TRANSIT

Not all observers were persuaded that accommodating the automobile was wise. In the late 1930s, renowned historian and social commentator Lewis Mumford, whose criticism of the automobile culture would become even more intense after World War II, scored highway engineers and urban planners for "allowing mass transit to deteriorate." In his view, building freeways and downtown parking garages "helped destroy the living tissue of the city." Mumford was joined by a few like-minded observers. An editorial writer for the *Los Angeles Times* called the automobile a "Frankenstein . . . spouting exhaust exhaust smoke and reeking of burnt gasoline fumes." The "liberation" that auto enthusiasts trumpeted was becoming "a mockery and a memory." However, the overwhelming majority of important decision makers in the United States responded to the automobile's increasing dominance of urban roadways with equanimity.

They accepted the automobile, in part because it was clearly a major contributor to the nation's economy. In addition to generating tens of thousands of jobs in the manufacturing sector, the car culture required an elaborate infrastructure of supporting services, which in turn created more jobs. These included automobile dealerships, gas stations, automobile repair shops, parts stores, and tourist services. The automobile culture also opened new opportunities for insurance underwriters and for teachers in the nation's schools offering new courses ranging from driver education to traffic engineering and management. Thanks to the automobile, government agencies added tens of thousands of personnel in law enforcement, automobile registrations, licensing, and other regulatory functions.

Perhaps no vision more clearly symbolized traffic engineers' supreme faith in technology than Norman Bel Geddes's breathtaking exhibit "Futurama," which opened at the New York World's Fair in 1939. Bel Geddes, an inspired, if glib, visionary, was hired by General Motors to provide fair goers a glimpse into a future dominated by the automobile. The designer outdid himself. During the summer of 1939, millions of Americans waited for hours in line to experience Bel Geddes's simulated airplane trip through America in 1960. The trip lasted just sixteen minutes, but the program packed an enormous sensory wallop. Viewers "flew" over model cities dominated by 100-story-high skyscrapers and multilayered roadways 8 and 10 lanes wide, over which cars would speed at 50, 75, even 100 miles per hour. In Bel Geddes's vision, there were neither traffic jams nor accidents, as drivers were automatically prevented from making erratic judgments by friendly electronic beams and sensors. Nor could pedestrians be hurt, since they were separated from cars by elevated or submerged walkways. In an early-day Jurassic Park scenario, technology would presumably take care of any eventuality. Most viewers of the "City of Tomorrow" failed to register the fact that the design almost wholly ignored mass transit. Bel Geddes clearly assumed that the automobile would serve the daily transportation needs of virtually all Americans in the near future.

If his vision appears narrow, or even cold-blooded sixty years later, in some respects it represented changing realities in the late 1930s. By then, the automobile was already posing a serious challenge

For most of the twentieth century, decision-makers in the United States have shared enormous faith in technological or design fixes to control automobility and bend it in directions of their choosing. The superhighway model laid out by designer Norman Bel Geddes in his "Futurama" display at the New York World's Fair in 1939 conveyed his optimism concerning the efficiency and ease of getting around in the metropolitan regions of 1960.

to mass transit. For decades, millions of Americans had relied upon trolleys to move them from home to work, on shopping expeditions, even on family excursions to pastoral parks and amusement centers on the edges of cities. The horse-drawn trolley, prevalent during and after the Civil War, had been supplanted first by cable cars and, in the late 1880s, by the electric-powered streetcar. Introduced by Frank Sprague in 1887, the electric trolley almost totally dominated mass transit in America's cities by 1900. By then, the average American urbanite took more than one trolley ride per day. Ridership on trolley lines continued to grow in the first two decades of the twentieth century; in 1926, Americans took over 17 billion rides.

Unfortunately, trolley company officials basically sowed the seeds of their own destruction. With tens of millions of urban Americans almost totally dependent on public transportation, trolley officials all too often treated their riders with contempt. Trolley rides were frequently downright unpleasant, particularly during peak commuting hours. A reporter for the Los Angeles *Record* painted a grim picture of local streetcar conditions in 1912:

> Inside the air was a pestilence; it was heavy with disease and the emanations from many bodies. Anyone leaving this working mass, anyone coming into it . . . force[s] the people into still closer, still more indecent, still more immoral contact. A bishop embraced a stout grandmother, a tender girl touched limbs with a city sport, refined women's faces burned with shame and indignation—but there was no relief. . . . It was only the result of public stupidity and apathy. It was in a Los Angeles streetcar . . . [any] old day you are in a mind to board a city street car between the hours of five and seven in the afternoon.

The evolution of such a state of affairs is not difficult to understand. In the late nineteenth century, urban leaders had to attract investment capital in mass transit. Cooperative politicians regularly offered capitalists potentially valuable municipal franchises to operate trolleys on city streets, some of them covering 50 or even 100 years either free or for ridiculously low fees. Many franchises allowed trolley operators to create monopolies. Later investigations revealed extensive, blatant bribery of local politicians by transit company officials in some cases. In many cases, transit officials used political influence to ratchet up fares. Numerous urban workers earning no more than ten or fifteen cents per hour experienced actual hardship when transit companies raised fares, doubling them in some cases from a nickel to a dime. In their defense, transit company officials claimed, with considerable justification, that, as trolley lines extended farther out to spreading suburbs, they needed additional revenue to finance construction. Unfortunately, they found too many ways to alienate customers. Typically, they resisted riders' efforts to liberalize "transfer" privileges. In some cases, patrons had to pay multiple fares in order to reach final destinations.

As a result, by the early twentieth century, trolley riders in many cities considered local company officials greedy and corrupt monopolists, heartlessly milking them for unconscionably high fares, in arrogant disregard for public welfare. Newspaper editorials increasingly criticized transit officials' cynical manipulation of captive riders. Noted American writer Theodore Dreiser produced two novels, *The Financier* (1912) and *The Titan* (1914), featuring a hard-bitten traction magnate named Frank Cowperwood. Knowledgeable readers did not miss the fact that his protagonist was a thinly disguised and generally unpopular real-life street railway monopolist, Chicago's Charles Tyson Yerkes.

By the first decade of the twentieth century, many urban reformers were calling for vastly increased public regulation of trolley companies. Some envisioned the end of privately owned mass transit operations, and they advocated municipal ownership of the lines. In an atmosphere of increasingly adversarial and poisonous relationships between patrons and transit companies, many urbanites began to seek their own alternatives to street railways. To large numbers of Americans, the big transit companies represented unfettered capitalism at its worst. By contrast, the little guys producing automobiles in bicycle-repair facilities and blacksmith shops epitomized rugged individualism at its best; and the American public was becoming increasingly interested in supporting legislation facilitating the spread of privately owned automobiles. Many Americans were attracted to the democratic image of individuals supplying their own transportation devices, rather than being subservient to insensitive, bureaucratic public utilities. Yet another attractive feature of accommodating automobiles was that they occupied less street space than horse-drawn conveyances, and they were cleaner. Historian Clay McShane estimated that, in the 1890s, horses dropped between 800,000 and 1.3 million pounds of manure onto New York City's streets every day.

Transit officials appeared totally unprepared to respond effectively in this rapidly shifting cultural and political climate. As cities spread farther horizontally, transit officials were under rapidly mounting pressure to invest huge amounts of capital to extend lines farther and speed up service. Rapid inflation in the 1910s came at the worst possible time, forcing transit companies to make increasingly frequent pleas to local governments for permission to raise fares. In cities where franchises were either expiring or were up for renegotiation, transit officials encountered increasingly hostile politicians. Earlier generations of urban politicians were perceived as either naïve or corrupt for being overly generous in awarding franchises. By the early twentieth century, mayors and city councils were wary of creating any impression among voters of giving transit companies a break. Not surprisingly, in most cases in which street railway companies had to appeal to the public for support, there was seldom any reservoir of good will. Transit officials usually discovered that their entreaties fell on deaf ears. Between the two world wars, trolley companies found themselves fighting for their lives.

By the end of World War I, rapidly increasing numbers of automobiles were already jamming city streets, particularly in central business districts. The fact that both drivers and downtown merchants demanded curbside parking effectively eliminated use of half the width of four-lane streets. Tripling of the numbers of cars nationwide during the 1920s only made urban congestion worse. For a time, public officials believed they could solve this problem through street widening, synchronized traffic signals, construction of more off-street parking, and other minor adjustments.

There were other efforts to deal with traffic congestion From the 1860s on, a few densely settled cities experimented with elevated rail lines in order to remove mass transit lines from streets that were already crowded with pedestrians and horse-drawn conveyances. Elevateds were, at best, a limited success, since steam-powered trains showered citizens below with sparks and soot. Electrification of mass transit vehicles solved part of the problem, but the elevated structures were still eyesores, and they were extremely noisy when in use. By the turn of the century, a handful of the nation's largest cities, including Boston and New York, had either placed subway lines into operation or had plans to do so. Unfortunately, subways were incredibly expensive and they made economic sense only in the very largest, most densely settled and congested cities.

In the late twentieth century, a number of American cities, aided by federal grants, spent billions of dollars building subways or light rail lines. Why didn't they do so decades earlier, when both acquisition of rights of way and construction costs would have been far cheaper? In the crucial period between 1910 and the end of World War II, only Chicago commenced construction of a new subway system. The answer is highly complex, but one major contributing factor was the fact that traffic engineers nationwide consistently underestimated the challenges created by automobile congestion. Many, if not most, sincerely believed in relatively quick technological or design fixes. Politicians seldom offered alternative visions, as few had either the vision to perceive it or the backbone to take the long view. In addition, most politicians were reluctant to commit huge amounts to projects whose benefits would not be recognized by voters until the lines were completed several years later. By then, the politicians might have been voted out of office. Another inhibiting factor was that the advantages brought by subways would not be spread out evenly between council members' districts. Though subway lines enhanced property values, only those urbanites living within convenient walking distance of stations experienced obvious benefits. Unfortunately, because tens of thousands of urban dwellers lived too far from subway stops to find them convenient to use, subways provided no perceivable advantages to many voters, even in the largest cities. Politicians found it far more politically expedient to fund street improvements, whose tangible benefits could be spread out more evenly and which could be completed far more quickly than subway lines. The widespread public adoption of the automobile, like the electric trolley before it, helped speed up the emerging sprawl of metropolitan regions.

Suburbia, associated initially with rail transportation, was clearly enhanced by the automobile, but it preceded World War II by decades. The first suburbs in the United States, springing up along steam railroad lines serving large eastern cities, dated from the early nineteenth century. In the late nineteenth and early twentieth centuries, many real estate developers built trolley lines to assure potential buyers easy access to urban cores, thus enhancing the value of their holdings. As late as World War I, when trolleys were still king, almost all residential development was within half a mile—or easy walking distance—from the nearest lines. Back then, advertisements for single family homes almost invariably emphasized convenient access to rail transit. In most metropolitan regions, trolley lines spread outward like spokes from a wheel's hub (downtown). Typically, the remaining vast stretches of undeveloped land between trolley tracks tended to spread farther and farther apart as distance from densely settled downtown areas increased. Automobility meant that the land between the trolley lines could be profitably developed. By the onset of the Depression, most advertisements for new homes dropped any mention of convenient trolleys; instead, they featured garages. During the 1920s, the nation's suburbs grew twice as fast as the central cities.

THE AUTOMOBILE CHANGES AMERICA

How did automobile use change over the first half of the twentieth century? As noted, the earliest cars were experimental devices. Once innovators showed automobiles could work, wealthy sportsmen—and not a few less-well-heeled imitators—became vitally interested in seeing how fast they could go. Almost from the beginning, auto men spent large sums attempting to set speed and endurance records. By the early 1900s, it seemed as if every county seat had a dirt-covered racing track. In 1909, Carl G. Fisher, the very same individual who later masterminded early development of the Lincoln Highway, spearheaded construction of the Indianapolis Motor Speedway. Although some of the first races Fisher sponsored were catastrophes resulting in multiple deaths for both drivers and spectators, Fisher and his partners later surfaced his 2.5-mile track with bricks, a more durable, far safer material. The first Indianapolis 500 race was held in 1911, and it has become a cherished American tradition.

Long before World War II, some Americans relied regularly on automobiles to take them even into the hearts of the nation's largest cities. Once there, however, parking arrangements were often informal, even haphazard.

Most Americans, however, sought considerably more practical uses for their cars. In small towns and rural areas, doctors discovered that cars provided them far more range for making house calls then did horse and buggy. Cars were faster, and they never got tired (even if they did experience frequent breakdowns). Farmers were less interested in speed than in versatility of uses, and they fell in love with the rugged, easy-to-maintain Model T Ford. "Tin Lizzies" not only conveyed whole families to town but could be hooked up to pull plows. Some farmers even built attachments that could convert Model Ts into tractors. According to one automobile historian, such units helped with light work but were not for heavy field work. Not even the durable Model T could be driven for long under full load in the heat and dust of fields. A more typical application was using cars for belt work. Rear axles could be elevated and pulleys attached to the wheels. The pulleys could then drive belts that powered feed mills, water pumps, churns, grindstones, washing machines, silage cutters, and portable grain elevators. No wonder that, after initial opposition, most farmers quickly adapted to the automobile. Henry Ford became a folk hero, particularly in rural areas; many citizens saw him and his product as symbols of the best of America. During a 1915 visit to the White House, Ford earned a laugh from President Woodrow Wilson by telling him about the eccentric farmer who stipulated in his will that he would be buried with his Model T: it had pulled him out of every hole so far, and he expected that it could pull him out of that one too.

However, small-town merchants running general stores were not always so enamored of the Tin Lizzie. They immediately sensed that the automobile was a threat, as farmers and small town residents could easily motor to larger towns and cities to buy lower-cost and often standard-brand goods from the chain stores that were rapidly emerging by World War I. In larger towns and cities, the first shopping centers emerged in the 1920s. With the exception of Jesse C. Nichols's tastefully designed "Country Club Plaza" in Kansas City, Missouri, and well-conceived shopping districts in a few other cities, shopping centers were generally nondescript strip developments along busy thoroughfares, offering ample free parking and easy access.

Automobile buyers were enthralled at the new sense of freedom they experienced. To early-twentieth-century Americans, increased personal mobility became a treasured objective. Urban Americans who owned cars were no longer tied to trolley schedules. Young men on dates did not have to interrupt romantic evenings to catch the last train home. Housewives could stop at numerous stores and carry heavy packages home in back seats; no longer did they have to pay multiple fares on the trolley and struggle on and off cars, bumping into unfriendly strangers with awkward bundles and perhaps soiling or damaging their purchases in the process. In an era when ethnic tensions and racial hostility appeared constant, automobiles provided their owners another extremely precious commodity: private space. When drivers slid behind the wheel, they avoided potential contact with those they considered "undesirables."

Nowhere did automobiles create more changes than in how Americans experienced leisure. As historian Cindy S. Aron has shown, in the nineteenth century, Americans enjoying vacations usually traveled to some type of resort, either by train or boat. The resorts ranged from posh, internationally famous retreats such as Saratoga Springs, in New York, costing upward of $100 per week, all the way down to inexpensive religious encampments, where families could enjoy a week's respite for as little as $10. However, from wealthy to working-class vacationers, unless they were avid horsemen, boatsmen, or hikers, almost all were limited to sampling attractions close to railroad or steamship lines. This invariably meant being confined to fixed schedules and, particularly for the well-to-do, taking meals in stuffy, formal dining rooms.

As social historian Warren J. Belasco has ably demonstrated, the automobile revolutionized Americans' vacation habits in the early twentieth century. To be sure, aristocrats still took European tours, where they visited the same spas and watering holes their fathers—even grandfathers—had. Once ensconced in famous resorts, they might or might not have enjoyed side trips via automobile. For Americans sightseeing in their own country, the automobile provided an attractive and exciting alternative to the conventional, predictable vacations they had experienced in the past.

Most importantly, motorists were confined to neither rigid schedules nor fixed destinations. They could get up when they wanted, eat wherever they wished, drive in any direction they chose, and travel only until they were tired. As Belasco astutely notes, ". . . [A]mong the ironies surrounding the car culture, perhaps the strangest is this: early on, the automobile industry became the backbone of modern industrial capitalism, yet it was born in a spirit of rebellion against that system." Automobile touring had drawbacks, however. Early automobiles experienced frequent mechanical breakdowns, and flat tires were daily occurrences for most travelers. Any man brave enough to take his family on an automobile vacation had to be handy with a wrench and pliers. When roads were still primitive, travelers often had to be pulled out of mud holes by farmers using plow horses—for a price, of course.

Early automobile adventurers called it *gypsying*. They took to the road and took their chances. Rear fenders and bumpers, sometimes even the tops of cars, would be weighted down with camping equipment, picnic baskets, and boxes jammed with food and cooking implements. At dusk, they would search for a scenic spot along the road and pitch camp. Wise travelers asked for permission from property owners.

However, it did not take long before many rural Americans grew tired of growing numbers of freeloaders. Too many campers failed to ask permission; or else they littered farmers' fields with trash, looted fruit orchards and corn fields, or sometimes left fires smoldering dangerously. As auto camping evolved following World War I, enterprising city councils in some towns, hoping to enhance business for local merchants, established free public campgrounds for motorists. For a brief period, each town tried to outdo its neighbor in providing amenities, which sometimes included running water, electricity, privies, laundry rooms, kitchens, and even cold showers. Under ideal circumstances, fifty or sixty families occupied campsites spread over fifteen or so acres, enjoying congregating around campfires and exchanging life stories and information about conditions on roads up ahead and those just traveled. Many middle-class and, particularly, working-class families appreciated being relieved of the necessity of paying for hotel rooms downtown and having to pass review of lobby patrons and get cleaned up before eating expensive meals in hotel dining rooms. Auto camps were both cheaper and more democratic; no snooty registration clerks looked down their noses at tired, grubby travelers.

The free municipal camps did not last long. By the mid-1920s, there was a shift toward private camps that charged fees. The free camps had become crowded, and some campers, particularly middle-class Americans, thought they were becoming *too* democratic. Many auto campers were loud and uncouth. Even worse, some poor campers did not spend a night or two and then move on; instead, they lingered for weeks, even months. Such undesirables usually failed to spend money with local merchants, much to the distress of civic leaders. Savvy entrepreneurs soon became aware that middle-class travelers would pay twenty-five or fifty cents per night for clean, functional campsites, even if mainly to escape from constant exposure to "riff-raff" who could not or would not pay.

"Cabin camps" evolved virtually simultaneously with "fee" camps. Automobile ownership multiplied threefold during the 1920s, and whole new groups of Americans were vacationing by car every season. Not all new automobile campers wanted to sleep in tents or under the stars; yet, they, too, yearned to bypass downtown hotels. One answer was small, rustic cabins, either in campsites or separate locations. These units were usually tiny, often no more than eight feet square. For fifty cents, or perhaps as much as a dollar, travelers got a bed and a sink with running water (usually cold). Although showers were usually free, they were typically communal facilities. Bed clothes cost extra, often another twenty-five cents. Cabin courts were typically mom-and-pop operations. Court operators often designed and built their own rustic units, although a few companies offered inexpensive "cabin kits" that could be set up by any competent handyman. As often as not, "mom" operated a lunch counter café, or diner, while "pop" ran the courts and made repairs. Cabin courts thrived even during the Great Depression, gradually fading out by the end of the 1950s.

The final step up the evolutionary roadside amenities ladder before World War II was the motel. The first facility to actually use the designation was James Vail's Motel Inn in San Luis Obispo, California. It was actually a hotel "with automobile facilities," which opened in 1925. Motels emerged slowly, in large part because of the stock market crash in 1929 and subsequent Great Depression. They would not be widespread on the American landscape until after World War II. However, the concept of chain motels was already in place. During the 1930s, several entrepreneurs established numerous separate motels featuring uniform, standardized exterior and interior decor, amenities, and identical nightly rates. In 1929, E. Lee Torrance founded the Alamo Plaza Hotel Court chain; by the outset of World War II, more than a dozen Alamo Plazas were scattered across Dixie.

With cabin courts and motels came the precursors to today's fast food. The first was Royce Haley's Pig Stand, opened in Dallas in 1921. By the early 1920s, hot-dog stands, greasy spoons, and, occasionally, more pretentious restaurants were popping up along the nation's roadways. (Standardized food chains would not really emerge until after

World War II.) Some of the early food stand architecture was bizarre. Imaginative designs far exceeded the typical giant hot-dog motif. Stands shaped like fruits and vegetables were popular: apples, oranges, watermelons, and corncobs. Animals, including fish, cows, dogs, and cats, were seen, as well as donuts, pancakes, and muffins. Unfortunately, almost all of this pre-war kitsch architecture has been destroyed.

Lunch stands were soon joined by drive-in movies. The first drive-in movie was opened in Camden, New Jersey, in 1933; the second on Pico Boulevard in Los Angeles in 1934; both by Richard M. Hollingshead Jr., who soon began franchising his idea to other proprietors for a fee of $1,000 plus 5 percent of their gross receipts. Start-up costs were low, a critical consideration in the Depression, and drive-in operators passed along some of their savings in the form of low admission prices. However, the big boom in drive-ins would await the post–World War II period.

From the earliest days, however, the emerging automobile culture had numerous negative impacts on the American landscape. Some roadside services were downright ugly, including tastelessly designed motor courts, shabby refreshment stands, and ramshackle gasoline and service stations, scattered haphazardly across forlorn landscapes. Environmental issues were not high on the public's collective consciousness, but many sensitive observers complained of the constant roar of poorly tuned engines, noxious exhaust fumes, thoughtlessly discarded trash, and oil-slicked public avenues. The proliferation of outdoor advertising offended the sensibilities of those Americans preferring pristine views along the roadside. Many farmers could not resist the blandishments of a new breed of marketing salesmen, who convinced them that a few dollars earned by allowing them to paint huge advertising signs on the sides of their barns would not hurt anybody.

While commercialization of rural landscapes offended some purists, at least one form of outdoor advertising delighted almost everyone: Burma Shave signs. The small, red, white, and blue notices, each containing part of a jingle, were spread out over several hundred feet. A motorist traveling at forty miles per hour could easily receive the message. One read

He married Grace

With scratchy face

He only got

One day with Grace

In an era less politically correct, another went

I plucked my beard

Said the Indian brave

Until I heard of

Burma Shave

Automobiles made a huge impact on family life and courting patterns well before World War II. Some fears voiced by social critics were general. As historian John Sears noted, ". . . [t]here were those who looked upon popularization of motoring as a miasma spreading over the land. Their objections were not that cars were dirty, noisy or frightening, but that they were too comfortable, too convenient and too seductive. In a way, it was the modern version of the puritan ethic that could countenance a horse modestly trotting but not flagrantly racing. In their book, fast meant loose, and you only had to look at the declining moral standards of the young to see." Typically, families owned a single vehicle, which in some cases comprised a key battleground of parental control. As early as World War I, young men pleaded with parents that lack of access to the family car would eliminate any chances they had of achieving popularity. Before the automobile, young people courting typically conducted their activities on front porches and parlors, under the watchful eyes of girls' parents. The car transformed Victorian courtship patterns, as young swains whisked their dates to secluded locations far from the prying eyes of nervous parents. Young and ambitious J. Edgar Hoover, newly ensconced as head of the FBI, raised the specter of couples sneaking off to cabin courts and motels, which, too often, rented rooms by the hour instead of all night. In his view, sleazy motel operators engaged in and actively promoted the sordid "hot pillow" trade. Numerous postcards and cartoons joked about sex and cars. One risqué postcard from the 1930s showed an attractive female hitchhiker holding a baby asking the motorist who pulled up beside her, "Aren't you the fellow who gave me a ride about a year ago?" Long before vans were introduced, car manufacturers offered vehicles whose front seats could be folded down to mesh with rear seat cushions. As early as 1925, the Jewett promised to sleep two persons in comfort, as long as neither stretched out to more than six feet six inches. Even with this feature, the brand failed to survive the Depression.

From the very beginning, songwriters celebrated the automobile. Other forms of transportation, including boats, trains, and horse and carriage, had long since found their way into the romantic lyrics of nineteenth-century music. Even the bicycle received attention, including a frothy song titled "A Bicycle Built for Two." But automobiles evolved simultaneously with ragtime and jazz, and many songs included references to the newfound joys of motoring. Without question, "In My Merry Oldsmobile" was the most famous song in the initial decade of the new century featuring motorized romance. By the 1910s and 1920s, the automobile was an important element in song lyrics. Titles of songs became much racier: "Fifteen Kisses on a Mile of Gas," "When He Wanted to Love Her, He Put Up the Cover," and "Tumble in a Rumble Seat" were typical entries.

Automobiles also occupied an important place in many of the offerings of famous journalists, poets, novelists, and other writers. As noted, it was central to the plot of Steinbeck's *Grapes of Wrath*. For Sinclair Lewis's unforgettable character, George F. Babbitt, the modern automobile, equipped with the most luxurious and up-to-date gadgets, represented the ultimate in modernity. John Dos Passos ends *The Big Money*, the last volume of his famous trilogy, with his *Vag* (vagrant or vagabond) standing on the side of the road trying to hitch a ride. He symbolized rootless poverty. As literary critic Cynthia Dettelbach noted, ". . .[T]he ultimate deprivation is to telescope one's sights, shrink one's horizons, and then have to depend on someone else's wheels to get there. For Vag, the car he does not own or cannot ride in represents a physical hardship as real to him as his hunger." No early-twentieth-century American writer used the automobile more effectively than F. Scott Fitzgerald. In his most famous novel, *The Great Gatsby*, most of the pivotal episodes revolve around the automobile. One of Jay Gatsby's prized possessions is a green-and-cream-colored Rolls Royce. "Money has bought Gatsby the car, as it bought him the house, the servants, and the style of life he creates. Because the car is the concrete embodiment of that money and a source of power and mobility as well, it becomes a phallic extension of Gatsby. . . . It is the vehicle that literally brings society to his parties and his badge of identity everywhere." It also played a key role in his tragic demise.

Movies and the automobile commenced a romance even before there was a Hollywood. As early as 1903, *Runaway Match*, a five-minute-long film, features a young couple eloping in a car. The bride's rich father chases them in a chauffeur-driven vehicle, which, undoubtedly to the delight of romantically inclined viewers, promptly breaks down. In the melodramatic *The Gentlemen Highwaymen*, filmed two years later, a villain in a big car tries to rob an upright young couple riding in a little runabout on a lonely road. However, the plucky couple in their more "democratic" little car manage to elude the would-be robber, and they even manage to knock him down with the runabout! A year later, in Biograph's *A Daring Holdup in Southern California*, both cops and robbers commandeer motor vehicles. Even the most casual students of film history have seen the hilarious *Keystone Cops* capers, which entertained millions of Americans even before World War I. Automobiles were prominently featured in many episodes. When the movie industry moved to Hollywood, dozens of full-length feature films with automobile themes were distributed to the nation's motion picture palaces. In the inter-war years, millions of Americans gobbled them up each week. Perhaps the most renowned was John Ford's screen rendition of *The Grapes of Wrath,* but movie patrons thronged to gangster movies featuring James Cagney and Edward G. Robinson in their powerful escape vehicles.

In fact, real-life gangsters relied heavily upon fast, dependable vehicles. By 1933, John Dillinger had tried any number of fast cars, including Essex Terraplanes, Studebakers, Packards, Dodges, and Buicks. He finally settled on a Ford Model A, powered by the first mass-produced, single-cast, flat-head V-8 engine rolled off the assembly line. Clyde Barrow was so impressed with the same model that he even wrote a fan letter to Ford: "While I still have a breath in my lungs, I will tell you what a dandy car you make. I have drove [sic] Fords exclusively when I can get away with one. For sustained speed and freedom from trouble the Ford has got ever [sic] car skinned."

In terms of production and sales, the 1930s and the first half of the 1940s were dreadful years for automakers in Detroit. From its prewar peak of 4.62 million units sold in 1929, car sales plummeted to 1.25 million just three years later. Output would not approach 1929 levels until 1941, when 4.43 million units rolled off Detroit's assembly lines. The nation's entry into World War II caused federal officials to suspend virtually all domestic automobile production for the duration of the war. However, the assembly line production methods developed in the automobile industry over the previous four decades proved to be an indispensable plus following Pearl Harbor. With the nation facing possible annihilation by the Axis powers, federal officials and Detroit auto men cooperated in near-miraculous fashion to convert huge plants to production of tanks, jeeps, aircraft, and other armaments. As one high-level automobile executive recalled, "In one night, I was applying thirty-five years of production experience to planning the layout for building not only something I had never put together, but the largest and most complicated of all air transport, and in numbers and at a rate never before thought possible." The United States did, in fact, become the "arsenal of democracy." In 1942 alone, the entire war industry turned out 40,000 planes and 32,000 tanks. By themselves, former automobile manufacturers produced over $29 billion in wartime goods, fully 20 percent of the nation's military hardware; this included 4 million engines, almost 6 million guns, nearly 3 million tanks and trucks, and 27,000 aircraft. Despite a delayed start, by 1943 the United States alone was outproducing all of the Axis powers.

On an even larger scale than during World War I, high-level automobile executives assumed strategic positions among the nation's policy makers during World War II. Perhaps the most important was General Motors President William Knudsen, who teamed with labor leader Sidney Hillman of the Amalgamated Clothing Workers to run the Office of Production Management (OPM). By mid-1942, the Allies had finally broken the forward momentum of the Axis powers. Although some politicians and opinion makers considered overoptimism regarding a victory over the Axis powers as tantamount to treason, from that point forward, increasing numbers of thoughtful analysts began thinking about postwar conversion. Economists were almost evenly divided between pessimists and optimists. The former believed that wartime prosperity was artificial: once the fighting was over and government spending was drastically curtailed, the economy would revert to something approaching its Depression-era level. Optimists, who obviously turned out to be right, grasped the fact that Americans had accumulated billions of dollars worth of wartime savings and had been denied access to their dream world of big-ticket consumer items for almost a generation. Once the final bombs fell on Japan in August 1945, optimists were determined to forget their nightmares and realize their material fantasies. Big, shiny new automobiles were in the middle of their visions.

In what ways had the automobile changed the United States in the half-century since its introduction? To be sure, only about half of all American families owned one. The primary beneficiaries of and participants in the automobile culture were white and middle class. Historian Virginia Scharff has argued persuasively that women enjoyed considerable access to automobiles but very low percentages of African American, Hispanic, Native American, and other minority families owned motorized vehicles. Almost everybody without a car wanted one. Virtually nobody questioned the appropriateness of accommodating motor vehicles. In addition, automobile-oriented symbols permeated the American landscape. The rest of this book deals with how these forces have ebbed and flowed since 1945.

Chapter Two

A LABORIOUS RECONVERSION

When V-J Day ended World War II, domestic production of automobiles had been virtually suspended for three and a half years. Before that, the Great Depression had also conditioned manufacturers to make very careful and, for the most part, extremely conservative decisions. Despite sixteen years of almost uninterrupted abnormal conditions, Detroit still dominated world automobile output. Before the war, most motor vehicles produced outside of the United States came from factories in Europe, many of which had either been leveled or suffered enormous damage during the war.

It may be hard for present-day readers to grasp fully how dominant Detroit was fifty-five years ago. In 1945, approximately 28 million passenger vehicles were registered in the United States. The remainder of the world boasted just 7 million automobiles! This meant that Americans drove four out of every five automobiles in the world! As for the world's 10 million commercial vehicles, Americans operated 60 percent. Overall, Americans owned more than 75 percent of all cars and trucks in the world. In 1945, Americans drove 250 billion miles in their automobiles. In 2000, they drove twelve times as far: 3 trillion miles! By contrast, in 2000, there were approximately 750 million cars and trucks worldwide, and Americans owned 30 percent of that total (almost one vehicle per American, compared to one vehicle per nine persons worldwide).

THE WAR EFFORT CONSTRAINS
THE CAR CULTURE

During the desperate fighting in the early months of the nation's participation in World War II, it had been considered by some as both unlucky and unpatriotic to talk publicly about postwar plans, or visions. Nevertheless, a few intrepid souls challenged this orthodoxy. In a nationally broadcast speech before the National Association of Manufacturers on December 4, 1942, Henry J. Kaiser, a renowned shipbuilder and a producer of cement, magnesium, and steel, advised policy makers to begin "planning for peace." Although Kaiser was one of the key contributors to the nation's evolution as the "Arsenal of Democracy," he received sharp criticism from some quarters. Several editorial writers responded testily, arguing, in effect, that Americans might dream all they wished about a postwar world filled with all the adult toys they desired, but talking about it might somehow distract both policy makers and ordinary working Americans from exerting their maximum effort to defeat the Axis powers.

During World War II, American consumers had learned how to "make do." In terms of production of consumer goods, the automobile and vital accessories had been among the first consumer items to be sacrificed for the war effort. This made simple, basic sense: automobiles and the products required to keep them running consumed a great deal of the nation's natural resources and required importation of critical raw materials. In December 1941, if responsible public officials had not anticipated the precise location of a Japanese attack, they had been acutely aware of rising tensions in the Pacific. They had also been thinking about how to respond in case of war. Just three days after the surprise attack on Pearl Harbor, government officials suspended sale of new automobile tires. Three weeks later, the Office of Price Administration (OPA) authorized production of a mere 35,000 tires per month, less than a tenth of normal demand. This proved wise, since an uninterrupted string of Japanese victories in the South Pacific early in 1942 deprived the country of 97 percent of its prewar supply of natural rubber. Likewise, government officials announced that virtually all production of 1942 automobile models would stop. The last civilian model rolled off Ford Motor Company's assembly line on February 10, 1942. General Motors had quit producing civilian vehicles a few days earlier. Between 1942 and 1944, less than 1,000 new passenger cars were built in American factories; predictably, most of them went to VIPs. Anyone lucky enough to have acquired a 1942 model of any brand before suspension of production was the envy of his neighbors!

Given the universal unpopularity of gasoline rationing, it was not formally instituted until December 1, 1942, nearly a year after Pearl Harbor. By the end of the war, civilian driving was reduced by approximately one third from its prewar level. Almost everyone felt pressure to conserve. Teenagers, in particular, must have felt incredibly repressed even on those rare occasions when they were permitted to slide behind the wheel in search of sheer pleasure. The driving Americans experienced was under a national thirty-five-mile-per-hour speed limit, deemed most "efficient" from the standpoint of fuel efficiency. As in the Depression, few Americans put their wheels up on blocks. They were so ingrained with the "automobile habit" that it seemed inconceivable to give up driving completely. Most licensed drivers did everything they could to keep their jalopies on the road. Americans with mechanical skills became valued friends, at least insofar as they helped their neighbors keep balky, aged engines running. By the summer of 1945, a lot of the vehicles still puttering about the nation's streets and highways were relics from the 1920s or even earlier.

"FUTURAMA": CARS GET THE GREEN LIGHT AGAIN?

No wonder frustrated American consumers pricked up their ears when, shortly after Germany's surrender in early May 1945, federal officials announced that automakers would be allowed to produce 200,000 civilian vehicles during the remainder of 1945. Feature writers for popular magazines captivated readers with visions of what postwar America might look like. They prophesied a technological utopia, with new automobiles prominently featured. Perhaps inspired by Norman Bel Geddes's "Futurama," writers for the *Saturday Evening Post, Colliers,* and other mass-circulation magazines envisioned modern, skyscraper-adorned cities boasting sprawling suburbs. Most future suburbanites would commute to jobs in the inner city via modern highways, perhaps in vehicles attached to electronic beams, which would in theory, eliminate any chances of accidents. Almost nobody envisioned a technological wasteland or even voiced significant reservations about potential social costs likely to be experienced by those who could not afford the new generation of vehicles.

For months before Germany's surrender, rumors had swirled around Detroit regarding when car manufacturers would be allowed to resume production of private vehicles. Before they received the green light from federal officials, automakers, perhaps aglow in the near universal approval they had received as "miracle men" in producing wartime goods, predicted that they could turn out fully half a million units during the remainder of 1945! Had Detroit lived up to its rhetoric, manufacturers might at least have benefited from economies of scale; unfortunately, they seriously underestimated the challenges of converting wartime plants back to peacetime production. Detroit managed to produce less than 84,000 units during 1945. Machinery used to manufacture civilian vehicles had been mothballed for nearly four years. Many parts were rusted or needed replacement; and, thus, carmakers required cooperation from dozens of suppliers before they could get machinery running again. In addition, carmakers had to orchestrate delivery of large shipments from dozens of raw materials suppliers, which, all too often meant making secret black-market deals to obtain just the right combination of essential but scarce supplies. Thousands of workers had to be recruited back into positions they had filled before the war, or new workers had to be hired, relocated, and trained All of this had to be done while following to the letter the provisions of complicated labor contracts negotiated years earlier. Labor leaders had faced ceaseless pressures of their own during the war, and many of them, like their managerial counterparts, were both suspicious and edgy. These myriad challenges extended time lines and strained budgets.

Consequently, there were immediate glitches as corporate America partially reconverted to peacetime production; equally predictably, Detroit automakers blamed almost all of them on the government. The most ridiculous problem, in the minds of automakers, was the government's obstinate resistance to unleashing free market forces. In an effort to stem worrisome inflation, the OPA initially required that prices of new vehicles be kept at 1942 levels. That meant, for example, that if all parties in the transaction scrupulously followed the rules, an economy-priced Ford model could be sold for only $728. Later in 1945, Ford dealers and executives claimed that following such unrealistic price guidelines would mean a $300 loss on every car sold.

Perhaps more than any other group of Americans, it seemed that military servicemen and servicewomen should have been placed at the head of the line waiting impatiently for postwar goods. The Democratic-controlled executive branch and Republican-dominated Congress had reached a rare level of cooperation in passing the GI Bill in 1944. This important legislative achievement profoundly shaped postwar America, as military personnel were given access to low-interest loans to purchase homes, generous support for higher education, unemployment insurance, and other benefits. Soldiers, seemingly well positioned, were determined to realize their dreams in postwar America. According to the "official" soldier's newspaper, *Stars and Stripes,* the material dreams of GIs returning from overseas almost always included new homes and new cars. Many GIs who married during the war had been forced to leave young wives and, sometimes, infants they had never seen, with extended families sharing cramped cold-water flats in blue-collar neighborhoods of large cites. These young couples and millions of other families would use low-interest Veterans Administration (VA) loans to buy cracker-box houses in mushrooming suburbs.

After a wife and a house, a new car was very likely high on many GIs' lists of desires. For some single men, a new automobile might be their top priority. In the flowery words of one historian, to them, as well as millions of civilians, automobility meant ". . . a direct enhancement of life, as an enlargement of life's boundaries and opportunities . . . so enormous, so radical a transformation . . . nothing less than the unshackling of the age-old bonds of locality; it is the grant of geographical choice and economic freedom on a hitherto unimagined scale."

Unfortunately, rather than occupying honored positions near the front of the lines of potential buyers anxiously seeking cars, most military personnel quickly found themselves at the rear. When GI Joe, recently returned from combat and accompanied by his new wife, showed up in automobile showrooms in the fall of 1945 or the spring of 1946 in hopes of buying one of the few new cars available, he witnessed strange sights. Perfumed, pomaded, overdressed salesmen with bored facial expressions contemptuously treated throngs of would-be buyers. Occasionally, one of the more worldly and aggressive customers might pull one of them aside, whisper some words in the salesman's ear, then slip a thick envelope into his fists. More whispered words, a few emphatic gestures, then, finally, nods followed by a handshake and a shared chuckle. Not surprisingly, in a profoundly unbalanced seller's market, savvy consumers quickly discovered that so-called waiting lists could be bypassed—as long as a customer was prepared to pay a "bonus" of several hundred dollars to be divided between the salesman, his manager, and perhaps the owner of the dealership; or, the customer might have bet the dealer $300 that he couldn't jump over a clothesline lying on the floor. The principled customer who refused to stoop to bribes and maintained his proper place in line might wait a year, or even more, before delivery of the vehicle he ordered. And, if upon the long-awaited and several-times-postponed delivery day his car was blue and slightly dented rather than the green tone he asked for and pristine condition he dreamed of, he was wise to accept it graciously before it was whisked away to a less-discriminating buyer.

Many GI Joes probably left dealers' showrooms angry and depressed. Was this what they had been fighting for? Among the crowd of prospective buyers were overfed, pasty-faced clerks and machinists, civilians who for several years had earned three or four times their paltry soldiers' salaries. Unlike most soldiers, they had probably squirreled away hundreds, perhaps even thousands, of dollars in savings bonds. Most civilians had never missed a meal or exposed themselves to any danger during the war, and they were going to get cars before fighting men would! This was unreal; it was worse than mockery. That, in a nutshell, characterized the topsy-turvy, chaotic automobile market in the months following V-J Day, 1945.

In Detroit, the pressure was on to meet the voracious consumer demand, and automakers scrambled to exploit what might be a once-in-a-lifetime opportunity. They realized they could sell virtually anything on wheels. Assuming that the government lifted the lid on price controls, as most industry insiders expected momentarily, the company that could convert its plants from wartime production back into civilian output the quickest and most efficiently would reap the largest profits. Established producers sensed an opportunity to enhance their standing against major competitors. The potential rewards were so breathtaking that several new companies entered the automobile sweepstakes.

However, huge hurdles complicated the reconversion process for established producers. Virtually nothing about conducting business in Detroit in the postwar period would be normal, if any such state of affairs could even be imagined by auto executives. Seasoned automakers were having enough difficulty adjusting to postwar conditions. For newcomers to the industry, the obstacles were daunting.

Unfortunately, voracious demand for consumer goods, the reality of a thriving black-market economy, and the gradual collapse of wartime price controls fueled rampant inflation within weeks of V-J Day. In 1945 and 1946, the OPA was desperately trying to maintain artificially low prices for enormous varieties of consumer products. The agency's well-intentioned but doomed efforts satisfied nobody and alienated almost everybody. Producers and many consumers considered the OPA a meddling, unnecessary bureaucracy that was impeding postwar recovery; it did not long survive the end of the war.

Patriotic Americans who followed the rules looked like suckers. To innocent observers, the marketplace seemed to be controlled by the sharp operators who brazenly cut corners and casually flaunted laws. Less-principled consumers scrambled after small amounts of expensive goods, many of them acquired through black-market dealings, and inflation quickly hit double digits. Within five years, Detroit would begin regularly cranking out 5 or 6 million units each year; but, to impatient consumers in 1945 and 1946, the wait seemed excruciating, interminable. Production of passenger vehicles increased from under 84,000 in 1945 to 1.8 million in 1946; a year later, total output almost doubled again to 3.4 million. The latter figure was barely enough to satisfy demand.

THE WORLD OF AUTOWORKERS

Given the chronic labor unrest on shop floors of most of the major automobile producers in the late 1940s, it is remarkable that Detroit increased output so rapidly. Among the nation's heavy industries, automobile manufacturers had ranked close to the bottom in terms of employee satisfaction almost from the very beginning. The reasons were not difficult to understand. The work itself was generally demanding and stressful. Once Henry Ford installed his vaunted assembly line and began production of Model Ts at his new Highland Park plant in 1908, workers on the line were subjected to constant "speedups." The work environment was noisy, dirty, and sometimes dangerous. The tasks were repetitive and boring. The typical worker on the line performed the same simple task several times a minute. The work required little if any thought, but the pace was quick and relentless. In the late 1930s, Detroit pastor Reinhold Niebuhr visited an assembly line in his parish and was appalled: "The heat was terrific. The men seemed weary. Here manual labor is a drudgery and toil is slavery. The men cannot possibly find any satisfaction in their work. Their sweat and their dull pain are part of the price paid for the fine cars we run."

The assembly line also aged men fast. Straw bosses doing the hiring preferred young men from their late teens into their midthirties. After that, physical stamina diminished and reflexes slowed. In slack times, more than a few fathers in their early forties found themselves out of jobs and on the streets while their sons labored on inside the gates.

The roots of Detroit's labor mess, which had been festering for decades, deserve close examination, because, both directly and indirectly, they profoundly affected evolution of the postwar car culture. In earlier years, Henry Ford had briefly appeared to be the savior of the working man. Ford had instituted the $5 day in 1914, which effectively doubled the average worker's paycheck. Not only that, but Ford cut the length of the work day by two full hours! At the time, Ford's initiative created a sensation, and workers stormed the gates seeking admission into Ford's mysterious domain. Rival producers, stung initially by the loss of some of their best employees to Ford, had called him a "traitor to his class."

Ford's initially benign image quickly faded. Inflation promptly ate up the temporary advantages of the $5 daily wage. More important, Ford's apparent magnanimity had a dark side. He was a rigid autocrat, who demanded conformity from those who benefited from such generous wages. Ford established modestly priced company housing, then sent investigators from his so-called "Sociology Department" to check up on whether or not workers were conducting themselves in ways the boss would approve. As automobile historian James Flink noted, company snoops "visited workers' homes gathering information and giving advice on the intimate details of the family budget, diet, living arrangements, recreation, social outlook, and morality. Ford did not like the common practice among many immigrants of taking in boarders to help pay their rents. Americanization of the immigrant was enforced through mandatory classes in English." Workers who resisted such interference soon found themselves either on probation or back out on the street. By today's standards, such involvement in employees' lives away from work appears incredibly paternalistic and repressive. However, as Flink put it, in the early twentieth century, such policies ". . . reflected . . . long-standing assumption of American businessmen that the employer had a right to interfere with the private lives of his employees. . . ."

Ford's motives for instituting the $5 day were a weird mixture of sincere generosity and cynical self-interest. Part of Ford's genius was that he instinctively understood that, if automobiles were to be mass produced, they had to be marketed not just to comfortably fixed professionals but to virtually anyone who was steadily employed. Unlike rival producers, he grasped the fundamental fact that workers would identify more closely with their tasks if they could afford the products they were making. However, Ford's deepest motive may have been to thwart efforts to unionize the Highland Park plant.

By World War I, the American Federation of Labor (AF of L) had finally penetrated many industries employing large numbers of skilled workers. Although the United Mine Workers and American Railway Union had established shaky toeholds in these heavy industries, the workers' tasks were also mostly skilled. Most industries using large numbers of unskilled workers were still unorganized. Henry Ford and his major rivals at General Motors and Chrysler were determined to maintain the status quo.

Management dominated workers in the automobile industry through the 1920s and deep into the 1930s. Changing social and economic times, however, finally caught up with Ford and the rest of Detroit's "gasoline aristocracy." Ironically, the Great Depression, which resulted in prolonged unemployment for millions of Americans, set the stage for revival of organizing activities in the nation's heavy industries, including automobiles. Under the leadership of liberal Democrats, and with the approval of President Franklin D. Roosevelt, Congress passed several laws authorizing workers to create their own bargaining units, which companies had to recognize. Subjected to a barrage of lawsuits from conservative businessmen, legal language had to be refined. However, the significant kinks in federal legislation were worked out between 1935 and 1937, allowing the newly formed United Auto Workers (UAW) union to begin organizing in Detroit.

In the mid-1930s, Ford, Chrysler, and General Motors may have been competing ferociously in the sickly market for new cars, but they stood shoulder to shoulder in their determination to ward off union organization. At Ford, Harry Bennett's "spotters" on the shop floor were constantly on the lookout for union organizers. Some suspicious foremen even prohibited conversation between workers on the assembly lines, fearful that they could be talking union. Cynical workers perfected what they called the "Ford whisper," by which they could converse quietly while barely moving their lips. On balance, it is difficult to escape the conclusion that, deep down, Ford felt contempt for his workers. Biographer Keith Sward observed that Ford publicly stated that most jobs in his plants held no appeal for "men with brains." They would be suitable only for the "majority of minds" who are blessed by nature to take the "drudgery of mass production and like it." At General Motors, management spent nearly $1 million in 1934 and 1935 to fund wiretappers and infiltrators. In the minds of some, repression at GM even outdid that at Ford. Senator Robert La Follette's investigating committee later condemned GM's tactics as "a far-flung industrial Cheka . . . the most colossal supersystem of spies yet devised in any American corporation."

However, by the late 1930s, management faced formidable opponents. Union organizers, led by the brilliant Reuther brothers, Walter and Victor, were determined to rectify what they considered inhuman working conditions in the auto plants. However, they sensed that publicly announced mass walkouts would permit management to organize effective countermeasures. Hence, they decided on a surprise preemptive challenge to management's control of the assembly lines. They ordered workers to occupy the work space, sit down, and refuse to budge. In a word, they took control of the plant. And there they stayed, week after week. Workers occupying the plant received food, fuel, and other necessities thanks to deliveries from family members and other sympathizers. If management tried to interfere with these supply chains, they confronted angry, menacing pickets, many of them women. Public opinion was overwhelmingly on the workers' side, and pressure against management mounted daily. They were desperate to get production rolling again. On February 11, 1937, after a forty-four-day standoff, GM capitulated and formally recognized the UAW. There were some important secondary issues, but legitimization of the union was by far management's biggest concession.

General Motors had surrendered, but over at Ford, the old man, Harry Bennett, and other hardened managers snorted in disgust; they were damned if they would cave in so easily. It turned out that they had several months to prepare their strategy. Big Labor had many other battles to fight in the early months of 1937, including organizing the steel industry. However, challenging Ford was never far from the minds of union leaders. On May 26, 1937, UAW organizers, including Walter Reuther, tried to distribute handbills to workers crossing an overpass to enter the company's huge River Rouge plant, which had been built in Dearborn in the mid-1920s. Their reward was bloody beatings by Bennett's goons; they even roughed up two females badly, one of whom vomited blood. Fortunately for the union men, photographers recorded the one-sided violence and published the dramatic evidence in several of Henry Luce's national magazines. Henry Ford retaliated by pulling all company advertisements from Luce's publications for the next year and a half, but the damage was done. The family's enterprise suffered a grievous blow to its public image, which it did not repair until Ford's grandson, Henry II, took over the corporate reins in 1948.

Despite Edsel Ford's anguished pleas with his father to enter the modern age and recognize the UAW, the elder Ford, Bennett, and their minions were still determined to defy Big Labor, and they managed to hold out for four more years. Bennett's men were particularly creative in suppressing union organizers. In one case, a suspected union representative had a spotless work record. Foremen could not work up a rationale to fire him; so one of Bennett's thugs spilled a pail or two of nails and oil at his workstation, whereupon the alerted foreman fired him on the spot for "keeping dirty floors." A more common tactic was deliberately provoking fights with suspected union men, then discharging them for fighting on company premises. On occasion, one of Bennett's men might casually brush against a target right before quitting time and drop a small tool into his bib pocket. The unwitting target would then immediately be searched and just as quickly be fired for theft of company property.

However, Bennett's totalitarian tactics finally backfired. After he arbitrarily fired eight men on April 1, 1941, some 1,500 workers walked out. Once again, Walter Reuther and his associates rushed to River Rouge to assess the situation. By the time they arrived, the whole plant—50,000 workers—had struck. Although he had been diagnosed with stomach cancer and had just two more years to live, Edsel Ford once again bravely beseeched his father to listen to reason. The senior Ford finally agreed to an election to be supervised by the National Labor Relations Board (NLRB). The old man was devastated when only 2.5 percent of the workers voted against unionization. He angrily vowed to shut down the plant, only to be talked out of it by his wife, Clara.

The war years brought both opportunities and prosperity but also posed challenges to labor unions. On the plus side, the enormous demand for able-bodied workers translated into full employment, high wages, plenty of overtime, and rapidly expanding union enrollments. The UAW, for example, grew from 165,000 members in 1939 to 1,065,000 in 1944. Tens of thousands of workers from Appalachia and the Deep South, both white and African American, moved up from farms and cotton fields to jobs in the war plants in Detroit. However, there were drawbacks. Race relations during the war were explosive. White and African American workers competed for much of the same cramped, expensive housing and inadequate recreational facilities. Forced to live close together, members of both races felt stress. Nerves became frayed, and tempers grew short. Nationwide, there were several serious race riots during the war, including one in Detroit in 1943 that resulted in 35 deaths and more than 700 wounded. The high cost of living also created tensions among civilians. Although federal officials tried valiantly to control inflation, prices for many commodities moved steadily upward. The cost of living was far higher for workers in Detroit than in the communities they had left.

Despite uncomfortable living conditions and inflation, union leaders realized they needed to keep workers at their tasks. In the wartime emergency, the American public was extremely angered by any work stoppages. Shortly after Pearl Harbor, leaders of both the AF of L and the CIO had signed a No-Strike Pledge, and, for all intents and purposes, the UAW lost its most powerful weapon. What incentive did management have to negotiate in good faith with the workers?

Some work stoppages occurred during the war, most noticeably a 1943 coal strike that culminated in a spectacular public showdown between United Mine Workers (UMW) chief John L. Lewis and President Roosevelt. For the most part, though, union leaders kept their word. However, by late 1944 and early 1945, as Allied victory appeared increasingly certain, union leaders geared up for the battle that they sensed was inevitable. For workers in the auto plants, the end of the war threatened the elimination of overtime and a potential cut of about 30 percent in take-home pay. Rising prices were already hurting many workers, and union leaders were under intense pressure to negotiate big raises in hourly pay. For management, the end of the war meant an end to the lucrative cost-plus contracts that had guaranteed fat profits. Given the fact that millions of GIs would be returning to seek jobs in the civilian sector, management was just as determined to hold the line on hourly wages.

By V-J Day, the stage was set for labor wars across the nation's industrial landscape, and nowhere was the situation more volatile than in Detroit. At GM, Ford, and Chrysler, managers were determined to take back control of the shop floor from union representatives and what they considered their increasingly unreasonable, arrogant, and confrontational grievance committees. In late 1945 and early 1946, massive strikes occurred in several big industries. The UAW initiated the strike season by calling workers out at General Motors on November 21, 1945. In response to GM's claims that UAW demands for wage increases were inflationary and a threat to the company's continued viability, Reuther and his associates challenged management to "open the books" not just to union officials but to the public. Flabbergasted executives at GM sputtered that they did not even let stockholders look at the books! Early in 1946, President Truman intervened personally in the UAW strike. He summoned both management representatives and labor leaders to the White House. Eventually, both sides won some of their demands. After extended dickering, Reuther won an 18.5-cents-per-hour hike in pay. Corporate officials received concessions in the form of union agreements to allow them more latitude in setting production quotas and standards and to discipline workers who violated labor contracts.

THE POSTWAR YEARS OF THE CAR CULTURE

A number of historians have argued persuasively that during the late 1940s and 1950s industrial workers lost much of their militancy and joined the burgeoning American middle class. The postwar economic boom meant steady work and higher wages. In effect, material abundance largely co-opted industrial workers' class consciousness and blurred the economic—if not the social—distinctions between themselves and lower-level managers. Workers moved to modest homes in blue-collar suburbs; bought televisions, second automobiles, and washer-and-dryer sets; and even began sending their children to state colleges. Yet the immediate postwar years also brought enormous challenges to union leaders simply to hold onto their wartime gains, let alone grow and prosper.

After a decade of Democrats controlling the federal government, public sentiment began to swing toward the Republicans, beginning with the congressional elections in 1942. In the postwar period, Republicans were determined to reinforce the shifting momentum. They were particularly anxious to reverse Democratic initiatives that had facilitated the emergence of large industrial unions. One of the Republicans' most important victories was passage of the Taft-Hartley Act in 1947. This epochal law, passed over Truman's emphatic veto, significantly reduced the power of unions. It was a complicated law, but union officials were most disturbed that it enhanced the likelihood of government injunctions against strikes, provided for lengthy cooling-off periods before unions could strike, and effectively outlawed the closed shop, in which workers in an organized plant were forced to join the union. Unions had always opposed situations in which workers could enjoy union wages without joining and paying dues to the organization that created their benefits. In addition, even before Wisconsin Senator Joseph McCarthy began his notorious witch hunts—raucous and highly publicized efforts to ferret out "known" Communists in the military, the State Department, and other vital American institutions—conservatives had successfully linked Communists and assorted radicals and "pinkos" (persons suspected of being sympathetic to Communism) with labor unions. The leadership cores of a few unions were indeed dominated or heavily influenced by Communists. During the immediate postwar years, conservatives effectively used a handful of sensational exposes as a public relations weapon against unions in general.

These developments affected the automobile industry, directly and indirectly, in the short run and over the long haul. What annoyed impatient automobile purchasers most was that these developments slowed production. As late as the spring of 1948, three years after V-E Day, consumers still had to pay "premiums" of $500 to $700 to avoid long waits for the most popular GM models. What's more, with a handful of exceptions, the early postwar offerings were warmed-over 1941 or 1942 models: bulbous, ponderous, generally unexciting. There were a few innovations. In 1945, Studebaker introduced its "Champion" series, designed by Richard Loewy. People either loved or hated these unique models, which were quite streamlined and had a bullet-shaped nose. Enthusiasts claimed that they were ahead of their time. Smirking critics said they looked like submarines and that you could not tell if they were going forward or backward. However, Studebaker managed to triple its sales between 1946 and 1949 from 58,051 to just under 200,000 units.

Nevertheless, the immediate postwar years saw few startling innovations in automobile design. Automakers concentrated on production itself rather than research and development for the simple reason that, at the time, consumers had little choice but to accept anything that moved. In subsequent decades, consumers would prove to be far more demanding and fickle. Old-timers in the industry would look back upon the "seller's market" conditions of the immediate postwar years with deep fondness. Obviously, the big achievement within the industry during those years was finally catching up to enormous consumer demand. By 1950, the automobile industry had not only recovered from Depression-era doldrums, the rechanneling of its efforts during World War II, and the complexities of reconversion to serve civilian needs but was also entering new uncharted territory in terms of production records. At midcentury, the domestic industry set an all-time record in churning out 6.6 million passenger vehicles alone, a figure the industry would match or exceed with regularity during the 1950s. This represented an almost eightyfold increase from production figures of 1945.

The transformation of the automobile industry in the half decade between 1945 and 1950 had been remarkable. Having been in the doldrums or under close government regulation for nearly a generation, by the summer of 1945 the domestic automobile industry desperately needed a shake-up. Some companies were in much better shape than others. For example, GM was blessed with a coherent managerial structure and had modern business systems in place.

FORD MOTOR COMPANY: ADMINISTRATIVE DARK AGES

However, it would have been hard to imagine a more dispirited, moribund operation than Ford Motor Company. Virtually unchallenged as the world's leading automaker just twenty years earlier, by 1945 Ford had fallen to a distant third among the "Big Three" producers in both leadership and profits. During the Depression, patriarch and founder

Henry Ford had become increasingly rigid, irrational, and paranoid. His business decisions, once brilliant, even visionary, bordered on the bizarre, and corporate fortunes were spiraling downward. In 1937, for example, GM sold $1.6 billion worth of cars and earned $196 million; Chrysler earned $51 million on sales of $770 million; Ford sold $848 million in merchandise, yet earned just $7 million!

Nothing was more symptomatic of corporate ills than Ford's lack of any coherent managerial system. Harry Bennett had achieved stifling influence over the direction of corporate affairs. In the words of one biographer, Bennett had, for all intents and purposes, become the senior Ford's Svengali: "He served Ford all this while in the multiple capacity of friend, advisor, spokesman, confidante, strategist, hiring agent, chief of personnel, production whip, political intermediary, informer, personal body attendant, captain of the guards, commander of the household troops, and, in a figurative sense, as prince regent and lord high executioner."

For years, Bennett engaged in a test of wills with Henry's son Edsel, who was dutiful and loyal and a fine automobile executive in his own right. Edsel had in fact been a driving force behind Ford's reluctant decision in 1927 finally to abandon the Model T and concentrate on the Model A (a choice both correct and long overdue). For a variety of puzzling reasons, the founder simply could not give his son free rein. As Edsel once lamented, he had all the responsibility but almost no authority. At wife Clara's insistence, Ford finally turned over the presidency of the company to Edsel; but, in hindsight, the decision may have shortened Edsel's life. With Bennett's connivance, the senior Ford systematically undermined his son's authority by countermanding his orders, reinstating ineffective or troublesome men Edsel had fired, and by committing countless other thoughtless—even cruel—acts. By several accounts, it was failure to win his father's approval and trust that drove Edsel to an early death in 1943.

By then, Bennett and his hired thugs, many employed in the euphemistically named Ford "Service Department," had long since gained near dictatorial control of the troubled company. There was no identifiable managerial hierarchy; decisions seemingly depended upon who had final access to Henry Ford himself. The old man had little grasp of and inherently distrusted the world of high finance. Incredulous auditors later discovered that he had millions of dollars squirreled away in non-interest-yielding checking accounts in banks scattered all across the Midwest. Ford insisted on paying workers in cash; allegedly, he had tried using checks once, but he was disgusted to discover that some workers had cashed them in bars and even whorehouses. He never explained how paying wages in cash would magically transform workers' morals. One newcomer in the managerial ranks, trying to get figures that would permit even the most rudimentary cost projections, discovered that old-fashioned bookkeepers kept piles of bills up to four feet high on their desks. They allegedly made rough estimates of accounts payable by measuring heights of piles with yardsticks! As one pair of historians aptly noted, "It was some sort of administrative Dark Ages."

Wartime contracts essentially resuscitated a dying company and kept the coffers reasonably full, but a reckoning was long overdue in 1945. Although he had shown little promise of being anything more than one more rich playboy at Yale in the 1930s, by the end of World War II, Edsel's son Henry Ford II had matured considerably. Young Ford was determined to gain control of the company and restore a sense of order and family control. With the support of his mother's 41 percent of family-owned shares, the twenty-eight-year-old heir took over the company's presidency in the fall of 1945. One of his first acts was to fire Bennett. Soon thereafter, Bennett's goons were likewise stricken from the payroll. When young Ford took over, it seemed that the company's fortunes could not get much worse. In 1946, Ford sold a total of less than 400,000 units. GM almost matched that figure in its Chevrolet Division alone with 329,601 cars sold. Ford did not know it yet, but better times for the company were ahead.

A REVITALIZED INDUSTRY

Few Americans outside of Detroit cared about the industry's labor and managerial problems. What consumers wanted was new cars, and they wanted them now! With hundreds of millions of dollars to be earned in providing cars for eager customers, several new players entered the automobile sweepstakes. Some possessed little but dreams and fiery imaginations. In 1945, outsider Preston Tucker galvanized public attention by announcing a revolutionary new model called the "Tucker Torpedo." The dazzling new offering would have a rear engine, a streamlined and low-slung body, a "Cyclops" third headlight over the middle of the front grill, and sporty fenders that turned with the wheel. This would supposedly redirect light more quickly in the direction the car was turning. The driver would sit in the middle of the front seat. Advanced safety features included disc brakes; seat belts; and a padded, crash-proof interior. With generous amounts of aluminum and plastic, the vehicle, according to Tucker, would weigh less than a ton and the promised marvel would be priced at under

Preston Tucker was one of several would-be entrants in the American automobile manufacturing derby in the immediate post-war years. His revolutionary designs captured the public's imagination. Unfortunately, economic realities soon caught up with him. Only four dozen hand-built 1948 model Tuckers were built.

$1,000! Not surprisingly, the audacious upstart generated a good deal of publicity in the early postwar years.

With neither capital nor collateral, Tucker somehow managed to lease a huge former airplane plant in Chicago from the government containing some $100 million worth of machinery. A rental deposit of $1 million would conveniently be postponed until he could sell stock and raise capital. Unfortunately, Tucker's dream collapsed almost as quickly as it emerged. Engineering problems and economic realities forced him to modify many of his most revolutionary design features. The Chicago plant only turned out about four dozen vehicles, all hand-crafted, and they did not arrive until 1948. By then, the Torpedo sports car had become the Tucker 48 sedan. It was no longer an economy car, as its price had mushroomed to over $2,300, placing it in the upper-middle price range. Within a year of offering his first shares, Tucker was under investigation by the Securities and Exchange Commission (SEC). He was eventually indicted on two dozen counts of mail fraud. Some of Tucker's most ardent supporters claimed that the charges were bogus, that they had been conjured up by rivals in the automobile business who were petrified at the potential threat Tucker symbolized. Although acquitted, he had obviously failed to produce enough automobiles when consumers demanded them, and his dream died.

Henry J. Kaiser and Joe Frazer mounted a more serious challenge to the Big Three producers. During the war, shipbuilder Kaiser, dubbed by some journalists as "Sir Launchalot," the nation's number one industrial production hero, voiced vague rumblings about building a postwar automobile for "everyman," priced at $400. Not surprisingly, industry insiders scoffed, dismissing Kaiser as an entrepreneurial "wanna be," who succeeded only when underwritten by huge federal contracts. These insiders had a point, since government contracts were critical in all of Kaiser's big projects. However, his partner, Joe Frazer, was an experienced and generally respected auto man with thirty years in the business, including stints in charge of Willys-Overland and, later, Graham Paige. The two men announced a partnership shortly before V-J Day. Kaiser had earned a national reputation as a road and dam builder, and later as a production genius, getting brand new operations up and running smoothly and quickly turning out huge volumes of ships, cement, magnesium, and steel. However, he knew nothing about producing cars. All he had were drawings of several somewhat innovative automobile concepts and dreams of challenging the Big Three. Frazer managed to convince his irrepressible partner that in order to exploit the enormous consumer demand that existed right after the war, they should concentrate on getting conventional models into production immediately; if conditions warranted, they could consider more experimental, futuristic models later on. This was one of the few contests of wills between the two men that Frazer won.

Once agreed on a strategy, they moved quickly. Within weeks, they had signed a long-term lease to take over Henry Ford's huge wartime plant at Willow Run. They could not turn out cars in 1945, but early in 1946 they introduced two new models, named the "Kaiser" and the "Frazer," at a spectacular extravaganza at New York's Waldorf-Astoria. Over four days, some 156,000 potential customers braved long lines to get glimpses of the new offerings. Even though they were not yet into production, salesmen took orders for 9,000 cars. Although some industry analysts doubted that the company would ever produce a single car, the ebullient Kaiser chirruped that they already had orders for 600,000 units and predicted that they would eventually produce 13 million vehicles. In the euphoria of the moment, nobody challenged his figures, which he had clearly pulled out of thin air; Kaiser-Frazer stock quickly surged to its all-time high of $24 per share.

Kaiser-Frazer produced 11,754 vehicles in 1946, losing some $19 million on just $10 million in net sales. In 1947 and 1948, however, the company entered the lists of major producers, passing older, more prestigious companies such as Packard and Hudson Motors and assuming, briefly, the number four position in total automobile output. In 1947 the company produced 144,507 cars, then topped that with 181,318 units in 1948, earning profits both years. That was the high-water mark. Thereafter, Kaiser-Frazer sales quickly tapered off. The major reason was that the company simply was not large enough to commit the tens of millions of dollars into product design and development that the Big Three did. In later years, Kaiser admitted that their biggest mistake was being undercapitalized; the partners raised only $53 million in their initial stock offering, when experienced underwriters estimated that they might have raised at least four times that much. As long as the automobile industry enjoyed a seller's market and buyers basically had to accept anything offered, Kaiser-Frazer did well. However, by the end of 1948, the Big Three were churning out millions of units each year, and supply had finally caught up to demand. Kaisers and Frazers were dependable and boasted some advanced safety features, but they were under-powered and decidedly stodgy. Consumer tastes had clearly passed them by. The company would limp along until the mid-1950s, when it transferred most of its operations to Argentina.

CHANGES IN DESIGN

The late 1940s and early 1950s brought revolutionary changes to the automobile industry, most noticeably in design. Henry Ford II had fired most of Harry Bennett's drones, replacing them early in 1946 with bright, energetic young men with new ideas, who were quickly dubbed the "Whiz Kids." These included Charles B. "Tex" Thornton, a statistician and a dynamic officer in the War Department, who in turn recruited some of his most promising young officers to aid in the resuscitation of Ford: Jack Reith, Arjay Miller, J. Edward Lundy, future Secretary of Defense Robert S. McNamara, and others. In addition to shaking up or totally replacing senior management, the "Whiz Kids" finally introduced modern managerial systems into corporate headquarters. No longer would Ford hemorrhage millions of dollars annually due to lack of the types of information that competitors had at their fingertips. Ford would finally be able to compete effectively with GM and Chrysler. Equally important, Henry Ford II also invested $118 million into a crash program to replace the stodgy, upright, boring Ford models from the immediate postwar period. Between 1945 and 1948, the changes were quick and dramatic; the 1949 Ford Custom was crisply styled, sleek, and almost totally new from the axles up. Between 1948 and 1950, Ford more than doubled its sales, topping one million units in 1950 and earning a cumulative net income of $260 million. During this surge, Ford regained its position as number two producer, ahead of Chrysler. The elder Henry Ford did not live to see the revival of his creation, having died on April 7, 1947.

General Motors experienced no such overnight metamorphosis in its identity, but big changes took place there as well. The corporation waxed fat in the postwar years; after-tax income jumped from $87 million in 1946 to $656 million three years later. Still, corporate leaders were acutely aware of the changing marketplace of midcentury. Their design "savior" was chief stylist Harley Earl, who had been smitten by the appearance of the Lockheed P-38 fighter plane, which had twin engines and . . . tail fins! Earl essentially reincarnated the P-38 tail fins in the 1948 Cadillac in the form of modest-sized bumps on the rear fenders. The positive public response was overwhelming, perhaps for reasons that were largely unconscious. By 1948, the postwar economic boom had been gaining momentum for three years; many Americans were finally persuaded that the Depression really was over, not soon to return, if ever. Americans may have *said* that they wanted safe, dependable, economical cars that would last for ten years. However, their buying decisions belied their words. After years of self-denial, after a generation of settling for economical, "practical" transportation, American consumers finally felt secure enough economically, free to indulge their material fantasies. Tail fins epitomized conspicuous consumption. Harley Earl was the right man at the right place at precisely the right time. He was aptly nicknamed the "Cellini of Chrome."

In recent years, some critics of the industry have suggested that postwar American automakers essentially forced large cars on a spineless, malleable public, but this simply was not the case. In fact, numerous producers offered a variety of alternatives, ranging from economical to merely comical. Even before the war, Powel Crosley Jr., an appliance and radio mogul and owner of the Cincinnati Reds, was determined to produce the nation's least-expensive automobile. In 1939, he marketed just over 2,000 small, 4-wheeled, 2-door units priced as astonishingly low as $210. Crosley accomplished this in part by eliminating "frills." He had no dealership organization; instead, buyers had to arrange for delivery at local hardware stores. Crosley continued production in 1940 and 1941, turning out approximately 2,700 units each year. He expanded his offerings to five models, priced between $413 and $581. In the early months of 1942, he built another 1,029 cars before the federal government shut down automobile production for the duration of the war.

Like many other auto men, Crosley had high hopes for the postwar period. Although he did not get back into production until June, 1946, his first postwar entry was a 4-door sedan priced at $905. Inflation and the high cost of materials had eroded his dream of offering a car far below the cost of competitors' models; but, in an era when anything on wheels would sell, he marketed 5,000 cars. When he managed to lower prices for most models by $100 or so, Crosley did even better in 1947, selling 19,000 units. Like Kaiser-Frazer, Crosley's high-water mark was in 1948, when he marketed 29,000 cars. As had been the case with Kaiser-Frazer, American consumers would accept Crosleys when they had little or no choice. However, when normal market conditions returned by late 1948, the handwriting was on the wall. Sales tapered off drastically, and Crosley closed his doors in 1952.

Other efforts to market "compact" cars occured right after the war. Having trumpeted his dream of a $400 car for "everyman" during the war, Henry J. Kaiser had originally hoped to lead a new generation of American consumers into the kingdom of small cars. Even when producing his bulbous, underpowered, conventional-sized sedans in the immediate postwar period, he never abandoned that idea. In 1949, with his older son Edgar at his side, Kaiser proudly unveiled the "Henry J" (corporate executives had toyed with the name *Mustang*), a diminutive, two-door sedan supposedly capable of seating five adults. Five dwarfs was more like it. Totally devoid of frills, it sported no chrome, no radio, not even a clock. Industry observers were generally unimpressed. As one put it, the Henry J was "a relatively small, stubby, poorly furnished, easily rusted fastback with ludicrous nubs of tail fins. . . ." Other than fuel economy, its only other attraction was price, as it sold for under $1,200. Still, the Henry J did better than the Crosley. Americans purchased 124,871 Henry Js over its four-year production span from 1949 to 1953.

There were other aborted efforts to market even smaller cars. In 1954, with typical hoopla, Nash Motors introduced yet another miniature car, the "Metropolitan." Like most of its economical and "practical" predecessors, it failed to generate a sizable following. Although it remained in production longer than the Henry J, from 1954 until 1962, Nash sold just under 95,000 Metropolitans, with 22,209 leaving showroom floors in its best year, 1959. A number of foreign manufacturers tried, with almost no success, to interest American consumers in small, economical vehicles: Fiat, Morris-Minor, and other producers offered cars whose features generated mostly yawns from American consumers. The smallest, and in some ways one of the most intriguing, was a three-wheeled Italian import called the "Isetta," which elicited mostly giggles when seen on America's streets and highways. Some observers claimed that it looked like an upright egg on wheels. It sported a tiny engine, either 250 or 300 cc, depending on model choice. Two wheels were in front, one in back. The driver had to use a left-handed gear shift, and the car's single door opened from the front of the vehicle. It seated two adults uncomfortably. The Isetta allegedly boasted a top speed of fifty to fifty-five miles per hour, although anything over forty or forty-five felt unsafe. The tiny engine delivered fuel economy of sixty miles per gallon. Realistically, it was satisfactory, even handy, for errands around town on city streets. On the open road, it would be a death trap. Americans adopted them by the hundreds; they were curiosities only. Another brand that failed to make a big impact at midcentury was Adolph Hitler's pride and joy, the Volkswagen. The German company exported its first "Beetles" to the United States in 1949: exactly *two* units! Not until Chevrolet introduced the Corvair and Ford countered with the Falcon in 1960—largely in response to increasing numbers of foreign imports and growing public acceptance of the Volkswagen in the late 1950s—would small cars generate any serious following in the United States. In 1961, Americans purchased 177,000 Volkswagens. Even so, these numbers paled compared with 1.6 million Chevrolets and 1.3 million Fords.

Clearly, Americans were not yet ready to consider seriously small, economical vehicles. Why should they? At three to four gallons per dollar, gas was cheap. Hardly anyone was even aware of—let alone concerned over—potential energy shortages or environmental damage caused by auto emissions. If they thought about it at all, typical midcentury American consumers assumed that petroleum reserves even in the United States were unlimited. At the time, the nation was still *exporting* millions of gallons of crude oil and refined products to other nations! Sophisticated oil men, of course, realized the long-term strategic importance of Middle Eastern oil, but even they underestimated future challenges. Most of them took the comfortable view that while the Middle East might occasionally be politically unstable, reasonably evenhanded treatment of various Arab states should ensure the continued flow of cheap energy to the United States for the foreseeable future.

Chapter Three

THE AUTOMOBILE, SUBURBIA, AND THE RESHAPING OF AMERICAN LANDSCAPES

From the perspective of the early twenty-first century, it is clear that automobility and suburbanization were closely linked from the very beginning. However, the profound shaping effect of their symbiotic connection was not plainly obvious until after World War II. As noted earlier, the first suburbs preceded the automobile, emerging initially alongside steam rail routes, then electric trolley lines. This meant that early corridor-like suburban development spread out from urban centers like very slender fingers from the palm of a hand, with large, undeveloped tracts of land between the lines. However, as increasing numbers of Americans adopted the automobile, huge amounts of land between the trolley lines became increasingly accessible—and valuable. By the end of World War I, providing access to streetcar service became less important to suburban developers than improving streets and highways. This chapter briefly traces the postwar decline in mass transit and the rapid development of suburbs. The automobile played crucial roles in both. These phenomena also had important ramifications for race relations in the United States. The emerging suburban culture became majority America.

THE DECLINE OF MASS TRANSIT

As automobile usage expanded and suburban development of land remote from trolley tracks surged, mass transit patronage flattened out and then declined, at first gradually and later precipitously. From its

DuPont corporation ad from 1943 selling the futuristic concept of postwar helicopters for the average American household: Some major American corporations oversold the idea that ordinary Americans would enjoy virtually unlimited personal mobility soon after the end of World War II. Executives of General Motors and Ford worried that such utopian visions were creating wholly unrealistic expectations and that they would reap a harvest of consumer resentment when they failed to deliver millions of personal planes and helicopters. Nobody, it seemed, even thought about regulation of air space over American cities.

beginnings in the nineteenth century, mass transit patronage grew steadily in an almost uninterrupted pattern until 1926, when Americans took 17.3 billion rides. Thereafter, patronage eroded slowly until 1940, with 13.1 billion passengers. The decline might have been even more precipitous had mass transit companies not replaced many streetcar lines with bus service. During World War II and immediately after, broken-down automobiles, combined with rubber and gasoline rationing, forced many reluctant Americans back onto streetcars and busses. In 1946, ridership on all forms of mass transit spiked back upward to its all-time high of 23.5 billion.

Some transit officials deluded themselves into believing that they had turned the corner, that public transit was headed toward a bright, new future. In hindsight, their optimism was clearly wishful thinking. By the mid-1940s, most transit companies were extremely vulnerable. For the most part, their equipment was decrepit; some of it antedated the First World War. Equally worrisome, very few investors were willing to underwrite modernization of mass transit companies; there were simply too many more attractive avenues for investment capital after the war. The long-term outcomes in decline of local mass transit systems were as similar as they were predictable. In one American city after another in the late 1940s and early 1950s, privately owned mass transit companies were forced into the often reluctant hands of municipal officials, who did little more than provide minimal service to the very young, the very old, and the very poor.

However, in the postwar years, the problems in the mass transit industry were becoming irrelevant to increasing numbers of Americans. They almost gleefully abandoned mass transportation at the first opportunity—just as soon as they picked up keys to their new cars. During the wartime emergency, they had been willing to "do their part" and ride in hot, stuffy mass transit vehicles, jammed with "foreigners" and others who perhaps did not practice the same levels of personal hygiene they did; but, with the return of peace, millions of Americans refused to put up with such cramped, unpleasant conditions any longer.

THE RISE OF SUBURBIA

The changing shape of metropolitan regions was another reason that mass transit shriveled. Among politicians, academics, social critics, and the general public, the "post–World War II suburb" has become a cliché. Listening to some commentators, the uninformed might even be led to believe that suburbs did not exist before the war. Although the suburban movement in the United States dates back at least to the early nineteenth century, and there is solid evidence that it was a dominant force in the reshaping of the nation's metropolitan landscapes well before the war, almost all contemporary commentators cite the postwar decades from the mid-1940s through the 1960s as the defining period in the emergence of a national suburban culture. In this quarter century, the suburb became the crucible in which many emerging, dominant, modern trends in American life were shaped.

As noted earlier, Franklin Roosevelt's New Deal had created an environment that encouraged suburban development. Although the New Deal financed programs that directly benefited urban dwellers, ranging from direct relief for destitute families to support for various practitioners of the fine arts, they were less supportive of initiatives that would physically transform the urban landscape. To the casual observer, it might have seemed that New Dealers were as much or even more concerned about encouraging improved living conditions in the inner cities as in outlying areas. Highly publicized slum clearance projects existed in a few cities, but they did not exert a major effect on the nation's urban infrastructure. By 1941, the United States Housing Authority had approved housing projects totaling 130,000 units nationwide.

The federal government might have built more except for intense opposition from private home builders' pressure groups and lobbyists, who branded such programs "creeping socialism." While the raw figures appear impressive, they paled beside the commitments by governments of other Western democracies to high-density urban housing for economically disadvantaged citizens. Public housing quickly became associated with racial minorities in the public mind, and most Americans resisted any thought of such developments in suburbs. Almost all of the projects were confined to the inner cities; and, therefore, they exerted comparatively little influence reshaping the urban landscape—or transportation patterns.

Other New Deal programs overtly encouraged the construction of single-family homes and, indirectly, the expansion of suburbs. In June 1934, the Federal Housing Administration (FHA) was created "to encourage improvement in housing standards and conditions, to facilitate sound home financing on reasonable terms, and to exert a stabilizing influence on the mortgage market."

The FHA and succeeding legislation profoundly influenced patterns of home ownership in the nation and the shaping of the metropolitan landscape. FHA-backed loans were a boon to prospective buyers. Institutions administering these loans could lend more than 90 percent of the value of the property, which meant that potential buyers had to come up with 10 percent, or even less as a down payment. Equally important, the FHA guaranteed loans over periods—typically twenty-five or thirty years—that significantly lowered average monthly payments. The Depression and World War II sharply curtailed new home construction, but a long-term seismic shift in patterns of home ownership was under way. In 1934, 44 percent of American families owned their homes. By 1972, that figure had jumped to 63 percent.

As influential Americans began planning for reconversion in the postwar, the stage was set for the rapid expansion of suburbs. Millions of GIs had left wives and girlfriends living at home—many of them jammed into cold-water flats with in-laws or extended families. Therefore, it was hardly surprising that building a nation of suburban homes became one of the most cherished postwar goals for many powerful interest groups. The new homes would be built in open spaces on the fringes of cities. That's where private contractors wanted them. The land itself was cheaper. They were not required to tear down existing structures. In a word, they could build entire communities from scratch and do things their own way.

Ambitious politicians dreaming of long-term futures insured by loyal constituencies were particularly anxious to accommodate veterans. The GI Bill, passed overwhelmingly by Congress in 1944, allowed potential home buyers to finance the entire cost of their property and stretch payments out over twenty-five or even thirty years. Thus, they could often purchase new homes for less than they had paid in rent. As one delighted new suburban resident noted, "We had been paying $50 per month rent, and here we come up and live for $29 a month. That paid everything—taxes, principal, insurance on your mortgage, and interest." In part because public policy in the postwar period was so favorable to construction of new houses in suburbs, there was little construction of new housing in the inner cities.

There were, however, some undesirable side effects. FHA underwriters were specifically trained to deny loans on properties in areas considered "high risk" or "undesirable." Naturally, this meant that prospective buyers of homes in inner-city neighborhoods in transition—translation: racially mixed neighborhoods where minorities were becoming predominant—stood virtually no chance of receiving FHA or VA loans. Administrators worried that large sections of cities could lose investment value if segregation was not maintained. Banks and savings and loan institutions likewise institutionalized the practice of denying mortgages "solely because of the geographical location of the property." Public officials and private lenders essentially conspired to maintain *de facto* segregation. Such policies eliminated complications for both lenders and public officials; it seemed like good business. Some real estate developers flatly refused to sell to minorities. In addition, they often inserted clauses in purchase contracts enjoining new home buyers from ever selling their homes to nonwhites. Few whites bothered to comment or even notice such discrimination. Many white GIs had fought with African Americans, Native Americans, and Hispanics in Europe and the South Pacific. Others had liberated Auschwitz or one of Hitler's other nightmarish extermination camps. Yet, when they returned to the United States and resumed their civilian lives, many white veterans quickly and casually eased back into a world where segregation and injustice prevailed. They apparently perceived little irony in having fought a war to preserve freedom and democracy and then refusing to demand racial equality at home. In the brand new suburb of Levittown, New York, there was not a single African American. As home builder William Levitt rationalized, "We can solve a housing problem, or we can try to solve a racial problem. But we cannot combine the two."

The impact of cheap FHA loans on suburban development was swift and dramatic. The housing market after the war closely resembled the automobile market: it was seemingly insatiable. In 1944, there had been just 114,000 new single-family housing starts. Two years later, there were 937,000; and the figure almost doubled again to 1,692,000 in 1950. In response to enormous demands after the war, thousands of developers entered the housing sweepstakes. Some were strictly small time, building no more than a handful of homes, selling them, then using the proceeds to build a few more units. However, several individuals built on a massive scale. None were more influential than Abraham Levitt and his sons William and Alfred, who ultimately built 140,000 houses. During its first four decades, the FHA guaranteed $119 billion in home loans. Roughly 90 percent of the loans were for homes in suburbs. Virtually all new home construction underwritten by all federal loan programs occurred in suburbs, excluding inner cities.

In laying out new suburbs and expanding older ones after World War II, the availability or lack of public transportation was an irrelevant factor in the calculations of almost all developers. To be sure, a few builders offered housing within short distances of steam railway or electric interurban lines, assuming that the majority of buyers would commute by rail into downtown sections of large cities. However, these suburban developments were typically geared to the upper-middle classes, who owned automobiles that they used for virtually all of their other transportation needs. Many of them owned comfortable—

J. R. Eyerman/Time Pix #227497

This obviously posed scene conveys both the positive and negative aspects of Americans' massive collective movement toward suburbs at midcentury.

even luxurious—homes, often built on lots of an acre or more. The real and imagined trials and tribulations of the affluent suburban commuter became one of the staples of magazines such as the *New Yorker*, which clearly served an upper-middle-class readership.

THE CENTRALITY OF THE AUTOMOBILE

Virtually every aspect of suburban development assumed the centrality of the automobile. Family breadwinners might commute into jobs in inner cities via steam or electric rail lines, but their wives often drove them to the station and met their trains at night. All but the most modest-sized suburban homes built after the war included a garage, or at least a carport, either detached or permitting direct entry into the kitchen. One of the most important developments affecting postwar American culture was that, as automobile production mushroomed in the late 1940s and early 1950s, many families owned more than one automobile. Thanks in no small part to aggressive and highly manipulative advertising by the automobile industry, this generation of consumers began believing that they not only needed but also deserved virtually unlimited personal mobility. These critically important cultural phenomena had profound and lasting effects on changing American lifestyles. Increasing numbers of commuters drove to work, exacerbating crowded road conditions during rush hours. Equally important, many suburban housewives had their own cars, which became their primary means of mobility. As more and more children's activities became formally organized, such as Little League and Camp

Fire Girls, mothers increasingly found themselves acting as chauffeurs. In the words of one astute humorist and social critic, a suburban housewife's life "was motherhood on wheels, [delivering children] obstetrically once and by car forever after."

For many newcomers to postwar suburbs, daily life was very different from their former lives in inner cities. Virtually everything about the new suburbs assumed automobile ownership. In the old inner-city immigrant neighborhoods, stores and small shops had been within easy walking distance. Because many immigrant families did not own refrigerators or, at best, had ice boxes with very limited capacity, many housewives shopped daily for family necessities. For many women, shopping trips on foot, replete with casual opportunities to catch up on neighborhood gossip, constituted a crucial segment of their social lives. Much of this serendipitous intimacy vanished in the postwar automobile suburbs. In the new suburbs, shops were usually clustered some distance away from homes, often a mile or more. There was far less casual window shopping in the suburbs. Most consumers were task oriented and single minded; they wanted to shop quickly and efficiently. When they ran errands, they often visited several stores and professional services on a single trip. Store owners arranged their enterprises under the assumption that most, if not all, shoppers would arrive by automobile. This was one of the major shifts in emphasis in retailing after World War II. Although the roots of standardized, more impersonal supermarkets, large chain stores, and even shopping centers preceded the war, they came into their heyday after 1945.

THE SUBURBAN NIGHTMARE

Some observers questioned whether suburbs had any effect on amounts and varieties of human interaction. New communication technology rather than changing demographics of settlement might have exerted an even greater impact. Numerous social critics pointed out that, whereas residents in many urban and small town neighborhoods in the early twentieth century regularly congregated on front porches, inviting casual contacts with neighbors and friendly passers by, the postwar family focused inward, subconsciously seeking more privacy and family togetherness. Some blamed the automobile. As numbers of vehicles rapidly expanded, so did levels of noise and air pollution. Porch sitting simply became less pleasant. For children, playing in the street became for more dangerous. But an equally powerful factor may have been television. As television became widely available and programming slowly expanded, this medium became increasingly popular as home entertainment. After dinner, families started gathering around the television set rather than on the front porch. One of television's significant downsides was that it cut down on time spent in casual interaction with neighbors—and often even with other family members. One 1950 survey discovered that, in homes with television sets, the average junior-high-school student already logged twenty-seven hours per week watching it.

Some contemporary observers were appalled at the monotony and uniformity the Levitts and developers like them created. They derided nearly identical homes on postage-stamp-sized lots. Lewis Mumford, one of the nation's most respected social critics, criticized the Levitts' "new-fashioned methods to compound old-fashioned mistakes." Even worse, Mumford found the postwar suburban environment stifling:

> In the mass movement into suburban areas a new kind of community was produced, which caricatured both the historic city and the archetypal suburban refuge: a multitude of uniform, unidentifiable houses, lined up inflexibly, at uniform distances, on uniform roads, in a treeless communal waste, inhabited by people of the same class, the same income, the same age group, witnessing the same television performances, eating the same tasteless, pre-fabricated foods, from the same freezers, conforming in every outward and inward respect to a common mold, manufactured in the central metropolis. Thus, the ultimate effect of the suburban escape in our own time is, ironically, a low-grade, uniform environment from which escape is impossible.

Another critic, Paul Goldberger, called Levittown "an urban planning disaster."

There is, however, a hypocritical ring to some of these jeremiads; many elitist critics lambasted the emerging suburbs from the comfort of their expensive—or at least very comfortable—custom-built homes in older suburbs, or pricey co-ops on Boston's Beacon Hill, or the East Side of New York's Central Park. They chided suburbanites for being umbilically connected to station wagons, even as they themselves took numerous taxi rides weekly and had luxury vehicles parked in nearby garages, available for weekend getaways to the country. They refused to acknowledge that these allegedly tacky developments created massive amounts of critically needed housing for millions of deserving Americans. What the Levitts and other large-scale developers created might have been eyesores to a sophisticated and condescending elite, but the houses represented a huge upward move for millions of Americans who had been relegated to cramped cold-water flats before the war. As suburban historian Kenneth T. Jackson succinctly observed, the "early Levitt house was as basic to post World War II suburban development as the Model T had been to the automobile."

THE SUBURBAN DREAM

Millions of second- or third-generation immigrants had worked for years, searching for escapes from the noise, grit, and disorder of inner-city slums. While some contemporary social critics voice nostalgia regarding the so-called quaintness and charm of the old ethnic neighborhoods of sixty years ago, the plain truth of the matter is that millions of ethnic Americans enthusiastically bought into the suburban ideal. They longed to move to the more open spaces promised by suburban developers' brochures. They had visions of green grass for their children to romp over, white picket fences, and flower beds and gardens next to a brand new, snug home in the suburbs. The automobile helped them realize their dreams. In individual, human terms, many newcomers to Levittown—and hundreds of similar suburbs in the postwar years— considered themselves unbelievably fortunate. As one descendent of first-generation Levittowners recalled, it originally comprised

> . . . working-class people . . . salt of the earth type people who
> saw Levittown as their dream. My mother always told me that for all
> the drawbacks Levittown had culturally, she still couldn't believe
> she owned her own house. She came from a family that didn't have
> much money, and so did my father, and here they were in their own
> house. It was a miracle to them. They thought they would never live
> anywhere but an apartment. . . . I think they saw it through the
> eyes of someone who was in love almost. They had found
> something and they made it even better than it was.

Millions of ethnic Americans happily joined the throngs of their countrymen heading to the suburbs. The elites, it seemed, would have preferred ethnic Americans to remain out of sight and out of mind.

Imagine a hypothetical midcentury suburban couple, Allie and Carmen Martinelli. They were on a very different social scale from the elite social critics living in swank urban high-rises. Allie was the oldest son of an Italian immigrant cigar maker. He had grown up in a crowded tenement on New York's Lower East Side. As he inhaled the smell of wet, freshly cut grass a couple of hours after daybreak on a warming summer morning, the freshly minted suburbanite glanced fondly at his wife, Carmen, framed in the kitchen window. Allie then looked over at his year-old 1950 Ford Custom parked in the driveway

In his inimitable style, Norman Rockwell captured the vicissitudes of a summer's day auto trip to the lake in The Outing, *a 1947 Saturday Evening Post cover painting. Grandma made the round trip stoically.*

and reminisced about how lucky he was as a Marine infantryman to have survived vicious jungle fighting at Guadalcanal and Iwo Jima. Leaning on the handles of his mower, he also thought about how far he had come from the days of his youth, when he and his buddies found relief from the summer heat only by swimming in the stench of the East River. Allie recalled the constant fear he experienced running with the Italian gang, constantly fighting the Polish and Irish, and sometimes even roving to the edges of Harlem to fight the African American gangs. He was grateful to have escaped, and he was proud to be the first in his family to graduate from high school. Allie had a good paying job on an AT&T assembly line, with excellent union benefits. The company even provided two weeks paid vacation each year! This year, he might take the family on a trip by automobile to visit his brother Vinnie's family in Chicago. Allie's reverie was interrupted by Carmen calling him in to breakfast. He looked forward to some time with his ten-year-old son Joey, whom he would drive to his Little League game at noon. Little League! Some things about suburbia weren't so good. The kids only got two or three at bats in a typical game. Growing up playing stick ball on the Lower East Side, a kid could get forty or fifty at bats in an all-day game. That's how you became a real ballplayer! Allie had to laugh. Life out here was so different, but overall it was pretty good. So what if Carmen had put on a little weight and he often had fantasies about that blond named Alice Flaherty who lived two houses down? He had it better than he ever dreamed about. Carmen called out again that breakfast was getting cold. Allie snapped out of his trance. Time to get inside, wash up, and enjoy that pancake and bacon breakfast.

On balance, elitist condemnations of suburban life and how the automobile shaped it appear decidedly off the mark. The dynamics of family life in postwar America, particularly in the suburbs, were more complicated than facile stereotypes of the 1950s might suggest. The snobs in their uptown penthouses might sneer at the poor slob "out there" in the faceless suburbs, chained to the mind-numbing tasks of mowing, weeding, and otherwise tending his tenth-of-an-acre grounds surrounding his pitiful castle, but it was highly unlikely that the suburbanite felt sorry for himself. To a remarkable extent, the automobile had helped create these new opportunities for enjoying life.

How much has life in cities and suburbs really changed in the half century since the initial big postwar suburban boom? In 2002, many Americans take personal privacy for granted—at least in a limited way. Houses are bigger, and tall fences often block neighbors' views into each others' yards. Most children, at least in the suburbs, have their own rooms. Once they have finished their workdays, many Americans retreat to the isolation of their homes and turn on their television sets or log onto the Internet. For many contemporary Americans, meaningful interaction with neighbors is almost an alien concept. They may know their neighbors on a casual basis, perhaps exchanging honks and waves as they drive their daily rounds. Most significant friendships are with peers at work or with those sharing similar interests. Some social critics blame the automobile for an apparent decline in any sense of neighborhood cohesiveness. Yet this phenomenon may be even more a product of increasingly frenetic postindustrial lifestyles than a result of suburbanization or the long-term impact of the automobile.

Chapter Four

THE FABULOUS FIFTIES
AND THE SOARING SIXTIES

It would be difficult to identify a segment of American culture that was not affected by the unprecedented spread of the automobile in the 1950s and 1960s. Perhaps chamber orchestra performances were immune but certainly not the broader arena of American music! Between 1950 and 1970, the number of automobiles on American roads grew almost 250 percent, from just over 40 million to just under 90 million. By the end of the 1960s, one in seven working Americans earned his living in an automobile-related occupation. Mere numbers do not begin to provide a sense of the motor vehicle's profound cultural impact. In addition to influencing where Americans lived, worked, commuted, and ran daily errands, the automobile helped shape many of their leisure activities. In the mid-1950s, singer Dinah Shore, hostess of the highly popular television show *Hit Parade,* urged Americans to "See the USA in Your Chevrolet." Millions did so annually; and, in addition to automobile manufacturers, entrepreneurs in the tourist, motel, and fast-food industries also thrived. American teenagers thronged to the drive-in movies; and this same young generation of consumers introduced their parents to drive-in restaurants. Whereas their grandparents had sung along with such tunes as "In My Merry Oldsmobile," teenagers of the fifties and sixties rocked to the lyrics of Chuck Berry, Buddy Holly, Elvis Presley, Little Richard, Jan and Dean, the Beach Boys, the Beatles, and dozens of other artists belting out mesmerizing tunes, many of them with compelling car themes. Movies, fiction, television, radio, and a host of other forms of human expression in the

United States were saturated with automotive imagery. The automobile culture and the emerging youth culture appeared to have a symbiotic relationship, but the former permeated the lifestyles and daily choices for almost all Americans. This chapter traces the more important of these changes.

AUTOMOBILES AND THE YOUTH CULTURE

To some critics, it seemed by the mid-1950s that preoccupation with the automobile was leading the nation's youth down dangerous paths. In high schools, thousands of young men cultivated highly personalized James Dean "rebel-without-a-cause" looks, complete with slick-back ducktail haircuts, and cigarette packs rolled into the sleeves of their T-shirts. They often appeared bored and insolent in the high-school classrooms; and their wisecracks, tough street language, and casual, sloppy dress appeared intended to offend teachers, parents, and most other adults. Many disdained academic achievement. However, many of these same insecure youths ruled the parking lots at high schools and local drive-ins with confidence that they lacked in classrooms and polite society. They arrived and departed in their powerful, gaudily painted, "souped-up" chariots amidst thunderclaps of noise, wildly spewing gravel, and engines usually at full throttle. Although their elders clucked disapproval, many of these teen rebels were sophisticated, knowledge-able car buffs. They frequently devoted far more time and effort to their vehicles than to their families and girlfriends. Nobody gained full acceptance into their fraternity until they could remove, rebuild, and reinstall an engine in their vehicles. Wearing the right clothes and talking the current car slang was a given. In the parking lots, or at garages of their homes, they sometimes instructed their less-informed peers on the proper care and maintenance of their hot rods, on how to double their engines' power, and perhaps even on the "coolest" mementos to dangle from their rearview mirrors.

The vast majority of automobile-obsessed youths had to make do with hand-me-downs: their parents' beat-up 1938 Chevrolets and 1940 Hudsons. A few youths took pride in fixing up antiques, such as 1929 Model-A Fords; they deftly turned adversity—the fact that their parents had had to nurse along an aging vehicle for twenty years before finally being able to afford a new or even a more recent used car—into a status symbol. Many young, underclass schoolgirls at mid-century may have dreamed of being chosen as homecoming queen and riding alongside a handsome football hero in a Model-A rumble seat, with all eyes upon them.

As one of my 1950s teenage chums said, reflecting on the male high-school culture of the times, "Knowledge of cars among teenage boys was somewhat akin to knowledge of sex. By that, I mean you were expected to know a lot about it, more was good, and you certainly didn't want to admit an ignorance or disinterest in the subject. With cars, unlike sex, however, some of us had to feign an interest because we really didn't care about how cars worked." He recalled "inheriting" a snappy-looking green and white 1951 Ford Crown Victoria when his family upgraded to a newer car and proudly driving it into the school parking lot. His joy quickly turned to chagrin when more worldly car buffs ridiculed him for driving a V-6 rather than a V-8. Far worse, would any self-respecting teenager drive an automatic? One sympathetic insider volunteered to help him rip out the automatic transmission and replace it with a stick shift.

Any number of teenage capers involved automobiles. In the mid-1950s, a group of boys in my hometown of Hinsdale, Illinois, planned an elaborate scheme to bollix up traffic on U.S. Highway 34, just north of town. For weeks in advance, they carefully "borrowed" barriers, directional signs, and other construction-site paraphernalia from locations of jobs in progress. They practiced setting up and taking down barriers and signs until they could create official-appearing detours in a matter of seconds. On Halloween night, 1955, the plotters struck. Within minutes, hundreds of cars and dozens of groaning semis were rumbling through the normally quiet streets of the cozy, upper-middle-class suburb. After winding tortuously through town, the vehicles were directed up a dead-end country road. It took local police hours to unravel the hoax and help semitrailers get turned around on the narrow, hilly country roads. The Hinsdale caper has undoubtedly been embellished by storytellers over the decades, but the alleged perpetrators gained heroic—even mythical—stature in the eyes of their more cautious and inhibited peers.

A VEHICLE FOR FREEDOM

To teenagers and, indeed, for virtually all Americans, automobility meant personal freedom. As historian George Pierson persuasively argued, personal mobility always has been and remains a cherished and peculiarly American value. Renowned economist Robert L. Heilbroner pithily described increased mobility as ". . . a direct enhancement of life, as an enlargement of life's boundaries and opportunities." Owning an automobile democratized such enjoyment. "This is so enormous, so radical a transformation that its effect can no longer be measured or appreciated by mere figures. It is nothing less than the unshackling of age-old bonds of locality; it is the grant of geographic choice and economic freedom on a hitherto unimagined scale." To be sure, there were some situations in which taking public transportation might actually be more practical than driving. However, to most Americans at midcentury, there was little hesitation over choice of conveyance. As one automobile enthusiast observed, ". . . I suppose the car represents a great system for having your own little world, a substitute for the country, if you will. You're able to order it any way you wish. . . . When I am alone in a car I have created a private world." The teenage hero of Henry Felsen's novel *Hot Rod* found similar release behind the wheel:

> When he was behind the wheel, in control of his hopped-up machine, he was king of the road. When he was happy, his happiness reached its peak when he could express it in terms of speed and roaring power, the pull of his engine, the whistle of the wind in his ears, the glorious expression of free flight.

In contrast, when he was unhappy,

> . . . the wheel once again offered him his answer. At these times there was solace and forgetfulness behind the wheel. . . . revenge against trouble was won through the conquest of other cars that accepted his challenge to race.

Automobile themes were central to many prominent novels, short stories, and even poetry of the period. Dean Moriarity, Jack Kerouac's protagonist in *On the Road,* discovers his very identity behind the wheel. Dean was even "born on the road when his parents were passing through Salt Lake City in 1926 in a jalopy." Literary scholar Cynthia Dettelbach observed that, on Kerouac's pages, "To be on the road driving at his speed is to 'zoom,' 'roll,' 'ball the jack,' 'blow the car,' 'go flying,' and 'roar on.' The Road is life, at its most exciting pitch." Further, she noted, "For Jack Kerouac and his beat friends, driving from one end of the country to another and back again is a never-ending, life-affirming process." For Dean Moriarity, the thrill was in the search for meaning.

In John Updike's famous *Rabbit* novels, automobile themes are omnipresent; his protagonist, Harry "Rabbit" Angstrom, is constantly seeking escape from his humdrum reality. Rabbit is constantly on the run, often in his automobile; only at these moments does he feel free. However, his search is tentative, fleeting, essentially fruitless. At the conclusion of *Rabbit Redux,* twenty-something Rabbit and his very pregnant wife Janice are cruising their blue-collar suburban Philadelphia neighborhood. Rabbit is startled to find himself on the street where his former mistress lived:

Because the liaison with Ruth had once opened up Rabbit's life and stultifying marriage, he now thinks Ruth's street will open onto a brook, and then a dirt road and open pastures; but instead the city street broadens into a highway lined with hamburger diners and drive-in sub shops, and a miniature golf course with big plaster dinosaurs, and food stamp stores and motels and gas stations. . . . The open pastures (real and illusory) have been preempted by big businesses catering to an automotive economy and mentality. Hence, the only animals are plastic replicas of the long-extinct dinosaur, the only thing that flows is out of a pump.

"DREAM CARS" OF THE 1950S

While their sons and daughters cavorted in hand-me-down jalopies, by midcentury, Mom and Dad nourished and then finally realized their dreams of choosing between wide varieties of dazzling new cars. By then, automakers had satisfied pent-up demand for the first wave of postwar cars. They next produced a whole new generation of powerful, snappy vehicles. The 1950s and 1960s marked a period in which Americans appeared to revel in the seemingly unlimited choices they had when they visited car lots. In future decades, the nation's automobile producers, often fearful of making huge marketing mistakes that could cost their firms hundreds of millions of dollars, would offer models that were similar in size and appearance. By the early 1970s, most of the models coming out of Detroit's design studios were both boxy and boring, in sharp contrast to the new models of the 1950s and 1960s, which had flair and individuality.

At midcentury, automobile designers instinctively sensed that while the public may have spoken as sober-minded, "responsible" adults and emphasized economy, durability, and reliability when interviewed about necessary qualities in their selection of new cars, they were actually children at heart. What they wanted—what would really dictate their ultimate buying decision—was adult toys, with pizzazz and sex appeal. They may have felt pressure to conform in many facets of their lives; but, on the road, many Americans longed to experience fantasies. If their new cars were not durable, so what? They could always trade them in for newer, even sexier models in three or four years.

In an era of generally widespread abundance, just about anyone, it seemed, could qualify for loans to buy new cars. Consumers had waited long enough; even those fortunate enough to finally purchase new cars two years or so after the war had had to settle for drab, clunky, warmed-over, prewar designs. By midcentury, many buyers wanted big, powerful, flashy new cars—not next year—*NOW!* They were fully employed. If they did not have money in their checking accounts, they were growing used to the custom of buying things "on time." Without question, they paid attention to sticker prices; but, once they found the new models they wanted, many consumers asked virtually no questions about the arcane mysteries of financing, other than wanting to know the size of the down payment and perhaps the length and amount of monthly payments.

If anyone appeared destined to lead this nation's revolutionary automobile redesign efforts, it was Harley Earl. Born into a prominent Los Angeles family in 1893, before there was a Hollywood, he grew up with Tinseltown. By the time the first generation of silent screen stars was emerging, the precocious twenty-something Earl was designing outrageously ostentatious, customized cars for the newly rich and famous. To many overpaid stars, cost was no object. For Roscoe "Fatty" Arbuckle, a popular Hollywood figure in the 1920s, Earl created a sensational rig priced at $28,000, which he called "the most streamlined vehicle anywhere. . . ." In the 1920s, Earl and a few other iconoclastic designers had experimented with futuristic body designs and they had introduced bold colors into the mix.

Back in Detroit, General Motors automobile executives William C. "Billy" Durant and Alfred Sloan were well aware of Earl's creations. Wedded by then to the brilliant marketing strategy of the annual model change, they realized they needed inspired, driven designers to keep the public constantly intrigued by what further delights might be around the corner the next year. In a word, before committing to new cars, many customers wanted to be sure that last year's model really was obsolete, at least from the standpoint of fashion. The lords of GM lured Earl east as their chief stylist in 1927. As long as both producers and consumers were in an expansive mood and business was high, wide, and handsome, he thrived. However, during the Depression and World War II, automakers, in part reflecting the nation's somber collective mood, had painted most cars in drab colors: black, brown, dark green, occasionally navy blue. Although Earl remained at General Motors, his natural creativity was temporarily stifled.

Surprisingly, Earl stuck it out. General Motors, after all, had sponsored Norman Bel Geddes's fantastic Futurama exhibit at the World's Fair in 1939, and Earl evidently sensed that he would be perfectly positioned to introduce daring automobile designs to the entire nation when good times reappeared. By midcentury, Earl and his peers were thoroughly prepared with dynamic designs. Many of the new models of the late 1940s and early 1950s reflected a mood of exuberant consumerism. Dazzling colors reappeared, embellished by two-tone jobs (kelly green bodies with beige hardtops). During the war, Earl had be-

Courtesy Mike Reschly

American automobile designs of the late 1950s included some of the nation's most revered, cherished classics. The 1958 Chevrolet "Impala" excited many enthusiastic buyers.

come fascinated with several fighter airplane designs, particularly the sleek P-38. He mesmerized his fellow designers by introducing tail fins, clearly derived from the P-38 airplane, to drawings and, later, clay models of the 1948 Cadillac. Despite some misgivings about patterning a car after military hardware, his bosses gave him the go-ahead, and modest but distinctive bumps first appeared on the rear bumpers. The 1948 Cadillac was a smash hit. Earl increased the size of the fins on the 1949 model Cadillac; that year was the division's best ever. Other divisions and designers picked up the trend. Bumper fins appeared on Oldsmobiles in 1949, Buicks in 1952, and rival Chrysler in 1955. Perhaps unconsciously honoring the obsession with design practicality of his grandfather, Henry Ford II held out until 1957. Earl stated on more than one occasion that design was like the entertainment business. To Alfred Sloan and later generations of GM executives, mounting sales of "hot" cars simply proved "the dollars and cents value of styling."

However, tail fins finally became victims of their own excess. By the late 1950s, it was clear that designers had gone overboard. By 1959, according to one historian, ". . . the tail fin had become so grotesque a motif that the rear of the Chevrolet Impala looked like a fan dancer's tantrum." Just when many other brands were adopting the most garish, exaggerated fins, Earl, determined always to remain in front of the pack, removed them from the 1960 model Cadillac. Earl was not the only "hot" designer in Detroit in the 1950s. In 1956, General Motors also hired John De Lorean, who had helped inject new life into both Chrysler and Packard. His task was to rebuild the Pontiac Division, which had been turning out boring, middle-of-the-market vehicles for years. Within a few years, Pontiac regularly dished out some of the most exciting models in the Motor City.

Many other automotive features made the Fabulous Fifties distinctive. Engines became bigger, faster, and far stronger. Standard models of some brands could compete in drag races with the souped-up hot rods of earlier years. Not surprisingly, fuel economy virtually disappeared, with some behemoths getting less than ten miles per gallon; but, with gasoline costing twenty-five or thirty cents per gallon and supplies seemingly inexhaustible, who cared? Other design features were more obvious visually. In middecade, Buick introduced its famous "porthole" look. Its hood featured either three or four (depending on the model) protrusions that resembled air vents but that served no purpose other than aesthetic. Car buyers either drooled or hooted, but *everybody* noticed Buicks.

Midpriced Fords and Chevrolets manufactured between 1955 and 1957 are today among the models most cherished by vintage automobile buffs. However, the two automobile giants most effectively tantalized buyers by introducing two fabled sports cars during the 1950s. Chevrolet's fabulous, low-slung, futuristic, fiberglass-bodied Corvette and Ford's dashing and dramatically styled Thunderbird—the latter sporting *real* porthole windows toward the rear of its diminutive hardtop—won rave reviews from both industry analysts and buyers alike. Today, almost a half century after they were introduced, these two sports cars still excite car buffs and collectors.

Some of the adult toys of the 1950s still possess a modern aura today. Perhaps this is in part because Earl and a number of other designers borrowed a page from Norman Bel Geddes after the war and began designing incredibly futuristic, utterly impractical "dream cars," then offering tantalizing glimpses to the public. The first significant dream machine of the postwar years was, in the words of one historian of design, "the astonishing Le Sabre XP-8, a phallic jelly-mold of a car with aeroplane nozzles and details," patterned after the F-86 jet, then being flown by American pilots. To publicize its forward-looking designs, GM produced a series of seven extravaganzas called *Motoramas* between 1949 and 1961. The shows were frankly designed to titillate potential customers, particularly the young. Sponsors also used them to test market-exaggerated design features being promoted by enthusiastic engineers. By interviewing visitors and asking them to fill out surveys, they could, presumably, gauge the public's response to them. However, the results were decidedly mixed. Market surveys have always been tricky and remain so even now. Back then, survey

At midcentury, American automobile designers almost literally indulged in flights of fancy, producing models sporting potential features of the future. Although never meant to be operational, full-sized models of "dream machines" reflected designers' supreme faith in technology and tantalized attendees at automotive shows.

techniques were far less sophisticated than they are today. Such informal takes on public reactions to specific car features could be highly misleading. A feature that appeared graceful on a fantasy vehicle and generated enthusiasm from relaxed visitors to motoramas might prove to be a dud when slapped onto a model intended for the mass market. Buyers usually experienced intense pressure at closure of deals for new cars, and one of their few defense mechanisms was rejecting expensive options on their cars of choice.

Although people attending motoramas were acutely aware that they were simply entering a fantasy world, the shows almost certainly stimulated future buyers eventually to convert vague fantasies into concrete needs. One automobile historian recalled coercing his father to take him to one such show in the mid-1950s: "All I can remember is that the cars under those bright lights had a sculptural glamour and desirability that in me inspired hysteria. In retrospect I know they were art—stationary objects in a museum-like environment—but I've never gotten that kind of a rush from a real museum." To one critic who charged that the shows and dream cars encouraged Americans to engage in wholly unrealistic fantasies, Earl commented, "You will never know what the industrial products of the future are going to be like, but the secret is to keep trying to find out." Another GM executive truly hit the mark when he commented, "We have not depreciated these old cars, we have appreciated your mind."

Domestic automobile manufacturers by no means abandoned mundane, practical models in the late 1950s. Americans still bought lots of station wagons for hauling around kids, groceries, and hardware supplies. It was hard to make a station wagon look glamorous, although a few sported ridiculous tail fins. Most vehicles had powerful engines. In the late 1950s, V-8s and powerful six-cylinder engines dominated under the hoods. Gas was cheap. Sure, sales of Volkswagens and a few economical imports were beginning to inch upward, but very few Americans worried about fuel economy back then.

If automobile executives in Detroit appeared on sure footing concerning Americans' desires for powerful engines, they were less comfortable dealing with women. Most advertising copy portrayed single women, usually blondes, driving convertibles; women driving station wagons were invariably accompanied by two or three children and, sometimes, a dog. Although advertisers paid condescending tribute to female buyers, automobile dealers seemingly had little clue about how to treat them. According to one historian, "The belief that women were influential in purchasing cars for their style, color and comfort turned out to be mostly a figment of male imaginations." In fact, some studies concluded that women had far less brand loyalty than men and that, when they shopped, they considered economy, reliability, durability, handling, and resale value.

There were a few bombs among the powerful, chrome-laden and tail-finned cars of the mid- to late 1950s, and none was as striking as Ford's ill-fated Edsel. Introduced in the late summer of 1957, its most distinctive feature was a horizontal front grille mounted over the front bumper that resembled a horse collar. The car was loaded with cheap gadgets, including push-button automatic transmission controls that sat on top of the steering column. Ford estimated that it would need to sell 200,000 Edsels just to break even. However, the model generated lukewarm reviews. Within weeks of its introduction, critics uncovered inferior paint jobs, low-grade sheet metal, and nonfunctioning accessories. After 11,544 units were delivered to dealers in September, only 7,601 left the factory in October, followed by even fewer in November. Although the 1959 model was adjusted in response to customer complaints, by the end of the second full year of production, less than 84,000 Edsels were on the nation's highways. Jack Parr, the host of the popular *Tonight* television show, skewered the Edsel as "an Oldsmobile sucking on a lemon." Dispirited Ford executives tried a third edition in 1960, but nothing helped. Only 109,000 Edsels were sold in less than three years of production. Total losses were a closely guarded company secret, and estimates ranged from $100 million all the way up to $350 million; by any measure, it was one of the biggest flops in automotive history up to that time. One Ford executive actually tried to blame its failure on the fact that the Soviets launched the world's first orbiting satellite, *Sputnik,* just a week after Ford unveiled the Edsel. However, a far more convincing explanation was penned by one astute industry analyst: "The Edsel was a classic case of the wrong car for the wrong market at the wrong time." The fact that, after months of confused indecision, Ford executives had named the car after Henry Ford's highly capable but tragically ill-fated son held bitter irony.

"MUSCLE CARS" OF THE 1960S

It would be impossible to pinpoint the origins of "hot" or "muscle" cars, but they achieved their heyday in the 1960s and early 1970s— before the Arab oil embargo of 1973. From the motor vehicle's earliest days, young men have been fascinated with power and speed. Racing was an important item in sports pages even before mass production of cars. However, after World War II, professional customizers began offering redesigned vehicles that held a magical appeal, particularly to young Americans. Perhaps the most famous customizer was George Barris, who came from the same general neck of the woods as Harley Earl: North Hollywood. Barris opened his business in 1945. At his "Kustom City" showroom, visitors soon realized that they were in a gallery rather than an automobile showroom. Barris built fantastic creations, which he exhibited in car shows all around the country. Novelist Tom Wolfe visited Barris's showroom and observed the sheer power of Barris's creations; but, basically, they were not built to be used. Rather, Wolfe noted, ". . . it's like one of these Picasso or Miro rugs. You don't walk on the damn things. You hang them on the wall. It's the same thing with Barris's cars. In effect, they're sculpture."

Just as Barris instinctively designed motor vehicles geared for a youthful market, so did Detroit designers like John De Lorean. By the mid-1960s, the first wave of baby boomers was reaching maturity—or at least an age when they would start buying new cars. De Lorean had headed up a team of young dreamers who had taken the Pontiac Division of General Motors from the doldrums to the number three position in the industry in terms of sales. Having already tasted success, De Lorean's team had no intention of losing momentum. The 1964 Pontiac Tempest was a midsize car that had achieved decent, if not exciting, sales. A bright young engineer discovered that a 389-cubic-inch V-8 engine had the same shape as a 322-inch V-8, which had initially been planned as an option for the Tempest. The bigger, more muscular engine fit under the hood, and it delivered sixty-seven more horsepower.

De Lorean and his men found themselves playing with a very hot set of wheels, which was fun to drive. For merely $296 more than the price of the Tempest, the customer got a muscled-up V-8 engine with dual exhausts and a four-barrel carburetor, a Hurst shifter, a heavy-duty clutch, stiffer suspension, and redline tires. The hood was also modified with a blacked-out grille and two fake hood scoops. These modifications, combined with the larger tires, provided the *Gran Turismo Omolgate* (an Italian phrase meaning approved for Grand Touring Racing), more frequently referred to simply by its acronym *GTO,* gained instant recognition among car enthusiasts. Pontiac executives initially had hoped to sell 5,000 of the conversion packages in 1964. Consumers snapped them up as soon as they hit showroom floors; company officials were hard-pressed to meet demand, which hit 31,000 in 1964. The next year, Pontiac sold 60,000 of the packages, then 84,000 more in 1966. Capitalizing on the GTO's popularity, the company produced shirts with GTO emblems. A discount shoe company brought out a shoe called the GTO. A rock group named Ronnie and the Daytonas, featuring high falsetto voices evoking images of Jan and Dean, quickly cranked out a popular single called "Little GTO," which sold a million copies.

The GTO lasted eight memorable years and attracted a dedicated cult following. Those lucky enough to own them reveled in their fortune; large numbers of people who did not own them lusted after them. The GTO reeked attitude! John De Lorean did not exaggerate when he claimed in his autobiography, "The most memorable product coup while I was at Pontiac . . . was the birth of the muscle-car craze." De Lorean had started something, and other car manufacturers quickly followed Pontiac's lead. Some of Pontiac's best competition came from other divisions of General Motors. The awesomely powerful Oldsmobile 442, the Chevrolet Malibu SS, and, later, the Buick Gran Sport all competed for attention from affluent baby boomers, as did Chrysler Motors' 426 Hemi Plymouth Satellite and the Dodge Challenger R/T Hemi.

Thanks in part to a fast-rising and ambitious young executive, Lee Iacocca, Ford Motor Company was not excluded from the market in self-indulgent vehicles. After a long and strenuous internal campaign in the early 1960s, Iacocca finally won approval to sponsor a new, sporty car to appeal to a younger consumer. Engineers began work in 1962. Since Iacocca hoped to list it at about $2,500—or roughly $1,000 below the price of the average American car—the new entry would not be loaded with power or luxury. The new offering, named the Mustang, was unveiled at the New York World's Fair on April 17, 1964. For those who could not make the Fair and see the car in person, Ford purchased advertising time slots on all three major television networks the previous evening. Some 27 million potential customers got their first glimpses of the Mustang, featuring a long front hood, short rear deck, and squared-off styling. Ford executives, with indelible memories of the recent Edsel fiasco, talked modestly about selling 100,000 the first year. Much to their delight, the company was swamped with 22,000 orders the day the Mustang was unveiled and they sold 417,000 units the first year! Iacocca had his smashing success and was on his way to much bigger things.

However, Ford also wanted to profit from the muscle-car mania. Its initial response was to beef up the sporty but lightweight Mustang. The 1964 model's standard equipment included a 6-cylinder engine rated at a mere 101 horsepower. A year or so later, options included an 8-cylinder engine with a rated horsepower of 271. By beefing up suspension and adding several other features, Ford offered customers a car combining American luxuries and European-style performance. In fact, equipped with a 271-horsepower V-8, the Mustang was a relatively lightweight but high-performance muscle car. Carroll Shelby's modified Mustang— named the Shelby 350—was a gutsy, buffed race car that could accelerate from zero to sixty miles per hour in just six seconds.

AUTOMOBILE RACING: STOCK CARS AND DRAGSTERS

Automobile racing had been a popular sport for a half century by the end of World War II; however, it had been largely dominated by upper- and upper-middle-class Americans. William K. Vanderbilt's *Vanderbilt Cup* races on Long Island between 1904 and 1910 had attracted as many as 250,000 spectators. After its inaugural race in 1911, the *Indianapolis 500* became the country's premier automobile speed and endurance competition. Following World War II, with suspension of wartime rationing of fuel and restrictions on the production of cars, the connection between motor vehicles and sports broadened and deepened. Stock car racing and drag racing became wildly popular, along with Grand Prix events. According to some sources, these endeavors combined became the most popular spectator sport in the United States, bigger than baseball, basketball, and even football, attracting as many as 75 million enthusiasts annually by the end of the twentieth century.

There are distinct differences between the sports. Drag racing is a test of sheer speed over a straight stretch, usually a quarter of a mile. From a standing start, the first car to cross the line wins. Stock car racing is almost always conducted around an oval track, measuring somewhere between a quarter of a mile and three miles in circumference. Grand Prix events combine sophisticated, very specialized cars and irregular-shaped race courses.

After the war, the technology of building dragsters evolved rapidly. In the early years, they were basically old vehicles, ingeniously modified by inspired mechanics to increase acceleration. In later years, drivers, mechanics, and automotive engineers created sophisticated vehicles powered by highly specialized new fuels and designed for a single purpose: to cover a quarter mile in the shortest possible time. For teenagers and many young men in their early twenties, racing powerful, noisy cars at maximum speed was a symbol of self-expression and, perhaps, a rebellion against the cautious, conservative values of their Depression-era parents. In one town after another, drag racers were driven off city streets by authorities. This did not even slow them down; they just moved to remote highways outside of town. Others found legal outlets for their races. The first formal drag strip opened in Goleta, California, in 1948; and, since that time, drag racing has gained both legitimacy and enormous fan support. According to one automobile historian, "Hot-rodding during the fifties became the common man's counterpart to the elite racing circuit that had been supported by rich men since the early days of the automobile." By 2002, the sport was rather loosely regulated and controlled by the National Hot Rod Association (NHRA), which sponsored approximately twenty major events annually. Predictably, as the technology of drag racing evolved, racing became enormously expensive. Ironically, the common man was once again relegated to the sidelines: he could watch, but he could seldom race—at least not on the big, highly publicized tracks. Unless an aspiring driver is independently wealthy or has sponsors with deep pockets, he or she finds it virtually impossible to compete on the NHRA circuit.

In the early postwar years, however, there were plenty of penniless mavericks. Back then, most of the "hot" dragsters were from southern California, but an occasional, gifted outsider managed to penetrate this fraternity. Don "Big Daddy" Garlits, from Tampa, Florida, first showed up at West Coast drag strips with a sorry-looking, beat-up dragster. His rivals were unimpressed. In a 1964 interview, Big Daddy recalled, "They took one look at my nightmare and they like to roll over laughing. . . . I cleaned up on them and they went home shaking their heads." Garlits dominated drag racing in the 1960s and 1970s. He became the first man to break the 200-mile-per-hour barrier in 1972, and he proved it was no fluke by doing it twice the following weekend. However, an even more unlikely success story was Shirley "Cha Cha" Muldowney. Born in Burlington, Vermont, in 1940, she was from a part of the country not known for drag racing; and, from the chauvinistic viewpoint of most dragsters, she was definitely the wrong gender. Soon after Shirley's father taught her to drive, she was hooked on moving fast. Her boyfriend (and, later, husband) modified her first dragster, a 1951 Mercury. A school dropout at sixteen, she gained experience dragging on the streets of Schenectady, New York. She recalled that, when she first joined the hot-rod circuit, crowds who saw no place for a woman on the drag strip booed her. However, Muldowny soon won them over. After nearly losing her life in a horrendous mid-1960s crash, she rehabilitated for two years, then got back behind the wheel. When asked why, Muldowney simply replied, "It's what I do. . . ." Evidently, racing fans of both genders admired her moxie; she became a crowd favorite and a winner. Muldowny won several regional titles in the 1970s, and she was the first female driver licensed by the NHRA.

The growth of stock car racing after World War II paralleled that of drag racing. According to several popular accounts, the origins of stock car racing can be found on the dirt roads of the rural South during Prohibition and the Great Depression. In remote and hidden hollows back in the hills, enterprising families distilled "moonshine" whiskey, then "ran" it to distributors, using specially designed automobiles. The business was, of course, illegal; yet, if one could avoid arrest, it was highly profitable. Producing moonshine continued to be illegal after Prohibition ended, just as it continued to be highly profitable long after the end of World War II. Supporters claimed that running moonshine reflected a time-honored southern and rural tradition of being suspicious of and defying federal authority. Many local police had little or no enthusiasm for enforcing federal laws. Some of their buddies engaged in the trade, so most small-town cops obligingly looked the other way. Matching wits against "revenuers" (enforcement officials) inspired "good ole boys" to build some of the fastest machines on four wheels.

Indeed, some of stock car racing's early legends, including Junior Johnson, learned to drive fast by outrunning federal agents over back-country dirt roads. Young Johnson regularly ran booze from his daddy's still in Ingle Hollow, near North Wilkesboro, in northwestern North Carolina. According to novelist Tom Wolfe, millions of dirt-poor southerners identified with Johnson, not just because he drove fast and defied "Yankee" authority but because he identified with them. Johnson ". . . is one of the last of those sports stars who is not just an ace at the game itself, but a hero a whole people or class of people can identify with." Johnson was finally caught, tried, and convicted; he spent about a year in prison in the mid-1950s. Upon his release, he returned to the oval racing tracks and soon earned a more-than-comfortable living racing legally.

In contrast to drag racing over uniform distances, there are several types of stock car racing. The most basic and primitive is over small-town dirt tracks, which are usually a quarter- to a half-mile oval. One step up are paved short tracks. At the top of the pyramid are the Grand National races at the biggest and best-maintained tracks, where drivers reach the highest speeds over the longest distances. Stock car racing became more formally organized in the years immediately following the war. In 1948, the National Association for Stock Car Auto Racing (NASCAR) was formed, and it hosted its first race in Daytona, Florida. A major turning point for stock car racing was the opening of the first superspeedway at Darlington, South Carolina, on Labor Day, 1950, when 30,000 fans showed up for the first major league stock car race. By the mid-1950s, there were about three dozen sanctioned Grand National races, fully half of them in Virginia and the Carolinas.

The ambiance surrounding each type of stock car event is unique, and the races appeal to very different groups. Grand National Races like the Talledega (Alabama) 500 are classic events. The Talledega track, a 2.66-mile state-of-the-art oval, is larger than the Indianapolis Motor Speedway. Racing fans begin arriving two or three days before the Sunday race, some to grab the best camping spots. Couples and families are generally well-heeled; many are equipped with motor homes costing upward of $60,000. Although seats in the grandstand are expensive, the race appears almost secondary in importance to the socializing; but those in the cheapest sections appear to have even more fun, and the action in the infield often rivals that on the track. As race time draws near, many families and groups appear to be trying to outdo each other in throwing elaborate tailgate parties. They ritually consume huge quantities of beer, chicken-fried steaks, and barbecue beef that strain fans' shirt buttons and belt buckles. Scantily clad females (who sometimes succumb to boozy but persuasive spectators to "take it off" and render themselves topless) parade in front of the grandstand until "detained" by leering security men. Despite all of the distractions, the races themselves are usually thrilling spectacles. Coming down straightaways, cars reach speeds exceeding 220 miles per hour, and the drivers are identified by colors, multiple advertising logos, and numbers. The drivers are all top-of-the-line, experienced professionals; as costs of maintaining and racing sophisticated stock cars are enormous, they are backed by corporate millions and well-staffed racing teams.

In contrast, at the other end of the racing spectrum, dirt-track races pit local "good ole boys" of all ages with some mechanical ability and a taste for speed, plus a few up-and-coming racers hoping to catch the eye of a sponsor. The drivers know their cars inside and out, often spending most of their free time during the week preparing them for the Friday night races. Hours before sundown, racing fans begin gathering at the track. Gates open at 4:30, and the races begin at 7:30. Wives and girlfriends, plus children, joined by buddies from nearby farms and mills, make up the crowds. In the late afternoon and early evening, plenty of hot dogs, hamburgers, and six-packs of Dixie beer are consumed. Basically, the mood is "family," and the crowds are usually raucous but friendly. In many ways, it is small town and rural South at their best.

Yet another form of fast, dangerous "action" has attracted large numbers of dedicated enthusiasts: demolition derbies. They were the brainchild of stock car driver Lawrence Mendelsohn. He was competing in a race on Long Island's Islip Speedway in about 1960, when a rival driver bumped him up into the twelfth row of the grandstand. Amazingly, Mendelsohn was not hurt, nor was any spectator. As the fortunate driver recalled, "That was what got me. . . . I remember I was hanging upside down from my seat belt like a side of Jersey bacon and wondering why no one was sitting where I hit. 'Lousy promotion,' I said to myself." Mendelsohn experienced an epiphany and soon converted from race car driver to race promoter. He sensed that, for every purist who came to see skilled racers, there were another five who lusted for wrecks. So why force fans to put up with monotony waiting for smashups? Why not offer a competition that was, in effect, nothing but violent collisions?

Thus was the demolition derby born. Mendelsohn figured that lots of drivers would enjoy careening around an area approximately the size of an overgrown football field in cheap "beaters," smashing into other cars: sort of a real-life bumper cars game for adults. The last car able to move under its own power was the winner. In the demolition derby arena, the area itself is fairly small, and there is too much chaos and congestion to permit any driver to reach dangerous speeds. By strapping drivers into harnesses attached to bolted-down seats, risks of serious injury were greatly reduced. The trick was to avoid being rammed by rivals, while inflicting serious damage on others. Most drivers learned to protect their front ends (radiators and engines were most vulnerable) and to ram competitors with back ends by driving in reverse. Once you delivered a blow, it was wise to get untangled and moving again as quickly as possible so as to not be a sitting duck for a third driver. Variations of the contest had actually surfaced earlier, including one in which drivers "raced" over a figure-eight course, with predictable mayhem occurring at the intersection.

Demolition derbies proved enormously popular. They struck a deep chord among race car drivers, perhaps even within the typical American motorist. How many drivers have fantasized about rear ending the knuckle-headed bozo who rudely cut them off in traffic and "teaching him a lesson"? Novelist Tom Wolfe called the demolition derby ". . . a sport that ranks with the gladiatorial games of Rome as a piece of national symbolism." Mendelsohn staged his first one at the Islip Speedway in 1961, and it was a rousing success. Other promoters quickly picked up on the concept. According to one source, 154 demolition derbies were staged in the first 3 years of their existence. By one count, 1.25 million fans witnessed them, and three-fourths of the contests drew capacity crowds. Inevitably, promoters sponsored the first "national" demolition derby at Langhorne, Pennsylvania, in the mid-1960s, with Don McTavish of Dover, Massachusetts, emerging as the first "world's champion." The sport continues to thrive in the twenty-first century; like stock car racing, demolition derbies remain a staple of regional and local fairs in small-town rural America.

CARS, KIDS, AND ROCK AND ROLL

One could certainly find evidence of serious attention being devoted to the automobile needs of older Americans. Auto companies happily supplied them with large-profit vehicles such as Cadillac Fleetwoods and Lincoln Continentals. However, in the 1950s and 1960s, the emerging automobile culture had an unmistakably youthful veneer. Nowhere was this more evident than in the field of music, particularly rock and roll. Much of this new form evolved from southern blues of the early twentieth century. Some of the earliest blues songs involved railroads, a primary means of mobility for poor, itinerant musicians. Many musicians, particularly African Americans, were too poor to own cars, and they had to "ride the rods" (sneak onto trains) to get from one poorly paying gig to another. Life along the railroad tracks was challenging; tales of hardship naturally found their way into blues and, later, rock and roll lyrics. By the late 1940s or early 1950s, cars were becoming more generally available; a typical small-time musician generally had one, even if it was a beat-up old Ford station wagon.

Many of the originators of rock and roll have been closely identified with cars since they first burst on the public scene. The legendary Chuck Berry's first-ever smash single, "Maybelline," exemplified a new wave of music in the mid-1950s. The song was pure genius; in three minutes of compelling, throbbing sound, Berry told a story about a poor young man "cruising" in his souped-up V-8 Ford. As automobile historian Warren J. Belasco notes, "Berry suggests that the inherent pleasure of moving is enough reason for getting behind the wheel; there need be no other rationale." Our hero just happens to see his sometime flame, Maybelline, riding in a Cadillac. The two vehicles engage in a spirited chase, which our hero appears to be losing until the penultimate moment when a rainstorm gives his engine new life: His vehicle finally "catches" his rival at the top of a hill. There are numerous powerful social messages in the song, some overt, others more subtle: poor boy chasing an ambitious, flirtatious girl with a wandering eye (the chorus repeatedly laments Maybelline's apparent fickleness) striving to get ahead, who is riding with a more affluent man in a Cadillac. Cruising is presumably a perfectly natural, innocent pastime, but is our hero really innocent? When he does catch up to her, what happens? This puzzle was one of "Maybelline's" biggest pluses; Berry's fans fantasized their own preferred endings. Another Berry hit song was "No Particular Place to Go," released in 1964. It's about "cruisin' and playing the radio." This time, our hero has the girl alongside him; he, at least, is looking for a place to make out, and evidently she is willing. However, once again our hero is frustrated. He is a bumbler rather than a smoothie, as he cannot figure out how to undo her protective seat belt! Millions of teenagers could identify with such adolescent opportunities lost.

Berry's personal life was filled with auto-related turning points. Before he became a popular recording artist, he was a twenty-eight-year-old blues player on weekends, but he had to support his wife and two children by working at the assembly line for GM's Fisher Body plant during the week. After he became a big star, he surrounded himself with Cadillacs and other fancy cars, usually powder blue. According to one social historian, "Berry's motivatin' brought disaster." Like turn-of-the-century heavyweight boxing champion Jack Johnson, another proud African American man ". . . who had dared [in virtually identical ways] to encroach on previously all-white turf, Berry infuriated racist authorities with his well-publicized love of fast cars and good times." He was arrested in 1959 for allegedly smuggling a fourteen-year-old Mexican prostitute in his car trunk. Berry's friends claimed he had been framed, but he was convicted of violating the Mann Act (transporting women across state lines for immoral purposes) and sent to prison in 1962. When released from prison, he made a mild comeback, but his brief years of stardom were over.

No rock and roller personified the 1950s and music's intimate connection with the car culture more than the self-styled "King of Rock and Roll," Elvis Presley. Like Chuck Berry, Elvis emerged from lower-class roots. By several accounts, he was deeply scarred by childhood deprivation in Memphis during the Depression. When Elvis began picking his guitar and singing, he was earning his living driving trucks for the Crown Electric Company. Once he cut his first successful singles and the money started coming in, Elvis felt compelled to distance himself as much as possible from unpleasant early memories by surrounding himself with gaudy, expensive possessions, including cars. As one observer astutely noted, "Elvis, like most Americans, saw the Cadillac as the quintessence of the social acceptability that had thus far eluded him." The observer continued:

> Flashy automobiles did indeed transport him, away from everything that stank of the immobile, inert indigence that had ruled his Depression upbringing. Presley's immense wealth, to say nothing of his *parvenu* urge to gild everything, shocked the nation as much as his pelvic thrusts, and his obsession with cars reflected the collective yearnings of an entire generation of formerly underprivileged Americans.

When cast in several Hollywood films in the late 1950s and early 1960s, Elvis reportedly stated that he did not want anyone in Hollywood to have a fancier car than he did. He hired George Barris to turn his dream into reality. The result was a grotesquely overstuffed Cadillac that defied description. Nearly every surface on the car was gold-plated, "from the headlight rims and hubcaps to the interior accouterments, which included a television, telephone, record player, bar, ice maker, and the obligatory electric shoe buffer." He dubbed the huge back seat the "Center Lounge." Seats were arranged in a semicircle, and Elvis's gold records decorated the roof. The floor was covered with white fur. His adoring fans loved it, and RCA, sensing a winning combination, sent the car on promotional tours, along with Elvis. At one shopping mall in Houston, the car alone attracted 40,000 gawkers. As one historian observed, "If Graceland was Elvis's Versailles, then the Gold Car was his Royal Phaeton, a hillbilly's dream come true." In Hollywood, Elvis starred in several movies with significant automobile themes. In *Viva Las Vegas* (1963), for example, he takes a job in a casino to raise money to compete in the Las Vegas Grand Prix. While on the casino job, he woos Ann-Margret, who, it turns out, is his chief rival in the local racing competition.

Elvis was so obsessed with Cadillacs that when he became enormously wealthy he used them as a form of personal currency. Tales abound of gifts to casual acquaintances, including bodyguards at concerts, maintenance women at Graceland, and many others. According to one story, Elvis once entered a large Cadillac dealership, purchased fourteen cars off the showroom floor from the dumbstruck dealer, and started giving them away, the last one to an elderly African American woman who just happened to be walking by! Many of Elvis's recordings paid homage to the emerging car culture. In "Baby Let's Play House" (1955), the proud hillbilly puts down his ambitious girlfriend who has "run away" to college. The lyrics warned that even though she had education, plus a "pink Cadillac," she was still in danger of becoming "somebody's fool."

To be sure, hundreds of wanna-be musicians offered tribute to "four on the floor," "love in the back seat," and other facets of the car culture, only to remain buried in obscurity. Still, the sheer number of songs with auto themes that were marketed by record companies is striking. Following the leads by Chuck Berry and Elvis, dozens of young rockers in the late 1950s and 1960s featured auto-oriented lyrics in their most popular songs. Some were indirect, aping—or mocking, depending on one's interpretation— car themes. Little Richard's object of desire, "Long Tall Sally," was "built for speed." Bo Diddley sported a rocket-shaped guitar with tail fins, which clearly was a takeoff on contemporary car styles. In one song, "Not Fade Away," Buddy Holly crooned that his love was "bigger than a Cadillac." The Playmates served up a cutesy little song, "Beep Beep," which improbably featured a Nash Rambler besting a Cadillac in a race. Even stories of grisly accidents and death on the road offered grist for songwriters' mills. Three of the most popular songs reflecting these themes were Mark Denning's "Teen Angel" (1960), Ray Peterson's "Tell Laura I Love Her" (1960), and Jan and Dean's "Dead Man's Curve" (1964).

The Beach Boys and Jan and Dean spearheaded the avalanche of recording groups pushing car themes in rock and roll in the 1960s. Many of their songs centered on the supposedly free-spirited and self-indulgent lifestyles of teenagers surfing in southern California in the early 1960s. And, of course, no self-respecting surfer could show up at the beach in anything but a "woody" (a beat-up old station wagon with fake wood paneling), with his surf board casually strapped to the roof. If the surf wasn't "up," he could pass the time cruising, trying to hook up with "surfer girls." The Beach Boys recorded at least a dozen songs about teenagers and cars. Among their most popular recordings were "409," "Fun Fun Fun," and "Little Duce Coupe." In addition to "Dead Man's Curve," Jan and Dean earned huge royalties with "Little Old Lady from Pasadena," "Move Out Little Mustang," and "Surfin' Hearse." Although lyrics of a few songs featured strong women, for the most part, song lyrics presented females as appendages or passive observers to be impressed by powerful machinery.

Finally, there were dozens of rock groups named after cars, including, simply, "The Cars," The Chevelles," "The Corvettes," "Flash Cadillac and the Continental Kids," "The Fleetwoods," "The Imperials" and "The Sting Rays." A common thread in naming of groups was that the vehicles so "honored" were either expensive, or fast, or both. As one historian concluded, "For the teen culture that emerged in the 1950s the fast car was inextricably linked with the new music hymning its praises. Both relied on new technologies, cared little for past traditions, and shocked older aficionados of travel and music." For teens, the last consideration was undoubtedly the most important.

CARS, DRIVE-INS, AND THE MOVIES

Perhaps no aspect of the youth culture of the 1950s and early 1960s offended older Americans more than their behavior at drive-in movie theaters. To be sure, leaders in the industry attempted to pitch drive-ins as "wholesome family entertainment." A case could be made for such a marketing device. Since many theaters charged a fixed price per vehicle, they traded on the idea that tired and overworked parents could take the whole family to double features at bargain prices. Equally important, they would be spared the hassles and expense of locating and hiring baby-sitters. If the children succumbed to routine bratlike behavior, they probably would not bother patrons in nearby vehicles, and parents would not be embarrassed by having to deal with them "in public." Although industry officials aggressively promoted sales of food and drinks at concession stands, families could further cut corners by bringing their own refreshments—in contrast to management policies in most walk-in neighborhood theaters.

By virtually any aesthetic measure, viewing a movie from an automobile was not as enjoyable as doing so from a comfortable seat in an indoor theater. Rows of cars sat in parking lots, facing giant screens. The driver pulled up to a stand containing a microphone, which provided the feature's sound. Acoustics through primitive microphone sets were often badly distorted. The picture projection on giant screens was usually blurred or grainy. There was little or no sense of shared audience experience: laughter, shock, fright. Although some drive-ins offered heaters, sitting for hours in a car was usually uncomfortable, unless weather was ideal. Rolling down windows for relief from heat on sticky summer nights could let in annoying insects.

For many teenagers, these considerations were of little consequence. Few went to drive-ins to see the movies. Some showed up merely to be seen, to interact with their peers, or to "fit in." Others, perhaps the majority, went there to smoke, drink, and explore their emerging sexuality in relative privacy. Once darkness fell and car windows fogged up from occupants' heavy breathing, it was difficult to see what was going on inside the cars. Comedians drew laughs with jokes about complaints from staid patrons of drive-ins that movie sound tracks were drowned out by the noise of zippers being opened. Another favorite line was that a young man proved his coming of age by learning how to un-

Drive-in movies offered both cheap family entertainment and opportunities for teenagers to explore their budding sexuality in relative privacy. They were enormously popular in the 1950s and 1960s, until gradually rendered obsolete by VCRs and co-ed dorms.

clasp a bra with one hand. The Everly Brothers' smash hit song "Wake Up Little Suzie" described a young couple waking up in the wee hours of the morning, having "fallen asleep" at a movie. The couple's (really, Suzie's) "reputation was shot." The lyrics make it uncertain whether the location was a walk-in or drive-in theater, but many listeners, if they thought about it, probably assumed the latter. Drive-ins earned various derisive nicknames within the teen culture, including "passion pits" and others that should probably be left for the reader's imagination.

Whether patronizing neighborhood theaters or drive-ins, moviegoers of the 1950s and 1960s saw countless films with strong or dominant automobile themes. The vast majority of them were eminently forgettable grade-B fillers, but a few were truly memorable. James Dean starred in the classic 1955 film *Rebel without a Cause*. Dean portrayed a troubled teen from the right side of the tracks, deeply alienated from both his parents and most of his peers. Clearly in search of himself, he attracted all sorts of minor trouble. During one brush with the law, he befriended costars Sal Mineo and Natalie Wood. The climax of the movie was when Jim Stark (Dean) and his rivals engaged in a game of "chicken" in which they raced their jalopies toward the edge of a cliff. The winner was the one who ditched his car last. It is a superb teenage "guts-and-glory" tale, immersed in the automobile culture. Ironically, all three stars met with real-life tragic deaths.

Although released in 1973, *American Graffiti* masterfully dissects the California "cruisin' " culture of the early 1960s. All of the action occurs in one hot summer night, when a group of recent, unfocused, directionless high-school graduates while away the hours, listening to DJ Wolfman Jack, cruisin' the "strip," and looking for "action." The movie features some of the most "boss" vehicles ever seen on the screen, plus a superb climactic drag race. One of the most unforgettable scenes was when one prankster crawled beneath a cop car, whose driver was waiting to pounce on any wayward teen, silently hooked up a thick chain to the rear axle, then crept back out and looped the other end around a telephone pole. Right on schedule, a few seconds later, his confederates zoomed past, whereupon the suddenly alert cop roared off in pursuit. A few dozen feet into the "chase," his chassis was yanked from underneath the body of his vehicle, and the wheel-less patrol car skidded down the street, generating nothing more threatening to teen transgressors than a shower of sparks. The movie catapulted Richard Dreyfuss, Harrison Ford, and Suzanne Somers into Hollywood's fast lane, as it were.

But even in real life, the "cruisin' " culture represented a lifestyle, sort of a permanent adolescence, for some. A group of cruisers at San Leandro, California's renowned "strip" along East 14th Street, observed a father and son "team" seated at a diner,

> . . . like salt and pepper, a matching pair in attitude if not in
> appearance. The father is darker than his son, heavy with a thick, oily
> mustache and the bulky muscles and drift of middle age. In both,
> even from a distance, you could sense some great impatience —
> some shared conviction that they've been waiting too long for
> something. They don't talk, they don't look at each other. The kid's
> bootheels tap out nervous energy on the floor; he fiddles with his
> coffee cup while his father stares out the window at the street. The
> old man looks like he's spent his best years here on East 14th Street;
> he probably has seen it all.

Fortunately, most former teen rebels found identities beyond the strip, but they still enjoyed the fast car culture vicariously. By the mid-1960s, Ian Fleming's James Bond movies tantalized viewers with fantasies involving fabulous cars and gorgeous women. *Goldfinger* (1964), the third of Fleming's Agent 007 movies, introduces James Bond's fabulous gadget-laden Aston Martin DB5, outfitted with machine guns, oil-slick dispensers, passenger-ejection seats, and assorted

No American institution of the 1950s and 1960s represented the heart of teenage culture more than the drive-in restaurant.

devices for thwarting the bad guys. The producers knew a cash cow when they had one, just as they recognized scenes that thrilled viewers. So James Bond movies continued without interruption, earning tens of millions for the studios. *Thunderball,* released the following year, received tepid reviews. However, in addition to acres of alluring female flesh, Director Terence Young added a surefire segment: a repeat performance by Agent Bond's imaginatively equipped Aston Martin. The late 1960s also marked the emergence of madcap, hair-raising car chases, greatly enhanced with spectacular special effects. Perhaps the most memorable of this genre was *Bullitt* (1968), starring Steve McQueen, Robert Vaughn, Jacqueline Bisset, and Donald Duvall.

A few movies are hard to label. One gets a sneaky hunch that the directors had something in mind besides merely making money. Viewers' reactions would probably depend largely on their moods when they entered the theater. One film, *Faster Pussycat! Kill! Kill!* (1966), had to be a spoof on virtually every aspect of southern California's underside, including the car culture. Three nubile strippers get their jollies hot-rodding in the California desert. The plot quickly sickens. After one car race gets totally out of hand, the characters find themselves wrapped up in kidnapping, robbery, murder, and (perhaps its sole saving grace) lust. One reviewer, undoubtedly handsomely compensated by the studio, called it "Easily the most watchable, fun and funny production to spring from the mind of Russ Meyer. Those who haven't seen it cannot truly be called 'cool'."

Lamentably, the vast majority of car movies churned out simply wasted lots of film. In *The Devil on Wheels* (1947), a teenager, inspired by his father's reckless driving, becomes a hot-rodder himself and wreaks mayhem and destruction. In *Dragstrip Girl* (1957), an eighteen-year-old girl supposedly comes of age competing against boys and grown men in drag races. In *Daddy-O* (1959), a drag racer (Dick Contino) traps the murderers of his best friend and (surprise!) wins the love of Jana (Sandra Giles), a race track bimbo. Although *Chitty Chitty Bang Bang* (1968), starring Dick Van Dyke, Sally Ann Howes, and Benny Hill, did reasonably well at the box office, it wins this writer's vote as a clunker. An eccentric tinkerer fixes up an old jalopy and magically transports his children to a world where (alas) the evil rulers have forbidden children! Special effects are poor; the plot is even worse. Delete!

THE BIRTH OF FAST FOOD

Before and after trips to drive-in movies, teenagers seeking peer approval spent hours at local drive-in restaurants. The teenagers' reasons for visiting drive-ins were very different from those of most other patrons. To teenagers, whose appetites were often legendary, food was important but it was often secondary. Teenagers really wanted to linger, to interact with peers. Their vehicles often jammed the cramped parking lots at local drive-ins. Teens were often loud, discourteous, and even rowdy. This often led to tense relationships between teens and restaurant managers. The latter recognized and respected the volume of business teenagers represented; without their loyal patronage, many establishments would quickly fail. On the other hand, they really wanted their younger patrons to behave nicely, eat quickly, and leave quietly: a fantasy usually unfulfilled. Young, working-class families also patronized drive-in restaurants on a fairly regular basis. They sought quick, inexpensive meals, which would fill up the kids and keep them quiet and, in the bargain, provide brief respites from kitchens for tired, overworked wives. A third source of patrons was travelers. In the postwar period, fewer travelers were affluent, genteel motorists who wished to savor a leisurely, expensive lunch or dinner at a quaint country inn. Increasingly, time was money. They did not want to waste time waiting for service in conventional, sit-down restaurants. Instead, most wanted cheap, quick, and filling meals before getting back on the road.

Although the first drive-in restaurants dated from the 1920s, they did not really reach their heyday until after World War II. In the immediate postwar years, there were few chains; most drive-ins were one of a kind, and their food varied widely in quality and cleanliness. Some featured attractive teenage waitresses who took orders, then brought orders to patrons in their cars. Typically, they would attach a small tray to the outside of the driver's window, then return to pick up empty trays when patrons were finished. Perhaps anticipating today's "Hooters" restaurants, some drive-in owners played the sex angle by hiring curvaceous young women, providing uniforms with revealing tops and tight shorts, and having the women work on roller skates.

By the late 1940s, the market was ripe for fast-food chains. More Americans were on the road driving longer distances. Obviously, they had to eat more meals away from home. An old saying noted that smart motorists should "eat where the truckers stop," but experienced drivers eventually learned that following such a strategy required a cast-iron stomach. To many Americans, the notion of the unpretentious, independent diner, graced by a garish neon sign simply urging passersby to "eat" conjured up images of "greasy spoons." Many a motorist also worried about cleanliness in the "mom and pops." In far too many diners, rest rooms were filthy and patrons had nothing to dry their hands on other than well-worn, suspicious-looking towels. Horror stories abounded about flies and insects buzzing frazzled customers and uninvited critters being found in blue plate specials. On top of all this, many customers resented being expected to leave generous tips for surly, unkempt waiters and waitresses.

In fact, the first chain restaurants began evolving around World War I, but none could claim a national reputation. Most historians award that honor to Howard Johnson, who opened his first restaurant on Cape Cod in 1935, where he dispensed hamburgers, sandwiches, and his famous twenty-eight-flavor ice creams. Johnson's Cape Cod establishment was spectacularly successful, and he quickly opened several dozen more restaurants. Each was built in a uniform architectural style, featuring a distinctive orange roof. Johnson's real break was landing a contract in 1941 to be the exclusive supplier of roadside food along the recently opened Pennsylvania Turnpike. By the onset of World War II, 150 Howard Johnson restaurants stretched from New England to Florida. Patrons were drawn to them for numerous reasons. They were attractive, clean, and well lighted. Most important, they offered basically the same food, prepared the same way, in every unit. Patrons knew in advance exactly what they were going to get and what they would pay when they stopped. This simple fact took much of the uncertainty and anxiety out of long trips, and some motorists in the East would not eat anywhere else.

Another early food chain was the White Castle, which copied Howard Johnson's formula but added another twist. White Castle's featured attraction was the ubiquitous hamburger, lovingly nicknamed the *slider*. White Castle sold them at low prices and in large numbers. Like patrons of Howard Johnson's, customers at White Castles knew exactly what they were getting. White Castle experimented in assembly line techniques of producing burgers. One of the slider's most distinctive features was that both the meat and bun were square rather than round. Experimentation had demonstrated that square burgers were easier for inexperienced chefs to cook on their grills. Another attraction was that White Castles were self-service. At some (not all) White Castles, one could drive up to a window, place an order, and wait in the car until the order was ready. Drivers did not have to leave their cars, nor were tips expected. Significantly, the dynamics of driving and eating out were merging fifty years ago.

To many contemporary Americans, the words *fast food* and *McDonald's* are synonymous. It all began with two brothers, Richard and Maurice McDonald, who moved from New England to southern California in the 1920s, seeking work in the movie industry. For them, like tens of thousands of other hopefuls, the silver screen yielded neither fame nor a pot of gold. In 1940, they set up a hamburger stand in San Bernardino, fifty miles east of Los Angeles, which they named after themselves. They were still flipping burgers in 1948, but they had converted the business to self-service so they could accommodate more drive-up customers. The brothers added several innovative features. Richard claimed that they were the first in the business to use infrared lamps to keep mass-produced French fries warm and crisp. In the postwar gold rush to southern California, business was so good that they built six more outlets by 1952, which they adorned with their now famous golden arches.

Their real break came at just that moment. Ray A. Kroc was a sales manager for the Lily-Tulip Company. This outfit had an exclusive franchise to the Prince Castle multimixer that could mix six milkshakes simultaneously. When Kroc got an order from the McDonald brothers for eight of his machines for a single restaurant, he sensed that something highly unusual was afoot. He flew from Chicago to southern California to check out the brothers' operations. Years later, Kroc recalled, "When I got there I saw more people waiting in line than I had ever seen at any drive-in. I said to myself, 'Son of a bitch, these guys have got something going. How about if I open some of these places?' "

Kroc and the McDonald brothers effected one of the most successful mergers in American business history. Over the next five years, Kroc set up a chain of 228 McDonald's outlets. With only minor variations, they were basically identical. Motorists soon learned to look for the distinctive, trademark golden arches, which were easily visible a block or more away. The partners quickly proved that ". . . less is more. McDonald's fired the car hops. They did away with . . . china, flatware, glasses, place mats, cloth napkins, and salt, pepper, and sugar shakers." Among other things, they "shook off the 'greasy spoon' image" of the typical quick-stop restaurant. McDonald's restaurants epitomized cleanliness. Most restaurants concealed food preparation behind swinging doors, which often had tiny, grease-stained windows into their interiors. This sometimes induced uneasy feelings in patrons, who feared that there might be good reasons for chefs to work out of their sight. In contrast, McDonald's exposed food preparation to full view of patrons. In addition to bargain prices, speed, and convenience for patrons, McDonald's emphasized cleanliness. Interiors of their outlets featured vast expanses of stainless steel and white tiling, which were easy to clean, as well as other important features. As one historian aptly noted, "Unlike the diners, where comfortable booths encouraged people to linger over their meals, McDonald's used hard plastic seats and bright colors to encourage folks to buy, eat up, and leave." The keys to profitability were fast, palatable, cheap food; quick turnover of patrons; and enormous volume. Unlike many other operators, McDonald's originally discouraged jukeboxes and cigarette machines, both of which, in their view, encouraged patrons to hang around after they had finished eating. Finally, McDonald's featured assembly line production and standardization of food delivery. Whether driving through Oklahoma, Illinois, or California, customers could rely upon the same quality and quantity of decent food, all at bargain prices. It was a winning formula in America during the postwar decades. Most importantly, it was food delivery ingeniously tailored to a nation of hurrying consumers on wheels. The McDonald brothers and Ray Kroc had hit upon a business formula that dozens of fast-food imitators would try to duplicate in succeeding decades, with varying degrees of success.

FAMILY VACATIONS: THE MOTEL CULTURE

Just as Americans were flocking to fast-food restaurants in the 1950s, so too were they taking to the roads to enjoy family vacations. Although the choices may have been heavily influenced by affordability, one survey discovered that vacationing by automobile was the preferred means of travel for four out of five families. As millions of families heeded Dinah Shore's invitation to "see the USA in their Chevrolets," increasing numbers of Americans preferred indoor sleeping accommodations to camping outdoors. In 1929, an American Automobile Association study revealed that three of four Americans seeking indoor accommodations patronized hotels. This trend was almost totally reversed by the end of the next decade. One study showed that, by 1940, hotels accommodated only 32 percent of all lodgers; the rest stayed in cabin courts and motels. A generation later, America had indeed become a nation of wanderers on wheels; by 1967, the average traveler spent 14.6 nights in rented accommodations. These trends stimulated an enormous boom in the motel business. In 1946, there were an estimated 20,000 motels in the United States; by the mid-1960s, there were more than 60,000. Even fiction writers developed motel themes. Vladimir Nabokov's racy, controversial novel *Lolita*, which appeared in the mid-1950s, opens with an exquisite depiction of the kitsch ambiance of the typical motel room of the period where he and his adolescent lover cavorted.

For many handymen, particularly retirees, the motel business appeared attractive. A couple could live for "free" where they worked. If Dad was handy and Mom could take care of the laundry and housekeeping, their overhead was very low. Before the rise of the big chains, some with hundreds of rooms, most motels were small, perhaps a dozen rooms. They were easy to build, and since cash returns were immediate upon completion, banks' loans and terms were usually liberal. The Tax Act of 1954 encouraged motel construction by allowing rapid depreciation of construction costs; this, in turn, encouraged builders to put up relatively flimsy units. These factors helped create a rapidly growing but quite volatile industry. Motel design was particularly ripe for experimentation, and most units quickly became obsolete.

Distinct parallels appeared between the fast-food and motel businesses. Although motel facilities were becoming a bit less rustic by the end of World War II, finding adequate, comfortable rooms at the end of a day's travel was still an iffy, hit-or-miss proposition. With a few exceptions, motels were individually owned and managed. Some motel owners went to extraordinary lengths to make guests comfortable. Others, perhaps possessing fewer people skills, basically ignored patrons' needs after they collected payment. Little, if any, standardization translated into huge differences in levels of cleanliness, service, and comfort provided.

Picture a typical traveling family at the end of a long, hot day on the road. Dad, as usual, is behind the wheel. These are the days before most cars have air conditioning. Despite the fact that the windows have been down, everybody is perspiring freely and collecting plenty of road dust. The three kids are all out of sorts, and Mom is pleading with Dad to stop soon. They enter a strange town. Traffic is heavy; so, at the very least, Dad has time to read the signs adjacent to the motels they pass. Mom finally sees a pretty sign for the Bo-Peep Motel and gets Dad to pull up in front of the office. Entering the office, Dad discovers that, yes, they have one room left. They are lucky, because there is a huge Shriner's convention in town. The room will be $5. Dad thinks this is a bit high, but he is inclined to take it. Still, he is no innocent greenhorn, and Mom has urged him to inspect the room. Dad asks to look at the room. Sourly, the lady hands him the room key and waves her hand in the general direction. Dad slouches across the hot, sticky asphalt parking lot. Opening the door of the room, he steps inside. Although there is little relief from the heat, the room looks clean enough, and there are two decent-sized double beds that sag only slightly. Dad is relieved that no mice or cockroaches are scurrying across the floor seeking hiding places. He returns to the office and says he'll take it. He feels lucky that they arrived when they did, since another worn-looking couple is now standing at the desk seeking a room.

Dad's sense of relief is brief. As he fills out the registration form, the lady informs him that there is an extra dollar charge for each child, including an extra cot. Local room taxes run a stiff 10 percent, so his $5 motel room has suddenly become $8.80. He's depressed, since he and his wife had thought they were being realistic when they budgeted $6 per night for motel rooms. Dad returns to the baking car and announces that arrangements have been made. His wife gives him a tired smile, and Dad maneuvers the car to the space in front of their room. She can think of little other than a cool shower. The kids are whining about the lack of a swimming pool. An hour earlier, they had passed through a town with several nice-looking facilities and had seen other kids frolicking in sparkling pools. Why hadn't they stopped there? He would have liked to indulge them, but he guesses that rooms ran as much as $9 a night, before "extras." Dad is relieved when the kids' attention is diverted by several other children grouped around a rusty swing and a slide in the weedy central courtyard. Perhaps they will be happy there for an hour while he and his wife freshen up for dinner.

After the kids squabble briefly over who gets to sleep alone on the cot, they get washed up, and the family heads out to find a place to eat. Dad had asked the desk lady for recommendations, but all of the places she mentioned sounded as if they would stretch the budget; so they find the local White Castle, buy a sack of hamburgers and some milk shakes, then have a family "picnic" at a local park as the sun sets. Being strangers in town, they do not have any idea what to do. They have already seen the double feature at the local drive-in, and Mom does not really care for demolition derbies at local race tracks. However, there is a television in the room, and at 8 P.M. they retreat to spend the rest of the evening watching sitcoms in the stuffy, small, uncomfortable motel room. With the three kids sleeping in the same room, Mom certainly will not be interested in romance. About 10 P.M., Dad announces that he's restless, that he's going to "take a stroll." Three blocks down the street, he enters a package store and furtively plops down $2 for a half-pint of Three Feathers bourbon. Returning to the motel, he finds that all of the lights are out in his room. He sits in the metal chair near the door and puffs on one cigarette after another while sipping from his bottle. Dad overhears the rustling of sheets and the panting sounds of a couple, probably young, in the room next door and tries to turn his thoughts to happier times. He has worked fifty weeks for this family vacation. Well, maybe things will get better when they get to the in-laws' home a mile from the beach.

This was the reality of automobile travel in the years right after World War II, at least for blue-collar workers who were enjoying their first paid vacations. As late as 1948, 98 percent of all motels were still "mom and pops." Only a small string of motels in the Southwest comprised a chain of establishments offering uniform standards of quality, service, and price. Alamo Plaza Hotel Courts was, in the words of historian John A. Jakle, "an ad hoc creation," the nation's first recognizable chain of motels, begun by Texan E. Lee Torrance in 1931. Originally, Torrance had no grand vision of opening a large group of motels, but by offering rates of a dollar for a single room, $2 for a double, along with clean, comfortable rooms, business even in the Depression was brisk. By adopting a standardized design and building at multiple locations, Torrance kept costs (and rates) low. He opened his first forty-three unit facility in Tyler, Texas, and he confidently announced plans to expand. However, several factors worked against him. Perhaps the most important was that Torrance had only immediate family members and a few intimate business associates to help him. He never thought in terms of building and training a competent management team. Torrance had a rigid notion of how motels should look, and he did not think in terms of more modern motel architecture. What was new and intriguing in the early 1930s was dated two decades later. Thus, expansion had inherent limits. At its peak in the early 1950s, there were twenty-two Alamo Plazas, but Torrance and his associates were not pacesetters.

Other modest efforts at building motel chains practiced varying degrees of standardization. In the late 1940s and early 1950s, some motel operators responded to the traveler's lament that it was difficult to guarantee acceptable accommodations in unfamiliar destinations. Duncan Hines published a useful guidebook evaluating restaurants, which was regularly updated; in the 1950s, this service expanded to include motels. The American Automobile Association (AAA) also offered its members tour books providing similar evaluations. Soon, restaurant and motel operators prominently featured these "official" AAA and Duncan Hines endorsements on roadside advertisements and signs.

The five-day, forty-hour workweek, accompanied by a two-week paid vacation, became the standard for millions of American workers after the war. Originally reserved for the managerial classes and white-collar employees, the annual two-week paid vacation became a staple in union contracts by the mid-1950s. As working-class families gained leisure time, automobile vacationing boomed. It was just a matter of time before the motel industry experienced the same standardization as the fast-food business, and the 1950s witnessed significant experiments in development of chain motels.

Kemmons Wilson was born into a poor family in Arkansas in 1913. He was smart, ambitious, and hardworking; after securing a foothold in local movie and jukebox enterprises, he became one of the largest real estate developers in Memphis, Tennessee. While taking a vacation trip with his family by automobile in the early 1950s, Wilson sensed enormous opportunity in the motel business. As he observed in a 1968 speech, "It didn't take us long to find out that most motels had cramped, uncomfortable rooms—and that they charged extra for children. Few had adequate restaurants and fewer still were air-conditioned. In short, it was a miserable trip." He was particularly irritated by surcharges of $2 for each child. "Our $6 room became a $16 room. . . . I told my wife that I didn't think this was fair. It wouldn't encourage people to travel with their children. I told her I was going to build a chain of motels, and I was never going to make a charge for children as long as they stayed in the same room as their parents."

Wilson's epiphany was critically important in the evolution of chain motels, and he moved quickly. Borrowing $325,000 from a local bank, Wilson built the first Holiday Inn Motel on the east side of Memphis, which opened in August 1952. His new motel offered all of the amenities missing in the places his family had stayed in the previous year: air conditioning, a restaurant, telephones in rooms, free ice, even kennels for family pets. His investment struggled at the beginning, but the intrepid entrepreneur had far bigger things in mind. Basically, he wished to replicate his establishment everywhere people wanted to travel. But how could he expand, yet at the same time guarantee the same level of quality and service at every location? Wilson decided to set up franchises. His challenge was finding investors willing to commit the large sums needed to effect rapid expansion, accept his property designs, maintain his quality of service, and provide the level of amenities he felt were necessary to distinguish Holiday Inns from their competitors.

Wilson recruited a partner, then incorporated Holiday Inns of America, Inc., in 1954. Initial progress was painfully slow. Most wealthy individuals are self-made, and few were willing to subordinate their egos to Wilson's. By the end of 1955, the company was $37,500 in the red and was operating out of an abandoned plumbing shop. However, Wilson eventually hit upon the idea of recruiting doctors, lawyers, and other professionals with large amounts of money to invest but little interest in running motels themselves. If such investors supplied the capital, Wilson and his men could provide the expertise on how to build, staff, and maintain the new facilities. After Holiday Inns were finished, the company retained small royalties from all services sold by each franchise.

Holiday Inns began expanding quickly in the late 1950s. In 1956, the company comprised 26 motels with 2,107 rooms and took in $1.6 million in gross revenue. By 1970, it had mushroomed to 1,271 motels with almost 180,000 rooms and gross revenue exceeded $600 million. There was no need for Dad to inspect the room, since guests checking in at the front desk knew exactly what they would get. Every Holiday Inn had year-round air conditioning, a swimming pool, and free advance reservations. There were televisions and telephones in every room, even baby-sitters and house physicians on call. It was, in many respects, home away from home. Holiday Inn billed itself as "The Nation's Innkeeper," and there was truth to the claim. Corporate advertisements gushed, "We build a new room in the time it takes most people to find one. Twenty-two minutes to be exact. We don't mean just a room. We mean first rate rooms. And people everywhere are reserving them just as fast as we can build and open Holiday Inns." By the early 1970s, there were numerous national chains.

Holiday Inn was by far the largest, but Best Western, Friendship Inns, and Ramada Inns provided spirited competition.

In addition, as millions of American families hit the road, numerous entrepreneurs consciously focused marketing efforts on budget-conscious travelers. Reacting against escalating nightly rates, home builders William Becker and Paul Greene opened the first Motel 6 in Santa Barbara, California, in 1962. The idea was to market clean, comfortable rooms with the bare necessities, which required little maintenance. They further cut costs by operating on a strictly cash basis. They initially offered rooms at $6.60 for a single. The concept caught on with many cost-conscious travelers; and, by the end of the decade, Motel 6 was joined by competing budget motel chains, including Econo Lodge, Super 8, and others. The United States had clearly become a nation of vacationers on wheels.

Of course, by then, vacationers could go virtually anywhere and enjoy almost any amenity in their automobiles, including church. In 1955, the Reverend Robert Schuller conducted his first sermon in a parking lot in Garden Grove, California, to a congregation of a dozen families. From the very beginning, he unabashedly proclaimed that religion was an enterprise, a "shopping center for God, part of the service industry." By the mid-1970s, Schuller had parlayed his initial effort into the Crystal Cathedral, a gaudy, star-shaped, futuristic church boasting 10,000 windows, and he ranked among southern California's most popular televangelists. Schuller never forgot his automotive "roots." He always stressed that churches had to have big parking lots: "You can be the greatest preacher in the world, but if people can't find a place to park, they won't stop to hear your message." In the quarter century after World War II, the automobile had penetrated virtually every facet of the national culture; it almost seemed as if Americans had added wheels to their anatomy.

Chapter Five

THE AUTOMOBILE, MASS TRANSIT, AND PUBLIC POLICY

In the postwar years, Americans demonstrated their allegiance to the automobile and bought them in record numbers. Registrations more than doubled between 1945 and 1955. As increasing numbers of American families enjoyed the luxury of more than one vehicle, they found more uses for them and average annual mileage driven per automobile escalated sharply. In short, Americans took to the road with a vengeance. Public officials were challenged to build the roads needed to accommodate more Americans. That officials responded so enthusiastically had profoundly important economic, political, and social ripple effects in the latter half of the century. This chapter addresses the issue of why public officials generally adopted policies that favored continued expansion of automobile use, as opposed to public transportation, until late in the twentieth century.

After a brief period of revival during the Depression and World War II, public transit experienced an extended decline. The vast majority of the steadily shrinking numbers of patrons of mass transit systems were poor; and, because they were less influential or organized than other interest groups, politicians gave short shrift to their needs. However, several million Americans still depended almost entirely on public transit, and, in most urban areas, politicians could not simply allow local systems to die. However, as their competitive position vis-à-vis the automobile deteriorated further, mass transit companies became increasingly dependent on public subsidies for survival.

TOLL ROADS

The decades following the war brought highway building and improvement on a massive scale. Thousands of miles of new road were built, and tens of thousands of miles of old road were improved. However, the dominant systems of financing the nation's highway projects that evolved by the 1950s might well have surprised a betting man in the mid-1940s. Although a few cities, such as New York and Los Angeles, had already poured millions of taxpayer dollars into modern parkways and "freeways," toll roads—or "turnpikes"—appeared to be the highways of the future. The latter, in particular, had already proven enormously popular. Sponsors of the Pennsylvania Turnpike estimated in 1939 that only 715 drivers would pay the required tolls each day. In fact, within two weeks of its opening in 1940, the actual figure was 26,000! Turnpike planners in the Keystone State quickly realized that they had a winner; they would be able to pay off principal on bonds and finance extensions and improvements far more quickly than projected by initial estimates. By the end of the 1950s, the Pennsylvania Turnpike stretched 470 miles and was the second longest turnpike in the country.

Road building almost ceased during the war; but, when hostilities ended, highway engineers and state-level politicians began an aggressive program of toll road construction. Although there were a few projects west of the Mississippi River, most of the turnpikes were in the heavily populated industrial states of the Northeast and upper Midwest. Some important pikes were built on a relatively small scale. For years, residents in scenic towns along the seacoast in Maine had been greatly inconvenienced by mounting traffic along U.S. Highway 1. The heavily used route went through downtown sections of every sizable seacoast town. Just as highway congestion inconvenienced locals, so too did it irritate tourists, whose tax dollars provided an increasing percentage of state revenues. In response, state officials created the Maine Turnpike Authority in 1941 and authorized it to plan a toll road that would bypass the heavily populated towns. Construction began after the war, and the first forty-seven-mile section between Kittery and Portland opened in 1947. Most of the users were from out of state: 60 to 80 percent during the tourist season and 60 percent over the whole year. Locals approved because it greatly relieved traffic congestion and out-of-state drivers financed most of the cost.

Toll roads were presented as technological marvels. Highway engineers were dazzled by the vision of potential savings of time, plus wear and tear on vehicles. Wouldn't it be wonderful if a driver could get on toll roads outside of New York City and not encounter a traffic signal or stoplight all the way to Chicago? In short order, in the 1950s, New Jersey, Ohio, and Indiana all authorized toll roads that would link up with the Pennsylvania Turnpike. The Ohio Turnpike was authorized in 1949; construction of the 241-mile route began in 1952 and was completed in 1956. The Indiana Turnpike was opened to the Illinois border in 1956. That year also saw completion of the 131-mile-long New Jersey Turnpike.

Hence, in 1956, the dream of an 840-mile, unimpeded drive from New York to Chicago became reality. Numerous traffic studies documented significant savings in time, gasoline, and wear and tear on vehicles. One study by the Indiana Toll Road Commission revealed that the roads were particularly valuable for truckers. Time of travel was cut by nearly one-third, gasoline consumption by approximately 10 percent. Turnpike travel probably added years to the lives of commercial truck and interstate bus fleets. The average number of applications of brakes between New York and Chicago was cut from 890 to 194, gear shifts from 3,116 to 777! Another huge advantage of toll roads was the safety factor. According to automobile historian John B. Rae, at a time when the national average for highway fatalities per 100 million vehicle miles driven stood at 5.6, most turnpikes averaged well under half that figure; representative annual fatality rates from the mid-1960s included the New York Thruway with 2.42; the New Jersey Turnpike, 2.17; and the Garden State Parkway (actually, a free road), an incredibly low rate of 0.66. Even if no study could accurately measure lessening of driver tension, no doubt many gear jammers silently gave thanks to the toll roads, as they eased their cumbersome rigs through the industrial flatlands of New Jersey and the mountains of western Pennsylvania.

The New York State Thruway is the largest single toll road in the United States, comprising a total of 629 miles, constructed at a cost of $1.13 billion. The road was first projected in 1942, and construction began in 1946. The 496-mile-long main branch runs north from New York City to Albany, cuts directly west to Buffalo, then skirts Lake Erie to the Pennsylvania state line. Construction of the main branch of the project was completed in 1956. Direct connection of the New York Thruway with the Ohio Turnpike would not occur until construction of linking interstate highways in the early 1960s.

The brief toll road building mania in the United States in the late 1940s and 1950s paralleled the canal craze of the early nineteenth century, which transformed the same region. Canals were essentially supplanted in significance by a "higher" technology, namely, railroads.

Toll roads were eventually phased out by a new form of financing: the massive, mostly federally funded Interstate Highway program. However, like canals a century earlier, the toll road movement had a significant impact on the nation's transportation infrastructure. In the 2 decades following the war, 21 states, 17 of them east of the Mississippi River, built almost 3,600 miles of toll roads, at a total cost of $5.5 billion. Once finished, they were extremely popular. Although some drivers griped about high tolls, the average motorist could perceive the basic fairness of the assessments. Those who benefited directly paid the costs.

A NATIONAL HIGHWAY PROGRAM

Ironically, just as toll roads were reaching their peak in popularity, a wholly different approach to road building took root. As highway historian Mark H. Rose ably demonstrated, the concept of a national system of integrated, federally funded, limited-access highways had been a cherished objective of a number of highway engineers for many years. Thomas H. MacDonald, head of the Bureau of Public Roads from 1919 until his retirement in 1953, was perhaps the first such visionary. The first federal highway program originated in 1916, albeit with modest objectives and limited federal financing. In the subsequent thirty years, federal decision makers had offered a variety of rationales for encouraging highway construction. In World War I, they promoted a system of national highways as useful and necessary for military defense in the event of invasion from abroad. During the Depression, on the other hand, the focus shifted to the fact that road building was labor intensive; such projects would help ease unemployment.

One reason for slow progress in effecting a national highway program was profound disagreement between competing interest groups over whose needs should take precedence and which interest groups should pay specific costs. Farmers were not that interested in a national system of roads; they still preferred local highways to help ease their physical and social isolation and to facilitate movement of crops to markets. Long distance trucking firms promoted national highways. Suburban real estate developers pushed highways connecting cities and suburbs, largely to enhance the values of their properties. Although public transit companies often fought such highway proposals as expensive, inefficient, and inherently unfair subsidies for their competitor, the automobile, officials in some of the nation's largest cities envisioned spending millions on elevated highways, which they perceived as a panacea for mounting traffic congestion. However, between the wars, rural interests had dominated decision making regarding highway routes. Very little road funding was expended on improving highways within cities. This emphasis prevailed until the 1960s and 1970s.

Not surprisingly, as during World War I, World War II refocused planning on highway building for national defense. The Defense Highway Act of 1941 did little or nothing for actual road construction; it simply designated specific highways for movement of troops, war materiel, and supplies. In 1944, Congress took another significant step toward a coherent highway policy in passing the Federal Aid Highway Act. This initiative was important for several reasons. First, it provided $1.5 billion, which would be available over the next three years. In addition, it specifically set aside funds for the extension and improvement of federal aid to highways located within municipalities. To be sure, earlier federal funds had been available for use in the cities but only at the discretion of the states; and most state legislatures, then as now, were dominated by rural interests. The heart of the legislation was the so-called *ABC provision* that earmarked 45 percent of funding for primary (A) roads between cities, 30 percent for secondary (B) roads in rural areas, and 25 percent for urban (C) arterial roads. Finally, although it did not yet provide long-term funding, the act envisioned a fully integrated 41,000-mile Interstate Highway System.

Who deserves credit as the founder of the nation's Interstate Highway System? It is impossible to single out a particular individual. Thomas H. MacDonald certainly merits consideration, having been an energetic, creative, and savvy bureaucrat, instrumental in promoting national highways since World War I. Any number of regional highway planners, including Robert Moses of New York, designer and chief promoter of New York City's elaborate regional system of limited-access parkways, also contributed valuable ideas that were eventually incorporated into the evolving system. Norman Bel Geddes aroused intense enthusiasm for futuristic highways through his compelling exhibit at the New York World's Fair. Others merit consideration as well; but, in April 1941, President Roosevelt set up the Interregional Highway Committee of seven men, including MacDonald, charged with devising a workable plan for future development of integrated national highways. Although they effected no actual construction during the war, the committee offered a fertile arena for debate and testing of new ideas.

Twelve years elapsed between passage of the Federal Aid Highway Act of 1944 and President Eisenhower's signing of an identically named law in 1956, better known as the Interstate Highway Act.

It was one of the most important pieces of legislation of the decade, perhaps even the century, as interstate highways profoundly affected rapidly evolving patterns of metropolitan development. The act outlined a national network of 41,000 miles of superhighway. One of the most crucial provisions was that 90 percent of construction costs would be borne by the federal government, just 10 percent by the states through which they passed. Funding was generated by taxes on auto parts and accessories, trucks, and truck parts and accessories, plus added levies on gasoline. The money collected was placed into a new reserve account called the Highway Trust Fund. To highway enthusiasts, the fact that, at least during its first years, no funds could be diverted from the trust fund to finance other government projects was an enormous plus. Thus, each special interest being taxed could rest assured that all revenues generated would be spent on projects that benefited them, either directly or indirectly. In crude terms, gasoline and tire tax revenues were not going to be siphoned off to support "welfare queens." At the time, creation of the Highway Trust Fund appeared inspired to many. Congress had established what transportation historian Stephen Goddard astutely labeled "a perpetual motion machine." Revenues were enormous; and, in the years of rapid expansion of the automobile culture, they were constantly increasing. Goddard also claimed that this funding mechanism basically allowed its administrators to operate in virtual secrecy, since they never had to appear before Congress to justify annual budget requests.

Final passage followed a tortuous struggle by competing interests, plus a great deal of political logrolling. A major reason it took a dozen years from initial authorization to actual implementation and funding of the Interstate Highway Act was profound disagreements over who should pay for it and how. A number of powerful individuals, including General John H. Bragdon, head of the Public Works Planning Unit in the Council of Economic Advisors, still believed that the highways should be toll roads. For a long time, President Eisenhower also preferred toll roads.

Other complicated issues revolved around the politics of financing. Some states had already made great strides in building through roads. In addition, some metropolitan regions had already spent tens of millions of dollars trying to solve congestion problems on their own. Why should political entities, which had supposedly failed to plan ahead and had thus made little effort to solve transportation needs, suddenly receive the benefit of state-of-the-art roads for which they paid just a fraction of the cost?

Eventually, broader, even more compelling political considerations tipped the balance toward federal funding for future integrated highway development. Eisenhower enlisted support of General Lucius Clay, a trusted aide-de-camp during the Second World War, to shepherd the interstate plan through Congress. Clay quickly discovered that numerous western states possessed a long-standing tradition of free roads, with virtually unlimited speed limits. In the South, already on guard against federal mandates concerning Civil Rights, some politicians were suspicious of possible federal Trojan horses. They feared that any federal grants for roads would come with unacceptable strings attached. Clay warned the president that he faced "revolution" if he tried to ram toll roads down their throats. Satisfying—or at least placating—a sufficient majority of aroused interest groups and securing passage of the Interstate Highway Act required a carefully planned campaign, carried out with the elegance of a minuet.

The economic and political stakes were enormous. When Congress established a subcommittee to gather testimony regarding the desirability of interstate highways, it was besieged, week after week, by lobbyists from virtually every known automobile, trucking, petroleum, long-distance carrier, tire and rubber, and automobile parts interest group, all enthusiastically backing what some critics have called the nation's biggest ever pork barrel project. Decades later, Helen Leavitt, one of the automobile culture's foremost critics, portrayed passage of the Interstate Highway Act in almost conspiratorial terms. She presented an elaborate flowchart of "interlocking organizations" forming an extremely powerful lobby, including the Associated General Contractors, the American Association of State Highway Officials, the American Road Builders Association, the Bureau of Public Roads, the American Petroleum Institute, the National Automobile Dealers Association, the National Highway Users Conference, and a host of other professional pressure groups and corporate lobbyists.

Leavitt had a point. Few among the dozens of speakers challenged the appropriateness of building roads in an effort to satisfy the nation's relentlessly increasing mobility "requirements," even within the highly populated metropolitan areas. Some urged Congress to go even farther in paving the nation. Not surprisingly, the Portland Cement Association favored an interstate system more than three times the size of the one already on the drawing board, some 128,000 miles in all! The association seemingly wanted to pave over urban America. Its industry report to Congress suggested, "That motorists have swarmed to use most freeways built in metropolitan areas during the past quarter century is a clear sign that the decision to build them was sound. Continuing traffic congestion, however, indicates that demand for such facilities is far from satisfied. . . . It is clear that the existing mileage of freeways in most metropolitan areas falls far short of present needs." As long as freeways were filled up to overflowing during rush hour, many of the automobile-oriented interest groups saw no alternative but to keep building them.

Powerful, occasionally crude lobbyists representing various trucking, automobile, and other manufacturing interest groups also worked hard to tweak forthcoming legislation to their sponsors' advantage. Mixes of rivals and potential allies were both complex and highly combustible. This was particularly true regarding financing. For example, while both truckers and auto groups enthusiastically supported the concept of "free" superhighways, lobbyists for the latter believed truckers should pay far higher license fees because the weight of trucks broke down pavement much more quickly. Trucking interests countered that this would lead to higher prices for thousands of consumer items delivered efficiently to markets. Restaurant and motel owners along busy U.S. highways initially licked their chops at the expected boost to automobile tourism, but they eventually discovered that newer chain establishments near interstate exits sapped most of their patronage. Tire manufacturers, petroleum producers, and parts suppliers all tried to divert attention from profits in their industries, pare down taxes on their products, and shift more of the road tax burden to others. In the political infighting, few fared better than trucking industry lobbyists; they reduced a proposed fifty-cents-per-pound tire tax increase down to a mere three cents! Almost totally lost amidst the cacophony of shrill voices demanding special attention was the complaint by mass transit providers that federal sponsorship of free superhighways was a naked subsidy for the automobile, whereas the transportation needs of millions of inner-city poor who did not own automobiles were totally ignored. If new limited-access highways penetrated to the cores of inner cities and the automobile siphoned off any more of their hard-core patronage, this would be ". . . the straw that broke the camel's back."

Even President Eisenhower questioned the efficiency of any program that encouraged one individual to travel into downtown areas in a 3,000-pound vehicle, requiring a considerable amount of parking space for ten or twelve hours each weekday. Some highway planners stressed that it would be preferable to emphasize circumferential routes, which would divert cars from urban cores. Powerful inner-city interests, however, would not be denied. Their support was critical for final passage of the legislation. During the months before key congressional votes on the Interstate Highway Act, there had been feverish real estate speculation in metropolitan regions around the country regarding likely routes. Although the exact amount of money required for completing the system remained a moving estimate, the first figures tossed about were roughly $27 billion. Some of the money would be needed for acquiring property in cities. Big-city mayors salivated over prospects of getting their fair share of the bonanza into their hands—or those of powerful supporters. It was a situation ripe for luscious real estate deals favoring well-positioned "insiders," which in turn encouraged naked political graft. In the first round of funded projects, numerous interstate freeways penetrated the cores of inner cities.

One of the reasons interstate highways had a long list of enthusiasts was that they provided an enormous boost to many segments of the economy. Obviously, manufacturers of the numerous products used in road building reaped fortunes. But the construction of superhighways, which greatly encouraged metropolitan decentralization throughout the United States, had an enormous ripple effect. By permitting automobile-oriented commuters far easier access (at least in the short run) to outlying areas, the interstates vastly expanded opportunities for real estate developers, furniture manufacturers, interior decorators, fast-food franchisees, and countless other service providers. These latter groups were not active in the original debates over interstates, but they benefited nevertheless. It was a repeat of the pre–World War II phenomenon but on a far more massive scale. Virtually all of the nation's population growth was occurring in the suburbs. In 1950, the growth rate there was ten times higher than that of central cities; with minor variations in percentages, these trends continued at least through the mid-1970s. The fact that millions of Americans were buying suburban homes with substantial yards, fences, barbecue pits, basketball backboards, or other recreational attractions meant a bonanza for hardware, home appliance, and sporting goods manufacturers. Suburbs were havens for young families with children, which created enormous demand for construction of new schools, which in turn generated career opportunities for teachers. Each positive economic ripple, it seemed, created important—if smaller—ripples of its own.

Opposition to the Interstates

However, there were losers. One astute observer noted, "On the local roads that the interstates replaced, small grocers, florists, and druggists had grown up over the years, their low land costs reflecting their relatively modest profits. Now they could only wave forlornly at their former customers streaking by on the new superhighways." By the 1970s, they were being driven out of business by the Walgreens and Wal-Marts, which were often located near the major interchanges. Closer to the centers of cities, many older neighborhoods were torn apart, many businesses demolished. Unquestionably, condemnation proceedings often resulted in disrupted lives and unfair settlements. When public officials planned the interstate route through Providence, Rhode Island, a welding business owner complained, "The appraiser didn't even look at my shop—all he did was walk in and walk out. I don't mind highways—We need them—but they took away my business and now I got nothing. It's not right. I used to have four men working for me, now I'm working for somebody else—it's no good. I was making good money then and I was my own boss—now I'm broke."

If the interstates became a powerful engine for expanding the economy, they were extremely ill-suited for delivering some projected benefits. Ironically, in part to enhance chances for passage of the legislation and acceptance by the American people, sponsors of the program named it "the National System of Interstate *and Defense* Highways." Once again, road building advocates revisited their strategies of the World War I era. When a workable coalition in support of interstates was being assembled by political insiders, the nation was in the midst of the cold war. Although the height of the "Red Scare" and "McCarthyism" was past, the public was intensely frightened about the prospect of nuclear war. Thus, sponsors of interstates attempted to convince potential supporters that the program was vital to the long-run security of the nation. In presenting its final report justifying passage of the enabling legislation, the Clay Committee claimed, "Large-scale evacuations of cities would be needed in the event of A-bomb or H-bomb attack. The Federal Civil Defense Administrator has said the withdrawal task is the biggest problem ever faced in the world. It has been determined as a matter of Federal policy that at least 70 million people would have to be evacuated from target areas in case of threatened or actual enemy attack" [emphasis added]. Amazingly, the report further claimed, "The rapid improvement of the complete 40,000 mile interstate system, including the necessary urban connections thereto, is therefore vital as a civil defense measure."

When called upon to explain such statements, General Lucius Clay almost immediately backtracked, testifying that he ". . . certainly would not want to be an advocate that you could possibly protect the people of the United States with any program of mass evacuation." Clay simply reinforced an obvious truth. To seize a strategic advantage, any nuclear strike would almost certainly have been a surprise attack. Civil defense authorities would have had minutes, or perhaps at best a few hours, to attempt to help civilians evacuate major population centers. Although Hollywood has done its best to present possible scenarios, the scale of gridlock, panic, and complete breakdown of civil order that would result from an actual attack challenges one's imagination. Nevertheless, overly enthusiastic advocates of the interstate occasionally offered arguments that totally defied common sense. One National Highway Users Conference pamphlet actually claimed that once the farsighted driver escaped the city leveled by nuclear weapons, one's car would become a ". . . rolling home. Persons can eat and sleep in it, keep warm and dry, receive all vital instruction by radio, drive out of danger areas and even be afforded some protection against nuclear fallout." Presumably, all needed roadside services required by the prudent motorist would still be functioning as usual!

Even the long-range usefulness of the interstates in strengthening the nation's defense capabilities was open to question. For example, when promoting the enabling legislation, backers of the interstate trumpeted its potential role in permitting military officials to move large, heavy, military equipment quickly and efficiently. However, when construction began, engineers set a minimum standard height of fourteen feet for overpasses, which permitted even the largest commercial trucks and buses to pass safely underneath them. Unfortunately, as a congressional investigation in 1960 later revealed, the Army, the Air Force, the Army Corps of Engineers, and the Navy all had weapons and other crucial items that exceeded fourteen feet in height when loaded onto transports. By then, some 2,200 bridges and overpasses had been built using the fourteen-foot standard. But that was not the worst of it, in terms of slipshod planning; as early as 1954, two years before passage of the interstate program, the Defense Department was building Atlas missiles, which exceeded the fourteen-foot standard. There was no suggestion of dishonesty or foul play, just lack of effective communication between military and civilian decision makers.

Few Americans voiced more opposition to freeways than representatives of inner-city neighborhoods through which new roads would pass. They often received support from liberal academics. These critics charged that urban freeways sometimes ripped the hearts out of "frayed, but stable" working-class inner-city neighborhoods. One academic study claimed that New York City's Cross-Bronx Expressway dissected 113 streets and smashed 159 buildings, displacing

5,000 people. Some of the most influential urban highway proponents even admitted as much. After a number of interstate projects were completed, Robert Moses addressed the issue with his usual bluntness in a 1964 speech: "You can draw any kind of pictures you like on a clean slate and indulge your every whim in the wilderness in laying out a New Delhi, Canberra or Brasilia, but when you operate in an overbuilt metropolis you have to hack your way with a meat ax."

A CONSPIRACY AGAINST MASS TRANSIT?

Other critics have argued that in another realm of public policy regarding private versus public transportation there was deceit, dishonesty, and even a massive conspiracy to promote the automobile at the expense of mass transit. Boiled down to its essentials, the so-called *conspiracy theory* runs as follows. As noted earlier, during the 1920s, automobile company executives worried that their market was becoming saturated, that almost all sales were replacements of old units. There were few new buyers of motor vehicles. At the depths of the Depression, new automobile sales plummeted to one-fourth of their 1929 level. Automobile manufacturers were desperate to enhance revenues through any corporate divisions that could market a viable product. National City Lines (NCL) was a transit conglomerate that had been formed in 1936 to own and manage numerous small street railway companies. Its operations were perfectly legal; and, between the late 1930s and mid-1950s, NCL scrapped almost all of the streetcars and replaced them with buses. Many of the buses were built by GM's Truck and Coach Division. Conspiracy theorists charge that in a diabolical, collusive effort stretching over decades, the two companies had attempted to rid the country of mass transit. During World War II, mass transit experienced a temporary boom, so the long-term effects of the conspiracy did not become evident until after the war.

The notion of a conspiracy against mass transit has some attractive features, plus just enough corroborating evidence to be intriguing. During the years NCL converted from streetcars to buses, with the exception of wartime, mass transit was in serious decline across the nation. In 1945, streetcars and buses each carried just under 10 billion passengers annually. Fifteen years later, buses were still carrying 6.5 billion passengers annually, but streetcar patronage had fallen to a mere 463 million! Some evil force must be behind it! Investigators also discovered that NCL purchased buses from GM without securing competitive bids. In addition, NCL entered into exclusive "sole-supplier" contracts with Firestone Tire and Rubber, Phillips Petroleum, Standard Oil of California, and Mack Manufacturing. Between them, the various corporate suppliers for NCL grossed in excess of $30 million through their contracts. Second, and more damning, between 1949 and the mid-1950s the Justice Department moved against GM on two separate occasions; one of the cases also involved NCL. Basically, the Justice Department was concerned that GM had a near monopoly in the bus market. Ultimately, GM signed a consent decree to supply needed components to other bus manufacturers. One supporter of the conspiracy theory observed that patrons disliked buses, which were foul smelling, noisier, less comfortable, and much slower than rail transit. However, his argument borders on intellectual dishonesty in failing to acknowledge that many bus routes that he used for comparison were originally neighborhood or "circulator" lines, designed as "feeders" for more direct, higher-speed rail routes. Since these buses traveled more circuitous routes and made much more frequent stops, they were obviously slower and less "efficient" than rail lines.

The conspiracy theorists also go too far in insisting that GM plotted to destroy mass transit. Some extreme versions of the theory suggest that GM executives, in collusion with their NCL lackeys, first converted NCL from streetcars to buses primarily to weaken mass transit, then encouraged bus service to deteriorate to the point that riders had little choice but to become car purchasers. By implication, streetcar lines were both viable and healthy before GM entered the scene and conversion to buses was the catalyst for a long downward spiral in mass transit. What this ignores is that, long before the chain of events cited in the NCL case, many mass transit companies were converting to buses. Some of these companies were healthier financially than others. Decisions about conversion to buses were complex, and numerous interests were involved. During the years when scores of transit companies were already losing money, many local-level politicians countenanced conversion from streetcars to trackless trolleys and buses. They determined that the latter were often more economical than rail lines in providing service to areas lacking inner-city population densities. Some traffic engineers also argued that, since they picked up passengers at curbside rather than in the middle of the street, buses and trackless trolleys created less congestion in crowded city streets than trolleys on rails. Also, bus service could be provided more quickly, and routes could be shifted easily in face of quickly changing traffic patterns and quirky consumer demand. Some conservative economists countered that, rather than being targets of a venal conspiracy, many mass transit operations received unusual numbers and varieties of "second chances," in the form of public sub-sidies. They also argued that it was rare when subsidies were given to any enterprises that "failed the market test."

Other factors sap the credibility of the conspiracy theory. Perhaps most important, by the time GM and NCL supposedly conspired to de-stroy mass transit, American commuters had long since embraced the automobile. Many commuters, even those whose routes between home and work were well served by public transportation, con-sciously chose the automobile. They loved their private space. Even minorities, whom most public policy analysts assumed mass transit would predominantly serve, overwhelmingly preferred automobility. For example, for the first two-thirds of the twentieth century, African Americans couldn't buy homes where they wanted. As one social critic observed, however, ". . . the car and its buying was one area where blacks could do as they damned well pleased. They could buy anything. . . . So when they bought cars, they also bought another kind of freedom, freedom from constrictions. They bought status. They bought success. They bought a sense of equality."

Particularly before World War II, there were few apparent ancil-lary costs to commuting by automobile. With the exception of less-than-typical cities like New York, even downtown parking appeared to be a manageable problem. In the driver's mind, after he owned his automobile, all he paid was out-of-pocket expenses: gas and oil, occa-sional parking, and infrequent bridge and road tolls. In the mid-1990s, auto critic Stephen Goddard challenged this view, claiming that when one takes into account long-term damage to public health caused by auto emissions, time lost in commuting, and other hidden factors, the costs to both individual buyers and the nation are enormous. Goddard claimed that "automobility costs Americans $2.75 more per gallon than they paid at the pump." However, most drivers simply did not think in these terms. It was far more immediately convenient to slip behind the wheel. No wonder "automobility" was winning the hearts and minds of the American public. If automobile company executives did consciously work to further weaken mass transit, it was needless overkill, like smashing a spider with a ten-pound sledgehammer.

EUROPE EMBRACES MASS TRANSIT

Advocates of mass transit routinely identify certain European nations, including Germany, Sweden, and France, as enlightened providers of state-of-the-art mass transit. True, a number of large European cities and even some smaller but densely settled population areas are served effectively by modern, efficient rail systems. In some countries, state planners have linked modern mass transit with "cluster communities": high-density enclaves, boasting most of the amenities needed for daily living. Residents live in imaginatively designed high-rises, attractive garden-type homes, condominiums, and assisted-living quarters for older citizens. In these communities, there are few, if any, single-family homes. Most amenities are within comfortable walking distance of homes, and automobile traffic, where not completely outlawed, is strictly regulated. Many residents who bother to own automobiles at all use them only on weekends. By the 1960s, a number of American social critics dreamed wistfully of similar developments on this side of the Atlantic.

By then, mass transit was far healthier in Europe than in the United States. There were several reasons. First, and perhaps most important, almost from the beginning Europeans had accepted mass transit as a vital public service that must be supported by the state regardless of its profitability. In the United States, mass transit companies originally entered the arena as capitalist ventures, whose primary objective was earning profits rather than providing public transportation. As noted earlier, many mass transit operators in the United States had thoroughly alienated patrons over many decades. A second critical factor was timing. Many European cities were centuries old; basic settlement patterns were firmly established when mass transit technology was new. Thus, in most European cities, street railways were originally grafted onto heavily settled and relatively stable urban landscapes. In many cases, they were a natural fit. In Europe, trolleys generally served densely settled areas. In the United States, on the other hand, urban settlement patterns were far more recent, malleable, and fluid. New transportation technology did not have to be shoehorned to fit existing settlement patterns. Modern—twentieth-century—transportation technology was a far more active, dynamic (critics would say destructive) shaping factor in urban growth patterns on this side of the Atlantic. In the United States, street railway companies worked in a political, economic, and social environment that encouraged promoters to focus primarily upon short-term profits. In providing mass transit, many entrepreneurs zeroed in on real estate speculation. Unfortunately, because they served more dispersed populations, most mass transit companies lost money in providing service.

Finally, Europeans appear generally more tolerant of dense living conditions than are Americans. This tradition goes back centuries. In Europe, as rural, farm-owning families grew, they had nowhere to expand unless they were wealthy enough to purchase a neighbor's property. In many countries, primogeniture (passing family farms along to the oldest son) forced younger children to look elsewhere for opportunities. Once the industrial revolution began to evolve, of course, some found jobs in factories. Many others, particularly younger offspring who did not inherit land, chose emigration to the United States. The "frontier" mentality in the United States might be a cliché, but it does reflect widely held public attitudes. One of the things immigrants found most attractive about the "New World" was the availability of inexpensive—or even free—undeveloped property; they, too, wanted their own space. This helps explain why Americans overwhelmingly prefer detached, single-family homes. It may also partly explain their penchant for driving their own automobiles, at almost any economic and social cost, rather than being crowded in with others in mass transit vehicles.

STAGNATION OF MASS TRANSIT IN AMERICA

Until the mid-twentieth century, public officials had usually felt reasonably confident that they were responding effectively to both the challenges and opportunities posed by mass transit. New technologies, particularly those with bright prospects, attracted intensely focused attention from investors and political decision makers. In the years following the Civil War, politicians in cities wishing to attract street railway operators had felt confident that granting generous franchises and providing other critically important concessions were wise policies. They believed they should do anything possible to stimulate development of an exciting new technology that promised to enhance the lives of their constituents. Later, when streetcar moguls achieved images as malevolent predators, many city politicians grasped the necessity of significant regulation of their activities. Some cities went much farther; losing faith in their ability to control street railways in the early twentieth century, they turned to municipal ownership.

However, when the fortunes of mass transit companies almost everywhere in the country spiraled downward—and they were becoming weaker by the month in the postwar years—public officials appeared far less surefooted in their responses. Once-powerful mass transit companies were now begging for relief. Earlier generations of politicians had often accommodated powerful traction moguls, who imperiously demanded favored treatment. Deals were often worked out behind closed doors. By the mid-twentieth century, the urban political landscape had changed dramatically. Politicians dealing with street railways generally negotiated with decidedly nonconfrontational, middle-level bureaucrats, often in public hearings. Even when economic conditions justified more favorable treatment, many city and state officials were unable to concentrate on and fully grasp the needs of transit companies. They appeared extraordinarily fearful of the possibility of negative responses by suspicious constituents to any concessions to mass transit operators. For these reasons, the responses of local and regional public officials to mass transit companies' desperate needs and requests were generally inconsistent, shortsighted, and weak.

One reason for the apparent stasis in public officials' responses to mass transit needs was that, in many cities, the fortunes of the service providers declined so quickly after World War II that some interested parties were caught off guard. Venture capitalists saw far better prospects in many other new industries, including specialty steel products, plastics, and electronics. They often refused to invest in mass transit. To many financial advisors, owning trolley company stock seemed outdated, appropriate perhaps for widows and "spinster" aunts but irrelevant for confident, aggressive investors. Unfortunately, many such supposedly conservative investments were no longer safe. As riders abandoned street railways, so did many shareholders, and many once-solid companies teetered on the brink of bankruptcy.

At midcentury, urban politicians in many cities faced uncomfortable choices. Acknowledging that they had a moral duty to maintain some sort of public transportation for the core of poorer citizens unable to afford or maintain automobiles, officials in many cities reluctantly assumed control of unprofitable companies with little capital, aging assets, surly and dispirited employees, and unsavory public images. However, few urban politicians were willing to undertake anything more than that. As a result, many cities refused to upgrade mass transit operations and virtually ignored them. Mass transit companies served mostly alienated, ungrateful, inner-city patrons, who resented the fact that they had to use public transportation. In the minds of some weary, cynical urban politicians, these constituents seldom voted, but they complained loudly about broken and aging equipment and discontinued routes. There was a seemingly interminable list of sticky management problems simply in keeping outdated, dilapidated equipment up and running. In addition, the transit companies hemorrhaged money, eating up precious tax dollars. What politician in his right mind would become closely associated with such unattractive services? Interminable meetings needed to resolve such boring technical issues as equipment repair costs consumed hours and produced little but minutes. These hearings often concluded with dry recommendations for modest equipment replacement, plus yet another transportation study. The press seldom covered such mundane matters. For most politicians, it was more politically expedient and much more fun to be photographed throwing out the first pitch for the local ball club's home opener; crowning a beauty contest winner wearing a skimpy bathing suit; or shaking hands with beaming, well-fed businessmen at banquets welcoming new businesses to town. If they worried about transportation issues at all, most urban politicians hoped their assistants could arrange for newspapers to photograph them cutting ribbons at official openings of new street-widening projects.

There was even less reason for advocates of mass transit to expect support from state-level politicians. One of the oldest axioms of American politics is that profound distrust between urban and "upstate" (or small-town and rural) political interests seriously divides most state legislatures. Representatives from rural areas and small towns often reflect the views of their suspicious constituents, who perceive themselves as being dominated and manipulated by unsympathetic, corrupt, big-city interests. Many thin-skinned, insecure, rural legislators resent the "phony pseudosophistication" of "city-slicker" colleagues, just as they react to less-than-flattering references to themselves as "rubes," "hicks," and "hayseeds." Urban legislators, on the other hand, frequently voice frustration at the numerical overrepresentation exercised by their rural counterparts. One rural legislator might represent 50,000 people, his urban counterpart 5 times that many. Obviously, political issues, including mass transit, appearing to benefit only relatively powerless urban residents could expect little support in most state capitols.

Even though the evidence supporting the conspiracy theory against mass transit is thin, there is no doubt that postwar federal government policy effecting highway construction helped encourage more automobile purchases and far more widespread use, at least until the worldwide energy crises of the 1970s. Although few federal decision makers thought in such terms at the time, such largesse toward Detroit's interests helped undermine public transportation. In contrast to the billions poured into building new highways and improving old ones, the federal government provided almost no support for mass transit. Between 1945 and the early 1970s, for every dollar federal agencies spent on any form of public transportation, they spent approximately 100 dollars on automobile-oriented projects.

One of the key provisions of the interstate highway legislation of the mid-1950s was the stipulation that revenues collected and deposited into the Highway Trust Fund were inviolate. This meant that they could not be diverted toward uses other than highway building. Almost from the beginning, critics blasted the Highway Trust Fund, claiming, with some justification, that automobile interests were receiving favored treatment, beyond that enjoyed by other highly influential interest groups. They came up with some rather interesting parallels, pointing out that liquor taxes were not used to encourage people to drink more booze and cigarette taxes were not put into programs trying to get more people to smoke. However, gas taxes were obviously being used for purposes that could only encourage more automobile usage.

What were the long-term effects of a national policy of encouraging automobility, whether or not it was deliberately at the expense of mass transit? Advocates of the automobile claimed that such a national policy simply reflected what the vast majority of citizens wanted. Sure, cars promoted suburban development. What was wrong with that? The United States was not Europe. Most Americans preferred wearing sandals, shorts, and T-shirts and entertaining friends at barbecues in their own backyards to attending "dress-up" outdoor concerts at pristine downtown parks. Critics retorted that Americans had acted impetuously, with little or no forethought or concern about how their choices negatively affected the lives of others, or the long-term impact on the environment. As one put it, "Traversing space now mattered more than creating space. . . . Few realized what they had incinerated on the altar of mobility. The automobile had become the master of their universe, and protest would come only slowly as the servants of speed and sprawl saw what it had wrought." By the 1960s, critics of the automobile culture became increasingly vocal and their objections became serious factors in political agendas from the local to the national level.

Chapter Six

THE AUTOMOBILE CULTURE UNDER SIEGE

As with any innovation exerting profound effects on humankind, the automobile and everything it came to represent in American life generated strong feelings, including persistent, often heated, criticism. Virtually from the initial hesitant sputter of the first internal combustion engine, critics gathered. Early skeptics confidently predicted that cars would never last. Others protested that, when operated at speeds exceeding ten miles per hour, they frightened animals and threatened human safety. Between World War I and the 1960s, the ranks of automobile critics grew steadily, but their complaints were comparatively muted, almost totally drowned out by the cacophony of demands for endless concessions and accommodation from increasingly powerful, sophisticated automobile interests. However, by the early 1960s, some excesses of the car culture had become so obvious and extreme that anti-automobile voices became louder and more insistent. They contended that the supposed benefits of the automobile had imploded upon themselves: the device intended to free humankind from crowded living conditions had instead created soulless, alien new landscapes, including urban regions more than 100 miles across. In the view of critics, the four-wheeled monsters had driven almost all other human activity off downtown streets; created traffic gridlock; further divided and alienated economic, social, racial, and ethnic classes; and, among other transgressions, profoundly and irrevocably damaged the earth's environment. In sum, critics claimed, the device intended to serve Americans had instead become their master.

A NATION ADDICTED TO AUTOMOBILES

Critics argued that, for many Americans, attachment to their cars had become addictive. This process began at an early age. One astute observer, A. Q. Mowbray, suggested that purchase of an automobile became a rite of passage into adulthood, particularly for young males. They would make all kinds of sacrifices, including committing half of their take-home paychecks to meet monthly installments. They would neglect their own health, girlfriends, and even wives and children. No wonder many feel so strongly about accommodating automobiles: "Once these sacrifices are made, he will defend with the ferocity of a mother lion his native-born right to drive his car anywhere, at any time, over any route, and to park it when he arrives. Any attempt by anyone to infringe these rights is, in his eyes, a serious blow at individual freedom." And such attitudes seldom soften with age: ". . . [T]he passion for this American freedom burns even more fiercely in the breast of the gray-templed, bay-windowed motorist. If he, as a law-abiding taxpayer wants to go from point A to point B and there's no road, he thinks in his own mind that they'd damned well better build one."

Many automobile problems revolve around the sheer numbers of cars in the United States: over 200 million in 2002. A second factor in the equation is that the typical American automobile owner is driving greater distances. In 1945, drivers covered an estimated 250 billion miles on the road. In 2000, total driving distance was estimated at *12 times* that amount: fully 3 *trillion* miles!

Particularly worrisome to some critics of the car culture was that Americans had lost the ability to imagine any alternative. Just as another so-called servant of mankind—television—had mesmerized millions of Americans to the point that many could not conceive of how they would entertain themselves in its absence, so too had riding in automobiles conditioned them to viewing the landscape through a windshield. These technological "marvels" shared other attributes. Both essentially isolated people from their physical surroundings and, perhaps to a lesser extent, from direct interchanges with other humans. Kenneth Schneider wrote of the automobile in organic terms; policy makers found themselves increasingly at the beck and call of its increasingly voracious needs. He concluded, ". . . [T]o the extent that our civilization becomes dependent upon the automobile we reduce ourselves and our character of mind to a new species of being, a society of invertebrates as clumsy as a convention of turtles."

By the beginning of the twenty-first century, the automobile no longer freed Americans but, rather, restrained, even regimented, them. In metropolitan areas at least, from the moment one slides behind the wheel, Big Brother's eyes and tracking devices monitor individual movements. Traffic police measure speed; surveillance cameras record violators running red lights. Drivers line up, then idle impatiently before stoplights at freeway entrances for electronic permission to join the glacial crawl to wherever they are going. In downtown areas, motorized meter maids relentlessly ticket violators whose hour-long shopping excursions extended to seventy minutes.

The growing dependence on the automobile became increasingly evident as it evolved from a luxury to a convenience and, finally, a *necessity*. By the early 1960s, if not sooner, some critics complained that Americans were trapped by the automobile. Borrowing from novelist John Keats, renowned urbanist and social critic Lewis Mumford launched a jeremiad against Detroit: "The insolence of the Detroit chariotmakers and the masochistic submissiveness of the American consumer are symptoms of a larger disorder . . . a society made in the image of machines, by machines, for machines." He claimed that the United States comprised ". . . a society in which any form of delinquency or criminality may be practiced, from meretriciously designed motor cars or insufficiently tested wonder drugs to the wholesale distribution of narcotics and printed pornography, provided that the profits sufficiently justify their exploitation."

How did automobiles entrap typical Americans? According to John Keats, author of *The Insolent Chariots,* a novel often cited by critics of the car culture, by midcentury, car owners had become easy prey for the automakers. Keats's fictional character Tom Wretch was stereotypical: "Tom is a member of the great middle majority that reaches from the upper-lower through the lower-middle class. In a word, he doesn't have much money and he is not too bright." Tom dutifully traded in his old car for a new model every three years and stoically paid huge monthly installments. According to car culture critics, by the 1960s, the tentacles of automobility were strangling any vestiges of resistance from the white-collar middle classes as well.

Picture another hypothetical American, living in any one of a hundred metropolitan regions. For Sharon O'Malley, a suburban dweller working downtown, there was no viable alternative to daily drives to and from work. Sure, she could take a bus; she had even tried it for a week, because she thought she might be able to get some reading done as she rode into town. But she found she couldn't concentrate. More to the point, the buses were seldom on time. One morning as she hustled to her bus stop at 7:40, she saw the 7:45 bus pulling away from the curb five minutes early. She'd had to stand in slush, literally cooling her heels for twenty-three minutes waiting for the 7:59, which finally showed up several minutes late. In addition, it was a half-mile walk from the bus stop downtown to her office, so even when the bus was on time, the trip from her front door to her office cubicle actually took longer than fighting traffic in her own car. Sharon might carpool, but that necessitated difficult compromises with neighbors or coworkers and cost her the freedom of impulsive last-minute changes in plans. So, five days a week she guzzled a cup of coffee, grabbed a jelly donut, eased into her car, and drove fifteen miles to her office in forty-five minutes. However, lately she found that because of increasing traffic volume, her driving time was lengthening to an hour.

Despite her driving hassles, Sharon might have been comparatively fortunate. Residents in outlying suburbs in California have been known to resort to extreme measures to beat traffic. Bizarre stories began to be heard in the 1960s, and, by the 1990s, they were common. The *Wall Street Journal* recently profiled a worker at a defense plant in El Segundo, near Los Angeles, who faced a 110-mile, round-trip commute from his home in Yorba Linda. Rather than face a two-hour drive each way every day, he hung out in his office until everyone had left for the night, then ate a brown-bag dinner, read, and wrote letters. At bedtime, he hauled out a sleeping bag and slept in his car. Nicknamed "The Owl," he repeated this daily routine several times a week! He admitted it played havoc with his family life. "The biggest mistake I ever made was not learning a skill I could use in a place like Montana, where you can really enjoy the time you've got on earth."

PAYING FOR THE AUTOMOBILE HABIT

Who hasn't fantasized about wider, more open roads when idling in traffic jams? But will more highways help? A half century ago, such expenditures generated little debate, but this is no longer true. Critics of the automobile rail at the enormous amounts of tax revenues from the local to the national level spent on services supporting the automobile. Until fairly recently, decision makers routinely built extra freeway lanes, ignoring the fact that such space filled to capacity with cars carrying only 3,600 passengers per hour. According to advocates of mass transit, if filled with buses or trains, the same space could accommodate 36,000 and 42,000 passengers per hour respectively. In the eyes of liberal critics, auto industry and highway lobbyists had even polluted the language of public policy debate. In their view, the public had been conditioned over decades to accept the idea that public agencies wisely invested in new highways but foolishly subsidized public transportation. In fact, public expenditures on facilities for automobiles vastly exceeded the combined revenues from license fees, sales taxes on automobiles and accessories, and gasoline taxes. One study revealed that Pasadena, California, spent eight dollars on services for automobiles for every dollar collected from motorists. Such expenditures went far beyond simply building roads. Some were obvious and direct, but dozens of line items in budgets were indirect subsidies for cars. Among the most direct subsidies were policing traffic flow; sweeping and cleaning streets; and erecting traffic lights, street signs, directional arrows, and stop signs. Automobile wrecks required prompt emergency attention from city police, fire department personnel, ambulance crews, and the emergency wards at city hospitals. Drivers' insurance seldom paid for more than a fraction of these costs; large portions of the rest were borne by the public treasury. As one critic observed, "Such tariffs hurt local government and public services. Policing for automobile infractions shortchanges other public services. . . . There is no free lunch—no free ride." Although snow removal and street sanding in cold-weather cities obviously helped the flow of public conveyances, the most direct beneficiaries were individual motorists. Pedestrians almost always had to fend for themselves, as virtually no public funds were used to clear sidewalks (except perhaps those sometimes walked by city mayors!). When motorists pass signs reading "Your Highway Dollars at Work," they would be well advised to think about just where the money is coming from. Was the junior high school's fine arts budget sliced yet again to pay for asphalt resurfacing or repairing an aging bridge over the interstate?

However, many large public expenditures are indirect subsidies to accommodate automobiles. At the national level, our nation has entered numerous armed conflicts in the Middle East over the past several decades, costing many billions of taxpayer dollars. Repeated forays into the maelstrom of Middle East conflict has harmed the nation's reputation among many nations. The indirect damage to our moral standing and strategic position is incalculable. Would we have engaged in such expensive and dangerous maneuvers were it not for our growing dependence on the region's oil?

At a more mundane, tangible level, how can one directly measure the damage to the nation's health caused by automobile emissions? Although perhaps not as toxic as secondhand cigarette smoke, breathing in automobile emissions on a daily basis for sixty or more years almost certainly exacerbates a wide range of lung diseases. In the mid-1990s, the American Lung Association estimated the negative health effects of air pollution costing the nation $50 billion annually. There are numerous other negative ripple effects on the economy. Taxpayers pay the cost of public hospitals; and increased incidence of death from lung diseases raises the cost of both life insurance and health coverage. Once again, American consumers, even those in good health and those

"Man, it really tears me to think that some squares want to pull down these lovely, beautiful signs!"

Late twentieth century critics of the car culture scored multiple facets of its alleged "excess." Visual pollution of metropolitan landscapes was near the top of the list of complaints, particularly among environmentalists.

without cars, help foot the bill. The Foundation on Economic Trends estimated in the mid-1990s that motor vehicle pollution caused crop yield losses in wheat, corn, soybeans, and peanuts alone of between 2 and 4.5 billion dollars each year. At the local level, construction of new state-of-the-art sports stadiums typically required extremely expensive extras, including dozens of acres of paved parking lots. In order to retain franchises and maintain good relations with team owners, city administrations often either provided partial subsidies for parking lots or underwrote their entire cost. One could easily compile a nearly endless list of other clear examples of how accommodating automobiles wreaks havoc on government budgets at all levels.

The pricing structure of many commodities and services appears rooted in the fact that, while Americans possess an enormous tolerance for hidden costs, they are outraged by increases in visible, direct costs. In Europe and Japan, gasoline costs approximately twice what Americans pay at the pump. While European drivers stoically pony up four dollars for a gallon of gas, their American counterparts complain loudly when the price approaches two dollars. Not surprisingly, the average American driver consumes five times as much gasoline per capita as his European counterpart, and *ten* times the amount used by typical Japanese drivers. By the mid-1990s, the average American family spent fully 20 percent of its annual income on transportation, *plus* hidden costs. This is not surprising, since Americans drive almost everywhere, taking only 5 percent of their trips from home on foot. In contrast, family members in Japan take up to *half* of their trips away from home on foot; actually using their expensive cars is a conscious decision rather than a reflexive action. Japanese families spend 9 percent of their income on transportation. European families did even better, spending just 7 percent on transportation.

SPRAWL AND MALL: ENVIRONMENTAL POLLUTION

As the twentieth century wound down, American consumers did not appear to be getting much for their money. Reliance on the automobile over public transit may have provided an edge in convenience for individual drivers, but commuting in general was becoming more stressful and time-consuming for everyone. The automobile's convenience advantage over mass transit was relative. Furthermore, both critics and defenders of the automobile had to confront the fact that the motor vehicle was creating many different forms of environmental pollution, either directly or indirectly. A good deal of the pollution was visual. Although Sharon O'Malley's particular housing development seemed pleasant enough, the route to work was ugly: endless dreary strip malls, auto dealerships and repair shops, gas stations, fast-food joints, discount liquor outlets, porno shops, and vacant lots littered with the detritus of modern materialism.

Social critics have been distressed with the visual pollution largely attributable to the automobile for some time. Yesteryear's negative commentary concerning its impact has decidedly modern overtones. In 1955, journalist Bill Gilbert described a particularly depressing stretch of "Highway Gothic" on U.S. Route 40 in eastern Maryland: ". . . a monument to the highway culture of America. . . . All the components are there: greasy food, venal mechanics, blackened foliage, tourist-court rooms, smelling of space heaters and linoleum; the sense of power, speed, double-clutching rigs, eight-cylinder beasts snarling with excess energy, pacing along hour after hour, day after day." Four decades later, social critic Edward Relph called such landscapes "uncomplicated in the extreme," which "declared themselves far too openly. There were none of the ambiguities, contradictions, and complexities that made landscapes interesting." These were "unifunctional landscapes: one building served one purpose."

By the 1990s, the automobile had created a whole new type of urban phenomenon: huge commercial developments that were virtually inaccessible by any other means of transportation. Automobile critic Jane Kay questioned, "Is it free choice when well-fed political action committees (PACs) and highway lobbyists keep the pork barrel full and deprive the poor, the old, and carless Americans of their mobility?" She continued, "Sprawl is space. Space eats dollars and megadollars to shift our nation from the city to the countryside, creating buckshot suburbs and mammoth coils of arterials to connect them."

Kenneth Schneider compared the damage to the inner city wrought by accommodating the automobile to that of World War II: "A parking map or aerial photograph of any American city center reveals devastation as obvious as that resulting from a London Blitz Saturation bombing is the only adequate comparison. Hundreds of buildings around the immediate center have been wiped out. In the photo the rubble seems to have been cleared by vast bands of glistening beetles who wait disciplined and ready in the empty blocks to clear the debris of unbombed sections."

Jane Kay lamented how the downtown sections of her native city, Boston, had retreated before the automobile onslaught. Although aggressive, assertive pedestrians might intimidate drivers who strayed forward a few inches into pedestrian walkways when stopped for lights by slapping their hoods, she "came to realize that the designs I saw often literally housed more cars than human occupants . . . every institution and every structure did obeisance to the automobile."

According to the automobile's critics, the billions spent, the wholesale reshaping of inner cities and building of massive freeway systems to accommodate the automobile didn't work. Building more freeways and parking garages simply attracted more cars, and more cars meant demands for more freeways and parking facilities. In their view, it was obviously a vicious cycle, a war with no prospects of victory. More freeways meant ever-increasing numbers of cars being dumped into downtown streets, which could only be "stretched" a certain amount. In many cities, streets and highways were no longer jammed just at rush hour but almost continuously, as "traffic pressures of one activity merged into those of the others." Between the end of World War II and the present, the nation has paved over an area equivalent to the entire land mass of Rwanda. Much of it is dark-colored "gasphalt," which attracts and retains heat, which in turn threatens the environment by contributing to global warming.

According to some renowned commentators, the postwar dominance of the automobile robbed the urban core of its vitality. Jane Jacobs' influential 1961 book *The Death and Life of Great American Cities* sounded the alarm. Jacobs may have over-romanticized the sense of

coherence and community in many inner-city neighborhoods in earlier years, but she nevertheless struck a responsive chord in describing the automobile's negative impact. "Traffic arteries, along with
parking lots, gas stations and drive-ins are powerful instruments in
city destruction." She continued: "To accommodate [cars] city streets
are broken down into loose sprawls, incoherent and vacuous for anyone afoot. Downtown and other neighborhoods that are marvels of
close-grained intricacy and compact mutual support are casually dis-
emboweled." Before the invasion of the automobile, neighbors would
gather on front porches or stoops, watch kids play on sidewalks, and
exchange gossip. There was little sense of hurry; most humans moved
by wagon or bicycle or on foot. After the automobile took over city
streets, that ambiance quickly vanished.

THE AUTOMOTIVE ASSAULT ON CITIES

Social critics began to refer to Americans' almost total dependence on
cars in terms conjuring up visions of serious illness, such as *automo-
bilism,* or *tyrannus mobilitis.* As they observed, when everything is
built for cars, everybody has to drive cars. They also lamented that in
many indirect ways the automobile-oriented configuration of the
American city discriminated against the poor, particularly those living
in inner cities. As automobility intensified after World War II, fewer
and fewer factories, retail stores, and services remained in downtown
areas. Most enterprises migrated outward. In Los Angeles, for example, the downtown had accounted for three-fourths of all retail trade
in the 1930s. That figure dropped to half by 1946, a mere 18 percent
by the late 1960s! A largely unanticipated effect was that thousands of
relatively low wage but stable jobs migrated outward from the inner
city. Inner-city residents owning cars had to drive longer distances to
keep these jobs. Commutes ate up a large portion of their earnings
and consumed precious free time. With mass transit in rapid decline,
the reshaping of cities provided a double hit to the poorest Americans; those who could not afford cars found it nearly impossible to
get to work, even when they could find jobs in outlying areas. One
critic called the central city "a sandbox for the refuse of society."

In addition, the penetration of many of the nation's urban cores
by huge superhighways exacerbated living conditions for those who
remained there. As builders bulldozed one fragile neighborhood after
another for superhighways, critics dubbed them "white men's highways through black men's bedrooms." In addition to the ceaseless
noise and fumes caused by constant streams of traffic, the inevitable

plethora of businesses serving the automobile invaded many marginal neighborhoods: muffler shops, car washes, spray paint services, tire marts, car parts stores, parking lots, and indiscriminately scattered junkyards. Some of these businesses generated their own pollution in the form of liquefied runoff that seeped into the ground or sometimes stagnated in putrid ponds because of broken or totally inadequate sewage facilities. It was no accident that six of New York City's seven carcinogen-spewing diesel bus depots were in Harlem. In the eyes of many liberal social critics, by the late twentieth century, some urban neighborhoods were becoming not-so-secret toxic waste dumps.

However, in significantly different respects, the landscape far away from urban cores, purposely designed in advance exclusively for automobile use, often appeared just as alien. Urban geographer Joel Garreau labeled the phenomena edge cities, by which he meant futuristic commercial clusters, usually near the intersections of interstates. Typically, they contained huge landscaped office complexes, numerous hotels and restaurants, perhaps a multiplex movie theater, and some giant discount stores. Often they lacked even sidewalks, since nobody was expected to enter by foot. French social critic Jean Baudrillar claimed that "All you need to know about American society can be gleaned by an anthropology of its driving behavior." He commented caustically about Los Angeles: "If you get out of your car in this centrifugal metropolis, you immediately become a delinquent; as soon as you start walking, you are a threat to the public order, like a dog wandering in the road. Only immigrants from the Third World countries are allowed to walk."

One historian observed cryptically in 1992, "We have built a transportation system, a great one, you know, only the entry fee is $10,000." That was roughly the price of a new car then. Today, that fee has almost doubled. No wonder large numbers of poorer Americans try desperately to lessen the escalating price of automobility by keeping gas-guzzling beaters moving and refusing to buy car insurance. If they hope to gain even the most modest toehold in the early-twenty-first-century American economy, they have little choice but to be auto mobile.

Even if they had once possessed social consciences, most elites no longer cared much about inner cities, in part because they had escaped to exurbia, many miles away from urban ghettos. As former Secretary of Labor and social critic Robert Reich observed a few years ago, many of them had seceded from the city. The social and economic classes were almost totally isolated from each other. Transportation historian Jane Kay observed in the mid-1990s that "Compassion fails in the antiseptic ambiance of the automobile environment. No sweat. No sight of the poor." We have been "quarantined by the car culture." As Kay put it, ". . . [P]ublic space, the stage of social life, is destroyed by our auto-oriented design that nullifies walking and intermingling. Sequestered by income, deprived of parks, bankrupting Main Street for malls, we no longer rub shoulders with our neighbors, rich or poor, deprived or thriving, that tousled mix of age, race and experience." Shopping malls, particularly indoors, offer little or no sense of community. Social critic Philip Langdon noted, "The focus is on consumption, on the pleasure of just being there." Sociologist Judith Coady identified a particular style of strolling she labeled the *mall walk.* "It's primarily a slower walk to the rhythm of music in the mall. The eyes are unfocused. Generally speaking, there's a kind of glaze on the eyes and a benign stare on the face." Individuals not meeting the conventional visual appearance of "licensed shoppers" attract close attention of security personnel. Should any "oddballs" or shabbily dressed "street people" somehow venture into these premises, they are quickly surrounded by security officers and quietly escorted back outside. Signs with large print warn that the indoor walkways between stores aren't really public space. "Permission to use said areas can be revoked at any time." How many shoppers actually think about who arrogantly assumes the power to "revoke"? If you're middle class and white, it obviously does not pertain to you.

Other hidden costs of automobility are not readily apparent, but businesses and individual Americans pay them nevertheless. In most cities, local building codes force developers to provide a certain number of off-street spaces for every unit they construct. One study showed that the typical apartment house builder had to budget in an extra $1,000 for every parking space included. These costs are invariably passed along to renters. However, in many suburban and unincorporated areas, governing entities are far less vigilant in making investors bear anything close to the true costs sprawling developments inflict upon the general public—most of them ultimately traceable to the automobile.

Americans profess to enjoy their wide open spaces. Unfortunately, sprawling development in America eats up another 1.5 million acres of irreplaceable open space each year. Thus, it is increasingly difficult to find the wide open spaces, and motorists have to drive longer distances to get to them. Daily driving for many Americans consists of numbing crawls along ugly freeways, idling in lines at fast-food outlets, and cruising crowded mall parking lots searching for a parking space. If they are fortunate, they do not encounter dangerously aggressive numskulls afflicted with deadly "road rage." As one observer put it, ". . . [T]axpayers pay more, far more, to scatter than to settle in tightly knit urban areas, more to heighten auto dependency

"Hey, Jack, which way to Mecca?"

This Peter Arno cartoon appeared at the New Yorker *at mid-century, but its sentiment resonates in haunting fashion a half-century later. Rich Americans in their fancy automobile reveal total ignorance of both the Muslim religion and Middle East sensibilities.*

through sprawl than to lessen it through close-knit settlement and infill." She concluded, "The meandering, outbound land [use] patterns . . . benefit their builders. Yet they cost their new users and drain their old ones of historic downtowns, small towns, and inner suburbs of shops and services, concentrating poverty and deconcentrating opportunity." According to one economist, the opening of a single "super-box" Wal-Mart outlet in a regional center will deprive the average small town merchant within a twenty-mile radius of nearly one-fifth of his business. Americans pay a heavy price for this perceived freedom.

CRITICS OF THE CAR CULTURE TAKE ACTION

The Arab oil embargo of 1973 and the concomitant energy crisis marked a period when criticism of the automobile culture peaked. In fact, a few voices questioned if the automobile culture even *had* a future. For the first time in the twentieth century, it appeared that the critics were in the driver's seat. Ralph Nader had fired the first shot across the automobile industry's bow in 1965 with his book *Unsafe at Any Speed,* a devastating indictment of General Motors' Corvair. Corvairs were not the only unsafe cars; the quality of most American cars was deteriorating. In addition, Americans were driving faster and more recklessly. Despite rapid construction of new interstates and widening of other highways, traffic deaths increased from 38,137 to a peak of 56,278 between 1960 and 1972. By the mid-1990s, the National Safety Council estimated that traffic fatalities alone cost the nation $176.5 billion annually. The added costs of dealing with damages and injuries resulting from nonfatal accidents obviously padded that figure even more.

Mounting highway carnage and what many considered assaults against the physical landscape were two of the most obvious negative aspects of automobility, but air pollution became another serious concern. As early as World War II, disturbing accounts of brown clouds rising over Los Angeles attracted national attention. By the early 1950s, a new word attributable to the emissions of tens of thousands of exhaust pipes in a concentrated urban area had entered the national vocabulary: *smog.* And Los Angeles was its national capital. In 1948, a chemist at California Institute of Technology, Jan Haager-Smit, began an investigation of its components. He eventually traced most of the problem to automobile emissions, which he broke down into four categories: unburned hydrocarbons that escaped in several ways; and three combustion products issuing from the tailpipe, including carbon monoxide, lead compounds from antiknock gasoline, and nitrogen oxides.

By the early 1950s, protests against foul air were beginning to mount. One early critic, Harrison Salisbury, described Los Angeles as "nestled under its blanket of smog, girdled by bands of freeways, its core eviscerated by concrete strips and asphalt fields, its circulatory arteries pumping away without focus . . . the prototype of gasopolis, the rubber-wheeled living region of the future." He concluded, "I have seen the future—and it doesn't work." Residents of the San Gabriel Valley, east of downtown Los Angeles, often went weeks without being able even to see nearby mountains; as for topographical variety and scenery, they might as well have been living in Wichita, where the air was much cleaner. At times, ground-level visibility for drivers was no more than a half mile. A wry piece of local graffiti from the 1960s read, "I shot an arrow into the air, and it stuck."

Long before then, California state officials sought redress in various forms from the nation's automakers. Essentially, midlevel public relations personnel in Detroit gave them the runaround. After promising to look into the matter, the Big Three "undertook low-priority research that produced little more than assorted technical papers." To be sure, the problem was complex, but industry foot-dragging was also due to its understandable reluctance to admit to the public that "Detroit's rendition of the American dream was flawed." Auto men naturally resisted accepting responsibility for foul air. Pollution controls would be expensive to develop, and costs would have to be passed along to car buyers in higher prices.

Fed up with stalling tactics from automakers, California officials finally acted in 1959, passing the first of a series of laws effecting emissions controls. By 1963, manufacturers had to equip all models sold in California with devices to recycle crankcase fumes in the engine for more complete combustion of fuel. In subsequent years, California passed increasingly stringent laws, and automakers grudgingly complied. In 1965, Congress followed California's lead, passing the Air Pollution and Control Act, making that state's standards nationwide on all 1968 or later models. But the real bombshell was the 1970 Clean Air Act, which decreed that a 90 percent reduction in air emissions had to be achieved within six years. This law may have been in part a residual effect of a huge recent oil spill off the coast of Santa Barbara and rapidly increasing public awareness of automobile-based threats to the environment. Although Big Three officials squawked that meeting such draconian timetables was totally unrealistic, the bill's primary sponsor, Senator Edmund Muskie (D-Maine) vowed that he wanted to "force technology to respond to public demands rather than, as had so often been the case, new technology bending the public to its will."

Environmentalists pointed out that air pollution was just one of the most obvious assaults on the delicate ecosphere attributable largely to automobiles. Extracting and processing the steel, plastic, rubber, glass, and other products needed to build cars also caused significant environmental damage and sapped the earth's limited resources. In fact, fully one-third of the total environmental damage caused by automobiles occurred before they were sold and driven. One study estimated that manufacturing the average car produced 29 tons of waste and 1,207 million cubic yards of polluted air. This information is significant because it calls into question the notion that keeping exhaust-spewing older vehicles, or "beaters," running is worse for the environment than trading them in for newer automobiles every three years or so. Junking used cars also places stresses on the environment. If vehicle life spans are inordinately brief, we risk even greater damage to the ecosphere. Finally, disposing used oil, transmission fluid, battery acids, and other automotive excretions caused further environmental damage.

Automobile accessories are also heavy contributors to pollution. Rubber tires are one of the worst. Each tire laminates a pound of rubber onto the nation's roads and highways each year of its life. Americans discard about 250 million tires each year, and, in 2000, approximately one billion still awaited proper disposal. This creates major problems. In Tracey, California, one huge pile of tens of thousands of used tires reached a hundred or so feet in height; locals nicknamed it Mount Royster, in honor of the entrepreneur who imagined rubber riches in recycling them. In 1993, air, rubber, and intense summer heat created spontaneous combustion, igniting a fire at Mount Royster that could not be extinguished for thirty hours. Nearby residents remembered "huge clouds of acrid black smoke [that] darkened the sky like lava-spewing volcanoes."

By then, environmental abuse, directly or indirectly related to automobility, was old news. In the summer of 1969, a massive spillage of 3.3 million gallons of crude oil from offshore drilling near Santa Barbara, California, outraged many Americans and briefly raised environmental consciousness. During the inevitable investigation that followed the disaster, Americans learned that drilling permits had been granted despite warnings from geologists that the area was dangerously exposed to potential disaster from earthquakes. Those who followed the proceedings closely also learned firsthand the raw power exerted by the oil industry to create special privileges and tax breaks for itself. For weeks on end, newspapers and television stories documented the plight of millions of waterfowl and fish killed by the waste, not to mention the miles of expensive beachfront property coated with grimy oil. However, media coverage all too often assumed a subtle, insidiously proindustry slant by treating each incident of this type as an ". . . *isolated catastrophe*, largely unexplainable and caused by misfortune or negligence" [emphasis added]. But the accidents, large and small, kept happening. Twenty years later, the *Exxon Valdez*, a huge oil tanker, slammed into a reef at Prince William Sound and burst open, emptying millions of gallons of oil into a major fishery off the coast of Alaska. Charges against boat captain Joseph Hazlewood hinted at drug or alcohol use and subsequent impairment of his judgment. Once again, Americans voiced outrage and demanded retribution. However, as one veteran environmentalist observer noted at the captain's trial, "It wasn't his driving that caused the Alaska oil spill. It was yours."

Equally appalling was the variety of pollutants associated with the automobile that Americans deliberately disposed of, usually in a careless manner. According to one study, car owners dump 100 million gallons of used oil into the ground and storm sewers and even down toilets every year. Each gallon of used oil seeping into the ground has the potential to contaminate a million gallons of potable water, virtually forever. Another damaging commodity is road salt. Used in prodigious quantities, particularly in the nation's snow belt in the Northeast and Upper Midwest, road salt is a major factor in the destruction of trees and roadside vegetation. Within a few years, road salt runoff will virtually sterilize soil and make it particularly vulnerable to hardy weeds, particularly ragweed.

From the mid-1960s forward, various government agencies effected policies that provided both incentives for compliance with new environmental standards and penalties for failure to comply. Billions of dollars in corporate profits were at stake. How well did new government regulations work? A combination of technological responses focused on the clean air campaign. Engine refinements, unleaded gasoline, and the catalytic converter all helped. One study showed that between 1966 and 1974, carbon monoxide declined 52 percent and hydrocarbon pollution dropped 65 percent in Los Angeles County. These impressive figures were reached despite a sixteen percent increase in registered vehicles. Between 1970 and 1995, PM-10 emissions dropped nationwide from 13 to 3 million tons; sulfur dioxide from 31 to 8 million tons; carbon monoxide from 128 to 92 million tons; and lead from 219 to just 5 million tons. Only nitrogen dioxide emissions showed a small increase, from 20.6 to 21.8 million tons. Nevertheless, there were numerous bumps in the road to cleaner air. Consumers complained that not only were catalytic converters expensive but they cut engine performance and decreased miles per gallon. Some public health officials worried that catalytic converters created problems of their own, namely introducing dangerous sulfuric acid mist into the air. Although both parties could be fined if they were caught, many motorists arranged with garage mechanics to disconnect the devices or they did it themselves.

Other environmentalists warned that some damage caused by the automobile was cumulative and that its effects were irreversible. According to one critic, "The car, its pollutants, its highways, its trips from shop to shop have a subtle but compound effect. We cannot define the threshold of human health. We play at the margin of safety for our persons—our planet. And where, what, and how much we drive heightens these personal and global perils." Despite what humans did to the environment, informed individuals could try to protect themselves. An environmentalist publication, *Earth Journal*, advertised "Greenscreen," a carbon-filtered sports mask that would allegedly filter out most of the dangerous elements still floating through the air. You could even look hip in a gas mask, as the manufacturer offered it in three styles! Nevertheless, there were risks everywhere you turned. Gas masks would not protect wearers from skin cancer, exacerbated by ever-larger holes in the earth's ozone layer, which were caused in part by automobile emissions. One group of physicians called skin cancer an epidemic, with a million new cases each year.

In the early 1970s, numerous books appeared with titles like *Superhighway—Super-Hoax, Dead End, Autokind vs. Mankind,* and *Paradise Lost.* According to the critics, the automobile was leading Americans nowhere. They spent ever-increasing percentages of their tax dollars building new superhighways, but traffic problems were intensifying. They committed more of their disposable income to motor vehicles and their accessories, but these devices seemingly produced only uncertainty, headaches, and aggravation. Emma Rothschild suggested that "[t]here [was] perpetually for the auto companies of the 1970s a danger that next year or next decade the limits of the car market may collide with the limits of human irrationality." Automobile historian James Flink observed that, by the early 1970s, the automobile was no longer "a historically progressive force for change in American civilization." Flink predicted saturated markets for automobiles. He also pointed out that the automobile industry was no longer the nation's leading employer; rather, the government by then employed more Americans than did the automobile and related industries. Equally important, television and computers were becoming more vital shapers of American culture. In 1972, John Jerome, an influential critic of the car culture, predicted, "When the history of the automobile is written, scholars will necessarily focus careful attention on the crucial period of the late sixties and the early seventies. . . . During that period the largest industry the world had ever known . . . peaked out. The automobile industry began to die." Obviously, none of these critics anticipated the spectacular emergence of the specialized recreational adult toys that became so popular late in the century.

By the late 1960s and early 1970s, some social critics believed that the excesses of the car culture had become so transparently evident that it would collapse of its own weight. David Miller, a well-known futurist based in San Francisco, described his conscious decision to try to live without a car:

> I'd begun to realize that time behind the wheel was bad time. You
> couldn't read. You couldn't write. You had to fight traffic, using
> plenty of energy. So I said, 'I'm going to try to give this up.' I'm sure

> the junkyard people thought they ripped me off because I wasn't
> trying to make any money. I was just trying to get rid of my car and I
> wanted to get shed of it while I was in the mood. I made myself a
> ground rule that since I didn't have a car, whenever the whim struck
> me, I would rent one or take a cab. And what happened was that I
> did do those things quite frequently in the early years. I do it less and
> less as time goes by. I've gotten adjusted to living without a car.

There were inconveniences, times when he wished he had never made the commitment. Miller recalled raw, rainy nights, when he and his wife stood for twenty minutes in windswept pickup zones waiting for late-night streetcars; at such moments, it was hard to resist flagging taxis. Consciously or otherwise, however, Miller stacked the deck to increase odds of a favorable outcome of their so-called experiment. The couple was childless, so they did not face the pressure of shepherding young children to or from school and between activities. And they chose an apartment in a neighborhood in a city that was well served by public transportation. One wonders how firm their commitment would have remained had they been parents of three children and lived in, say, Los Angeles or Houston, profoundly alien environments for those without wheels.

Some opponents of the automobile naïvely imagined that the nation's youth would lead the fight against the automobile and for attractive options in transportation. As Ronald A. Buel observed in the early 1970s, "The times they are a-changing. . . . There is increasing openness among the young. . . . The last decade has seen a large portion of American youth seriously question our materialistic values." However, another critic, Kenneth Schneider, writing about the same time, questioned the notion that the nation's youth would stand up against automakers. "Consider how each successive wave of hippies glory in rebelling against the entire establishment. Yet they have failed to rebel against the most pervasive and restrictive department of the establishment, the auto/highway/service complex." The "flower children" may have gathered in Haight Asbury in San Francisco for the "summer of love" in 1967, but many of them arrived by car. In fact, one of the most cherished symbols of hippiedom was a beat-up Volkswagon bus painted in psychedelic rainbow colors and festooned with peace signs and radical bumper stickers.

Yet if Schneider questioned American youths' ability and commitment to lead the revolt against the so-called tyranny of the automobile, he did believe that enlightened activists representing various racial, social, and economic classes and other people of all ages could incorporate certain techniques of youthful protest on behalf of their causes. He envisioned tens of thousands of pedestrians tying up freeway traffic by staging mass sit-downs during rush hour. Such coordinated efforts would clearly dramatize the vulnerability of the car culture. The downside? "Some persons may be taken prisoner for a time, but the authorities will always hesitate to take on the welfare of large numbers of detained demonstrators." He continued, "When pedestrians tie up vehicle movement the pressures become unbearable. Then pedestrians will get their improvement. Persistence, clear demands, and the threat of escalating immobility will force the concessions." In short, Mahatma Gandhi's passive resistance techniques, employed with dazzling effectiveness so recently in the Civil Rights movement, might bring about the downfall of the overstuffed, arrogant gasocracy.

Are there any solutions to the sprawl and "mallification" of the nation's urban landscapes? Some public policy analysts and social critics urge revival efforts in central cores. However, mere "gentrification" and throwing large amounts of money into huge downtown civic projects could be counterproductive. Jane Kay urges doing relatively easy, inexpensive things first, such as loosening the grip of the automobile. ". . . [W]e must strengthen and redeem the settled city street. . . . The agenda is not reinventing streetscapes but retrofitting them with the amenities that make for the welcoming corner café, the handshake that keeps Main Street's walkers from driving to the mall." Kay urges "transforming the so-called brownfields, the vacant lots in our cities, instead of obliterating the greenfields of our countryside."

Kay saw more than a little irony in the fact that the struggle against the automobile sometimes created strange, if temporary, bedfellows. In protests against downtown freeways back in the 1960s and 1970s, society matrons sometimes rubbed shoulders with members of the Black Panthers. However, all opposition to the downtown dominance of the automobile need not be confrontational. Two decades later, Kay advocated aggressive traffic-calming techniques, designed to make neighborhood streets more pedestrian friendly, in part by making them less efficient for automobiles. Planners could add speed bumps and unnecessary jogs. They could widen sidewalks and plant trees, which would interfere with drivers' sight lines and, presumably, force them to slow down. If all else failed in the fight against the automobile and its excesses, then follow the tough love example of Bill W, founder of Alcoholics Anonymous. Without supplying specifics, she suggested, "For some years an Automobile Anonymous Association might assist those who are susceptible to automobility to inaugurate a new pattern of life and to experience genuine freedom at first hand."

However, hatred of the "four-wheeled monsters" caused some automobile critics to lose touch with reality. Like John Jerome, who confidently anticipated the "death" of the automobile culture, Kenneth Schneider succumbed to wishful thinking and expressed optimism that it had peaked: "It may be too early to say, but perhaps the 1960s saw the climax of the tyrannous grip and the 1970s will witness a powerful reversal." In his view, Autopia would be a distant memory by 2000. "And so, one day about 1994, the roars, whines, and rumbles on Forty-second Street will just fade away. Decibels will drop to the human scale in the revived hearts of our cities. Curbs will lose the fright of cliffs. Collisions between bodies in motion will be resolved by apologies accompanied by smiles, for human bodies are not themselves very lethal."

Amidst laments among academics and inner-city intellectuals about soulless, postmodern suburbs, a few brave contrarians have challenged the seemingly universal condemnation. Historian Robert Fishman contended in the late 1980s that *technoburbs* had emerged as "viable socioeconomic units." They were, in effect, independent of central cities. "Spread out along its highway growth corridors are shopping malls, industrial parks, campus-like office complexes, hospitals, schools, and a full range of housing types. Its residents look to their immediate surroundings rather than to the city for their jobs and other needs; and its industries find not only the employees they need but also the specialized services." These technoburbs have more direct contact with other technoburbs around the country than with nearby urban cores. Traditional commuting patterns are obsolete. Fishman concedes that, in contrast to ". . . the rich and diverse architectural heritage of the cities, the technoburb has been built up as a standardized and simplified sprawl, consuming time and space, destroying the natural landscape. The wealth that postindustrial America has generated has been used to create an ugly and wasteful pseudo-city, too spread out to be efficient, too superficial to create a true culture." Fishman then reverses gears and makes a case for the technocity: ". . . [W]e can hope that its deficiencies are in large part the early awkwardness of a new urban type." He continues, "All new city forms appear in their early stages to be chaotic." He reminds us that ". . . even the most 'organic' cityscapes of the past evolved slowly after much chaos and trial and error." Early-twenty-first-century technoburbs have many obvious flaws, but Fishman predicts that humans will eventually learn how to make them better.

Most critics of the automobile are deeply committed, sober-minded people who take their self-appointed roles as watchful guardians of their versions of the public's interest very seriously. On rare occasions, however, even these earnest souls grasp the humor in unusual situations. One auto critic was attending a seminar in Boulder, Colorado, which had attracted numerous advocates of alternative forms of transportation. A speaker was droning on and on about the evils of the automobile and the hidden costs of our "hypermobility." It was a gorgeous, crisp October day, and some of his listeners no doubt daydreamed about sampling the area's renowned hiking and jogging trails or repairing to the Oasis brew pub for some cold refreshments. In an instant, however, the entire room woke up. There was a frantic squeal of brakes, followed by a car crash right outside the window. One vehicle caught fire. Sirens screamed. The fire department arrived. The intersection was soon overrun with police cars. Ambulances came and took away the victims. Tow trucks cleared away the wreckage, and city crews swept up the shards of broken glass and small auto body parts. As the last well-paid public employees departed the scene, silence enveloped both the street outside and the seminar room. Somebody asked the speaker, "Did you stage that?"

Ironically, the initial wave of studies lambasting the excesses of the automobile culture crested just before the Arab Oil Embargo of 1973. After the Middle East dramatically exposed this nation's vulnerability to energy shortages, debates about the viability of the automobile moved in significantly different directions. Before the energy crunch, however, defenders of automobility, coolly confident of their dominant position, generally dismissed their opponents as longhaired, bleeding-heart liberals. When a band of protesters representing numerous constituencies united to stop the Jones Falls Expressway in Baltimore, highway engineers dismissed them as Cassandras, "petunia-planting esthetes, bird-watchers and do-gooders."

Critics of the automobile culture could dismiss such reactions as defensive, small-minded, even childish. However, some industry spokesmen provided observations that may have made opponents squirm. In 1975, B. Bruce-Briggs charged that many critics of automobility were of a "New Class," self-appointed guardians of gentility and righteous living, comprised largely of academics and "literary intellectuals." This class airily dismissed "vulgar" middle-class values, which they stereotyped as best epitomized by gas-guzzling, chrome-plated automobiles. "The New Class prefers restorations to new houses, antiques to modern items, sailing to power boats, backpacking to cross-country motorcycling, and in general rejects all of the cultural artifacts of the industrial revolution." Bruce-Briggs claimed that arrogant elitism had permeated their thinking from the start. In particular, he singled out Lewis Mumford, who had repeatedly decried the automobile's impact ever since the 1930s. Bruce-Briggs argued that Mumford's writings were ". . . shot through with his hatred of modern civilization in general and American democracy in particular, which he would prefer to destroy in favor of some sort of idealized medieval, decentralized, 'nonmaterialist' society—where the peasants and workers would presumably know their place."

Bruce-Briggs also claimed that protests against the automobile were virtually nonexistent, or very muted, *as long as ownership was confined to elites and the upper-middle class.* That changed dramatically after World War II. By then, prosperous motorists had to share the road with blue-collar workers, and they didn't like it at all. Bruce-Briggs argued, "It is no coincidence that both the agitation against the automobile and the promotion of mass transit began when the urban workers switched from mass transit to the car. At its most vulgar level, the anti-automobile crusade is simply the attempt to drive the other guy off the road, particularly when he is not as sensitive, well-educated or prosperous as we are." He concluded, "That lower-class slob has some nerve jamming highways in his junky old Chevy with his wife in curlers and his squalling brats beating on the rear window. People like that belong in mass transportation, in subways or buses, not clogging up roads and slowing us down."

Bruce-Briggs scored some telling blows, but his defense against automobile culture critics frequently misfired. He ignored the considerable opposition to upper-class automobiles on city streets early in the century. In addition, he was just as guilty of stereotyping and oversimplifying realities of the past as were the so-called elitist critics of the car culture. For example, he dismissed federal laws mandating installation of emissions control devices and advanced safety features, largely as devices to drive up the cost of owning a car and force the poorest Americans off the roads and back into mass transit. He appeared bewildered when the Federal Energy Conservation Act of 1975 mandated that all new cars average 27.5 miles per gallon by 1985, concluding that such legislation would force drivers into small cars. "Of course, when millions of consumers go down to the showrooms and discover that there is nothing larger than kiddie cars, they will howl to heaven, rudely reminding Congress once again that the New Class is not the entire electorate. All this nonsense will be swept away to oblivion. . . ."

When Bruce-Briggs wrote in 1975, his cynicism appeared justified. Americans didn't much like small cars. Voices were shrill on both sides of the debate over the future of the automobile. At this critical moment, the domestic automobile industry, the linchpin of the American economy for decades, had fallen on hard times. Almost across the board, automobile executives appeared inept, indecisive, and almost totally incapable of responding effectively to comparatively gentle shifts in market forces, let alone insistent demands from critics and, particularly, government regulators that they change their menu of offerings seemingly overnight. How could an industry that had appeared all-powerful—even arrogant—as late as the mid-1960s have fallen so far and so fast in just a decade? Pride goeth before the fall; and we address these issues in the next chapter.

Chapter Seven

THE AUTOMOBILE INDUSTRY UNDER SIEGE

It is impossible to pinpoint a precise moment when the American automobile industry lost its previously almost unchallenged position as the world's leader in both production and innovation. However, overweening self-satisfaction and colossal arrogance on the part of top-level auto men in Detroit, increasingly evident ever since the end of World War II, contributed to the industry's gradual decay. When a styling engineer at Chrysler designed a low-slung, smaller car during the boom years of the 1950s, company president K. T. Keller huffed, "Chrysler builds cars to sit in, not piss over." Even as small, economical, and well-built foreign models made significant inroads into the domestic automobile market later in the decade, Henry Ford II contemptuously dismissed them as "little shitboxes." This chapter traces the decline of the domestic automobile industry between the 1960s and the mid-1980s. Before it experienced a remarkable revival in the late 1980s, it seemingly hit rock bottom.

ATROPHY IN THE AUTO INDUSTRY

Almost from the beginning, certainly long before World War II, leaders in the American automobile industry had developed a culture of denial, a tendency to dismiss or at least gloss over long-term problems. Because the public's demand for their products was so strong, for decades this attitude had few obvious negative consequences.

Despite occasional downturns in demand, for the most part the industry experienced almost uninterrupted good fortune until the mid-1960s. Raw materials to build cars were almost always available. Buyers generally accepted Detroit's products. Gasoline was plentiful and cheap. Government policy aided the industry. If assembly line workers were not always tractable, their level of productivity was generally acceptable. It almost seemed as if there was universal approval of corporate president Charles E. Wilson's oft-misquoted postwar dictum, "What's good for General Motors is good for the country."

However, from the mid-1960s until the mid-1980s, the American automobile industry experienced an almost uninterrupted series of poor choices, bad timing, less-supportive public policy, negative publicity, and bad breaks. For those twenty years, Detroit auto men collectively resembled the Keystone Cops or the gang that couldn't shoot straight. Long-festering public resentments assaulted them just when they appeared most vulnerable, and it appeared as if the industry came under attack from every angle. It seemed that nothing went right.

For decades, buying a car had been a distinctly unpleasant experience for almost all consumers, who had generally accepted abuse stoically. In the 1960s and 1970s, the media seized the opportunity to document and publicize how manufacturers and dealers manipulated buyers. Industry critics simultaneously zeroed in on the atrocious quality of some American makes. In addition, some products were highly unsafe on the road, almost moving death traps. Amidst highly publicized conflicts with management, workers in the auto plants rebelled against the mindless repetition of their tasks and their lack of input into quality control. They found job satisfaction nearly impossible to obtain, and newspapers and television enthusiastically reported their discontent.

After decades of being cynically manipulated by western countries, particularly the United States, major petroleum exporters in the Middle East flexed their collective muscles and limited the West's access to gasoline. Critics challenged Detroit to respond with smaller, more fuel efficient cars, and automakers eventually responded; however, the results were decidedly mixed. Government policy was no longer knee-jerk support of the automobile industry. Construction of some new freeways actually stopped. New environmental laws forced manufacturers to address fundamental causes of air and other types of pollution, and some tax dollars were diverted from the Highway Trust Fund into mass transit. As David Halberstam, an astute historian and social critic, observed, "The postwar years, the immense material strength and physical might, two generations of unrivaled prosperity—it had all lulled America into thinking it had attained an economic utopia, a kind of guaranteed national prosperity, like a concession

won in some marathon bargaining concession with God." By the mid-
1970s, it all seemed to be unraveling. According to American financier
Felix Rohatyn, "In just twenty-five years, we [had] gone from
the American century to the American crisis. That is an astonishing
turnaround—perhaps the shortest parabola in history."

INSOLENT CHARIOT MAKERS

During the boom years following World War II, top-level managers in
the automobile industry had enjoyed such uninterrupted success and
gotten their way so consistently and for so long that they had grown
collectively soft. Keller's arrogant remark about small cars was a
symptom of an attitude, common in Detroit's executive suites, that
Americans knew all there was to know about making and marketing
cars. In retrospect, a fundamental problem was that Detroit's "gasoline aristocracy" had essentially insulated itself from both criticism
and the real world. Not long before he was either fired or resigned in
frustration from GM in the early 1980s—the version depends on the
sympathies of the teller—brilliant designer John De Lorean wrote a
single-spaced, fourteen-page assessment of the corporation's problems. He observed, "We seem to forget that a cloistered executive,
whose only social contacts are with similar executives who make
$500,000 a year, and who has not really bought a car the way a cus-
tomer has in years, has no basis to judge public taste."

Auto men in Detroit were seldom exposed to those who might
disagree with them, particularly within the corporation. Almost without exception, ambitious, driven men who worked their way up corporate ladders at the Big Three got there by toeing the company line.
That included not questioning the operating assumptions of their superiors. As an article in *Fortune* aptly summarized, going to work for
GM was like "entering the priesthood. . . . GM executives are products of a system that discourages attention to matters far outside the
purview of their jobs. And they are captives of a camaraderie that
keeps them much in each other's company—on the golf course and
around the card table as well as the conference room. While this gen-
erates an *esprit de corps* that constitutes one of the organization's
great strengths, its effect is to insulate GM's managers from many contemporary currents of thought."

Since he departed from GM under a cloud, De Lorean emphasized
the flaws in the system. He described in excruciating detail an ossified
bureaucracy at GM. Nobody dared to make decisions alone; even the
most minuscule issues were assigned to committees. At one high-level

meeting, a nervous junior-level manager, through no fault of his own, had managed to put a dozen or so top-level executives asleep detailing with slides and graphs a minor problem that obviously should have been resolved much farther down the line. Corporate president Richard C. Gerstenberg, clearly bored with the details, snapped, "Goddamnit! I don't like to be surprised." He continued, "We can't make a decision on this now. I think we ought to form a task force to look into this and come back with a report in 90 or 120 days. Then we can make a decision." He then rattled off the names of a dozen or so men to comprise that group. Fortunately, one of his higher-level associates had the courage to inform Gerstenberg that the presentation was the product of a task force he had appointed some months ago, including some of the very men he had named to the new one! If GM's managerial hierarchy attracted the most negative attention during these years, working conditions in executive suites at Ford and Chrysler were very similiar.

By the 1970s, as the domestic automobile industry's troubles mounted, critics noted that most of its leaders' backgrounds were in finance rather than design and production. Armed with advanced degrees from the nation's most prestigious business schools, the post–World War II generation of automobile executives experimented with the most "modern" business theories. The so-called "bean counters" were clearly more comfortable with organization charts, "information flows," and balance sheets than with design blueprints and production challenges. Many older, experienced auto executives had worked their way slowly up the managerial ladder, starting with varied and extensive experience in production. If they had not actually worked on the assembly lines themselves, they were at least familiar with the frustrations blue-collar workers faced, and they could talk with the union representatives. They enjoyed working on design problems and exulted in a beautifully crafted clay model of a futuristic new car model. But the bean counters' focus was almost exclusively financial: cost analysis, balance sheets, quarterly reports, and dividends for stockholders.

Through the 1950s and 1960s, as the domestic automobile industry's profits increased to all-time records, Ford's "Whiz Kids" and their like-minded rivals at Chrysler and GM represented both a new generation and a completely different style of corporate manager. God forbid that they should risk getting dirt on their $400 suits by actually showing up on the shop floor itself! Behind unified corporate facades, the rivalry, even antipathy, between young financial wizards and older, more traditional product-oriented managers was fierce. Industry analyst Brock Yates scored the "numbers-oriented executives" who "came to dominate industry thinking at all levels . . . who were obsessed by the financial structure of the car business and viewed the product mainly as an abstraction out of which profit or loss would be generated." When hard times came to the industry in the 1970s, managerial teams in several big companies, severely weakened over decades by rigidity and internal stresses, buckled and fell apart.

DEALERS VERSUS CONSUMERS

Unless one is quite wealthy, the act of purchasing an automobile is never—and never has been—pleasant. From the moment when the first automobile buyer realized that a price posted on the windshield of a vehicle was not all that firm, the inherently adversarial relationship between dealer and buyer became increasingly evident. Since dealers worked at these transactions full-time and most buyers entered showrooms once every few years, the former almost always gained the upper hand.

Although consumer resentment was naturally directed against those with whom they dealt directly—local dealers—the latter in turn blamed manufacturers in Detroit for forcing them to unload large numbers of slow-selling vehicles if they wanted sufficient numbers of desirable models. The Big Three, along with most other manufacturers, awarded franchises to retailers of their new models. Since franchises could be withdrawn from uncooperative dealers, the manufacturers generally held the upper hand. Automobile dealers banded together to form associations like the National Automobile Dealers Association (NADA) to protect their interests. But who would speak for consumers? Publication of Ralph Nader's exposé of the Corvair, *Unsafe at Any Speed,* in 1965 seemed to loosen a floodgate of negative coverage of unsavory industrywide practices. Although used car dealers attracted the most unfavorable publicity, numerous attacks against middle men documented rip-offs of new car buyers. As prices rose and product quality in Detroit declined, American consumers' long-simmering discontent became more obvious and vocal.

Even some auto men admitted that inherently exploitative relationships between sellers and buyers of cars devolved from the top of the industry. Although his judgment may have been somewhat skewed in that he had some scores to settle, as John De Lorean reflected back on his aborted career at General Motors some years after he had left the company, he questioned the entire morality of the Big Three's marketing system. In De Lorean's view, the chief objective was ". . . to take some American wage-earner who was working his fanny off trying to pay for a car and, just about the day he got it paid off, convince him that he should start the payment process all over again. His 36 months were up." However, it was usually dealers who got the rap. Popular magazines featured articles describing a long list of misleading and unsavory practices by dealers, first to lure prospects onto showroom floors and, later, to take advantage of buyers.

The variations in dealers' shell games were seemingly limitless. In addition to the uniformly accepted high-pressure sales tactics, many retailers routinely used the switch. This was luring prospects into showrooms with vehicles advertised at tantalizingly low prices, then claiming that the last cars at that price had just been sold. Prospects were then offered more expensive units with overpriced add-on features. Customers who wanted one particular feature often discovered that it was only available as part of a much larger, overpriced package containing many features they did not particularly want. Some buyers were lulled into believing they had negotiated good deals with seemingly inexperienced salesmen, only to be confronted at the moment when fatigue was setting in by tough-talking "closers" who bullied them into accepting much less favorable prices and terms. Even focused, wary customers, who dickered for reasonable prices, might find a long list of unjustifiable charges for dealer preparation of cars for delivery on their final contracts. Buyers who successfully avoided all of these snares could still get caught in the finance pack trap— outrageous rates of interest on installment sales that sometimes included kickbacks to dealers from the finance companies. One critic concluded, "Few customers walked out of a salesroom without feeling that they had been victimized, and many people still shop for a new car with trepidation."

SALVOS AGAINST THE AUTO INDUSTRY

For years, ever since designers in Detroit went overboard with chrome and tail fins, increasing numbers of observers had criticized the industry's products. One of the first salvos came in the late 1950s from an unlikely source: Bishop G. Bromley Oxam, head of the Methodist Church in the United States. He raised a pertinent question, "Who are the madmen who build cars so long they cannot be parked and are hard to turn at corners, vehicles with hideous tail fins, full of gadgets and covered with chrome, so low that an average human being has to crawl in the doors and so powerful that no man dare use the horsepower available?" In 1966, Hal Higdon wrote in a *New York Times Magazine* article, "Last year a Yale University physicist calculated that since Chevy offered 46 models, 32 engines, 20 transmissions, 21 colors (plus nine two-tone combinations) and more than 400 accessories and options, that the number of different cars that a Chevrolet customer conceivably could order was greater than the number of atoms in the universe. This seemingly would put General Motors one notch higher than God in the chain of command."

With the emergence of the powerful, gas-guzzling, low-slung muscle cars of the 1960s and 1970s, such acerbic criticisms continued to be largely ignored. Still, Detroit's products began attracting increasing amounts of criticism, some of it even coming from generally friendly sources. Automobile reporter Brock Yates labeled American products of the mid-1960s as "oversized, overpowered, with soggy suspension, vague steering, weak brakes and low-grade tires; the average Detroit automobile of the day was a true ocean liner on the road." He tested what he called a "typical" General Motors product, the 1967 Cadillac El Dorado. Gadget-laden, with a "feather-pillow" ride and priced at $6,277, "it plowed through tight corners in an ungainly fashion, got only ten miles to the gallon, and would run 109 mph in a short burst like an ill-trained athlete."

Far more problematical was the steadily declining quality of American cars. To begin with, some recent American models were manifestly unsafe. Ralph Nader's broadside against Chevrolet's Corvair in 1965 was just the most publicized of consumer groups' complaints, leading to congressional committees' investigations into automobile safety. Before Nader's exposé, decision makers in the automobile industry, with few exceptions, had invested very little in safety features. One of the hoariest industry maxims was that safety didn't sell cars. In 1965, the same year Nader's book appeared, a Senate investigation revealed that GM had earned $1.7 billion in profits the previous year but had invested a paltry $1.25 million in product safety. Even worse for the industry, respected journalists for the *New Republic* and the *New York Times* broke stories that hirelings of GM had conducted extensive surveillance of Nader, attempting to uncover personal dirt that might compromise his integrity and, more important, his credibility. Although corporate president James Roche knew that his legal department had assigned its own investigators to follow Nader's trail, he insisted initially that their queries were limited to discovering his background, expertise, and possible connections with attorneys handling Corvair lawsuits against his company. However, subsequent *Times* stories claimed that Nader had received threatening telephone calls "and that women he did not know had attempted to place him in compromising situations." Roche publicly deplored "any type of harassment to which Mr. Nader [had] apparently been subjected," but mere apology was insufficient. Nader sued the corporation for $6 million in compensatory damages and $20 million in punitive damages. The two sides eventually settled out of court for $425,000, which Nader's attorney claimed was the largest such settlement for invasion of privacy to date. The damage to Detroit automakers as a group and GM's reputation in particular went far beyond a modest cash payout by the latter. By the late 1960s, increasing numbers of Americans questioned the notion that what's good for the domestic automobile industry was good for the country.

If Nader's campaign against the Corvair had a long-term salutary effect, it was bringing the whole issue of automobile safety front and center before the public. For decades, the industry and its allies had generally succeeded in thinly veiled efforts to blame accidents on careless drivers and poor roads rather than on defective vehicles. The Automotive Safety Foundation had been formed in 1937, essentially as a public relations arm of the industry. Its studies were funded by the auto companies, parts suppliers, and the petroleum industry. To combat spiraling accident rates and fearful death tolls, the organization almost invariably recommended more effective and extensive driver training, beefed-up law enforcement, and more modern roads and streets. President Eisenhower lent the enormous prestige of his office in forming the President's Committee for Traffic Safety in the 1950s. Its first chairman was none other than Harlow Curtice, at the time president of GM. Not surprisingly, almost none of its pronouncements dealt with the limitations of vehicles themselves.

By the early 1960s, however, more and more incidents compelled reluctant experts to examine motor vehicles with a more critical eye. Some cars were inherently dangerous even when standing still. In the summer of 1961, a teenager chasing a fly ball in a sandlot baseball game ran into the tail fin of a parked Cadillac. The sharp fin penetrated his heart, and the youth died. Two years later, a thirteen-year-old girl was riding her bike in Washington, D.C., and somehow ran into the rear fin of another parked Cadillac. She was impaled; although her father ran from the house and freed her, she died in a hospital two hours later.

Automotive safety was, and remains, an emotional, volatile, and highly complex issue. Safety statistics can be employed to justify virtually any desired position. From the first traffic fatality, recorded just before the turn of the century, annual traffic deaths experienced an almost constant rise, reaching a record of 56,278 when they peaked in 1972. Critics emphasized the irony that the public appeared indifferent to domestic carnage that took more American lives each year than were lost during the entire Vietnam War. Spokesmen for the automobile industry countered that death rates per capita have experienced a fairly constant decline over the course of the century.

Statistics gathered over the period from 1933 to 1937 revealed an average number of automobile deaths per 100,000 vehicles at 28.6 per year. The figure remained relatively level until the mid-1980s, then declined significantly to a low of 16.3 in the late 1990s. They claimed far more spectacular results if one considers deaths per vehicle mile driven. From a peak of 18.2 deaths per 100 million miles driven between 1923 and 1927, the number declined to seven in 1950, and less than two by the late 1990s. Moreover, by the early 1980s, the United States actually boasted the best safety standards in the world. Its figure of 3.1 deaths per 100 million miles driven compared to 3.4 in Finland, 3.5 in the United Kingdom, 4.3 in Canada and Denmark, 4.7 in Japan, all the way up to 6.3 in Germany, 7.1 in France, and 11.4 in Spain.

While defenders of the automobile industry would like to take credit for these results after the fact, much of the impetus for improvements in automotive safety was a by-product of aggressive public policies that basically coerced the industry into paying attention to safety. In 1966, Congress passed the National Traffic and Motor Vehicle Safety Law, which set safety standards for new cars, beginning with the 1968 model year. There were seventeen new standards, including seat belts, padded dash board and visors, recessed control knobs, safety door latches and hinges, impact-absorbing steering columns, dual braking systems, standard bumper heights, and glare-reduction surfaces. Eleven more standards were introduced in the 1969 model year, along with mandated recalls for any potentially serious design shortcoming. Television watchers became familiar with automobile advertisements showing in slow motion how added safety features protected life-sized dummies during real and simulated test site crashes. By the mid-1980s, there were numerous additional layers of government regulations related to automotive safety, including requirements that air bags be provided in ever-increasing percentages of new units sold.

Given increased public awareness of auto-related environmental issues, the dreadful timing of GM's conflict with Ralph Nader, and the precipitous decline of their collective corporate images, the Big Three had little choice but to go along with many of the new requirements. Many auto men grumbled about the oppressive business environment wrought by a new era of government regulations; but, given the dismal recent performance of the industry, most consumers welcomed consumer protection, at least initially. Industry spokespersons scored some public relations points when they emphasized that federally mandated safety and environmentally friendly features ratcheted up prices for new cars.

Automakers had a point. For example, in the early 1970s, GM originally estimated that full front seat air bag protection would cost

$1,100 per unit if installed in 250,000 cars per year, versus just $45 for front seat belts. The company introduced air bags as an option on 1974–1976 Cadillacs, Buicks, and Oldsmobiles. The company spent $80 million to produce 300,000 air bag systems. Even though GM charged only $300 for the option, customers ordered just 10,000; thus, each unit ended up costing the corporation $8,000! Their experience with air bags was extreme, but it symbolized how complicated decision making was becoming for automobile executives.

In the early 1970s, John De Lorean had complained that American automobile manufacturers had not come up with a really significant product innovation since the automatic transmission in the late 1930s and power steering in the 1940s. By his account, they had been too intent on chrome, tail fins, and glitzy marketing. And, to be sure, government regulation had made building cars more expensive.

One of the most serious problems Detroit automakers faced was deterioration of product quality. In the early 1970s, the Chevrolet Vega won *Motor Trend* magazine's "Car of the Year" award. Perhaps the award itself was an evil omen; a few years earlier, the magazine had selected Chevrolet's ill-fated Corvair for the same honor. The Vega was a sawed-off compact car, hastily produced in an effort to fend off increasingly serious competition from Volkswagon and other small, well-built foreign makes. Within months of winning the prize, Vegas were being connected to all sorts of problems. Their brakes were unreliable, and they vibrated. When brakes were applied hard in test drives, the vehicle often veered in a frightening manner. Vegas were difficult to start and often conked out in traffic. There were problems with the electrical system, which often failed totally. Gearshift levers fell off. One owner complained that his roof leaked: "It is extremely difficult to drive home from work with FOUR INCHES of water surrounding your feet." He must have prayed that his electrical system stayed on the fritz.

In response to these and numerous other complaints, Chevrolet began recalling Vegas. One recall of 130,000 units equipped with optional 90-horsepower engines was in April 1972. Deficiencies in the carburetor and muffler could ignite fires in the gas tank. As the recall letter noted, "After the muffler has ruptured . . . fuel spillage may occur. . . . [F]ailure of the fuel line hoses . . . [and] subsequent backfires then can ignite the spilled fuel and cause your Vega to catch fire." That was just the beginning of problems with the Vega. Another recall of 350,000 units with 80-horsepower engines just one month later meant that 85 percent of Vegas were faulty; a third recall in July included 95 percent of all Vegas. The third, and final, recall involved checking rear axles, some of which were "a fraction of an inch" too short, meaning that a wheel could easily fall off! During 1972, many Vegas spent more time in repair shops than in owners' garages. More than a few cynical Vega owners suspected dealers, who earned no profits from recall work performed under warranty, of trying to recoup some benefits by strongly recommending additional expensive and unnecessary repairs.

Amazingly, some dealers actually tried to turn recalls into positives. One automobile writer described an encounter with a salesman at Midtown Chevrolet in New York City. Asked about Vega recalls, the salesman replied, "That was last year." He suggested that the federally mandated recall program was the "best thing that's ever happened" to the automobile industry, that "otherwise the [defective] cars would be driving around." Even Rolls-Royce had experienced recalls. He actually seemed proud that Chevrolet led the Big Three in recalls with 4 million in 1972, followed by Ford's 3 million and 2 million by Chrysler! This car salesman at least could give politicians lessons in "spin doctoring."

TURMOIL ON THE SHOP FLOOR

Some of the problems surrounding deteriorating quality of American brands may have originated at the shop floor. Before World War II, management had generally held the upper hand in relations with workers on Detroit's assembly lines. Until at least the 1930s, relations between blue-collar workers and management were permeated by resentment, hostility, and mutual suspicion. When confrontations occurred, management usually won. A power shift began during the Depression, after Congress passed the National Labor Relations Act. This law forced management in heavy industries to recognize unions chosen by the workers. The United Auto Workers (UAW), under the able stewardship of Walter Reuther, became one of the most aggressive and farsighted industrial unions. After World War II, the UAW became one of the most militant, powerful, and successful big unions in the nation.

On the surface at least, the 1950s and 1960s were great years for workers in the automobile plants. The UAW was nearing the peak of its influence and power, with total membership topping out at 1.5 million in 1973. Previous generations of unorganized factory workers had usually been exploited members of an economic underclass, held down by ruthless business owners. However, the new working class enjoyed levels of security, affluence, and even leisure beyond the dreams of their forebears. The UAW negotiated paid vacations in new bargaining agreements with employers. In 1958, the average hourly wage for autoworkers was $2.64, compared to a national average of $1.95 for all production workers in nonsupervisory positions. By 1970, average wages had risen to $4.42 per hour. The average autoworker earned almost 50 percent more than his peers in other areas of manufacturing.

Economists, sociologists, and social critics were fascinated with the new so-called blue-collar middle class. A 1967 study revealed that almost three fourths of all industrial workers lived in suburbs, and most were buying their own homes. More important, in addition to paid vacations, this new class of workers enjoyed free or inexpensive medical coverage for themselves and their families, plus generous pensions. They owned television sets, washers and dryers, and even second automobiles. As one labor historian commented, "For a hundred years, the proletariat had loomed as an avenging force in Western society, forever erupting into protest, always threatening to storm to power in behalf of the downtrodden." That image was rapidly becoming obsolete in the postwar decades, particularly in the United States. "How odd, really, it now was to contemplate a working class so smoothly integrated into the system, so prosperous, so lacking in the bitterness and frustration that had led workers to radical movements and system-threatening protest in the past."

Such rosy commentaries suggesting a working-class utopia in post–World War II America are not altogether convincing. If automobile workers enjoyed unprecedented material abundance, perceptive critics found trouble lurking behind a prosperous facade. Some things had not changed since Reinhold Niebuhr's devastating commentary on factory life in Detroit in the 1930s. Investigations discovered that "dull, unrelenting, and fragmented jobs exacted a physical toll on autoworkers, depriving them of opportunities for rich and satisfying emotional lives." Few blue-collar workers had any realistic chance for meaningful promotions. Many worked twenty-five or thirty years in the same dead-end jobs, where their only reward was the paycheck. Since they had to follow orders from foremen who were often abrasive and intolerant, and since they had almost no say about quality control, workers seldom identified strongly with the products they turned out. Most jobs in the plants were mentally unchallenging, requiring little or no thought. In addition, most autoworkers experienced periodic layoffs, which lasted weeks, months, or sometimes even years. These uncertainties exacerbated stress levels. Several studies suggested that fifteen or twenty years of repetitive work in an unhealthy, unpleasant environment aged workers far beyond their chronological years; and problems extended far beyond just the workers themselves, affecting families, even whole communities. Sociologist Mirra Komarovsky concluded, ". . . [W]ork, school, and family patterns made working-class marriages bleak and bereft of emotional warmth, virtual prisons for wives of blue-collar workers."

Individual autoworkers grimly hanging on in cities like Detroit, Flint, and Hamtramck encountered additional stresses in the workplace. In the 1960s and 1970s, the Civil Rights and feminist movements created lasting changes in American life, which eventually filtered down to the shop floor. Some automobile producers, most noticeably Ford, had integrated their workforces decades earlier. However, almost all minority workers had been restricted to the least pleasant and lowest paying tasks. They had virtually no chance of rising to supervisory or managerial positions. Many foremen treated their sections as personal fiefdoms; union representatives often cooperated in keeping certain undesirables out and maintaining stable mixes of compatible ethnic groups in each location on the assembly line. African Americans, Puerto Ricans, and Hispanics might be largely confined to low-paid janitorial positions or forced to work in paint rooms that were permeated with unpleasant or even dangerous fumes. However, the 1960s brought a broad array of federal legislation mandating equal opportunity and affirmative action. Much to the disgust and discomfort of many older white ethnic males on the shop floor, minorities and women challenged their authority, even their seniority. All of a sudden, their easy, familiar racist and sexist banter could get them into fights, legal trouble, and perhaps even fired. To their shock and dismay, some veteran white workers found themselves taking orders from minority foremen for the first time in their lives.

However, job frustrations affected almost all workers on the auto assembly lines, including women and minorities. If the "rivet heads" could not do much about the tedium and monotony of working conditions on the shop floor, they also realized that it was difficult for companies to fire them, since they were protected by a strong union. Idle minds needed something to occupy them during seemingly endless, crawling hours and minutes on the job. Most lifers on the assembly line, at least those interested in mental survival, instinctively sensed that they needed distractions. What may have been good for GM was definitely not good for them. Some workers created ingenious ways to goof off on the job and otherwise kill time. They found imaginative ways to fake injuries or ailments, which would free them from the line, sometimes for hours. Enterprising workers ran betting pools or other sideline businesses on the shop floor. Experienced employees in some sections discovered that one worker could basically handle two side-by-side jobs. While one worker found a convenient hidden location to read, sleep, or even drink, his partner handled his responsibilities on the line. An hour or two later, they would trade places. More than a few workers sneaked beer, hard liquor, or even drugs into the workplace, although the practice was very risky in that apprehension could lead to almost instant dismissal. In their own minds, at least, assembly line jobs were so dehumanizing that they fully deserved any relief they could generate for themselves. Some foremen, realizing that a stable workforce was better than one with constant turnover, looked the other way.

A major confrontation at General Motors' Lordstown, Ohio, plant early in 1972 typified the increasing estrangement between management and labor. This Vega assembly plant, located just south of Warren, had been opened in 1966 and employed about 8,400 workers. This highly modernized, state-of-the-art factory had a young workforce, including Vietnam veterans and a lot of baby boomers who had not been hippies or worn flowers in their hair in the 1960s. Some were even college graduates who settled for jobs on the line because they paid well. Worried about declining worker productivity and wise to what they considered obstructionist tactics of the men on the line, management wanted to eliminate unnecessary jobs and extract more effort from each worker. They decided to speed up the assembly line from its usual pace of 60 or 65 cars per hour to an output of 100 units. This aggressive, confrontational move allowed management to lay off 700 workers.

There were two major problems with this strategy. First, the speedup caused a quality control disaster. Vegas quickly gained their unshakable reputation for being poorly built rattletraps. This was hardly surprising, since each worker now had just thirty-six seconds rather than roughly a minute to perform an assigned task. The speedup attracted national attention, almost all of it unfavorable for GM. In a rare pro-union editorial, even the *Wall Street Journal* allowed that, for the average worker confronting the prospect of a thirty-year career working at such a pace, the "soul must panic." Equally important, union men did not meekly accept either the speedup or the layoffs. In the words of two astute observers, "They'd grown steeped in the pugnacious traditions of the great steel and auto unions. That old fighting spirit and the rebellious attitude of the times created an explosive situation." In March 1972, they walked off the job for three weeks, crippling output of Vegas. Management finally dropped the 100-car-per-hour plan, but even when production began once again, problems remained. Quality improved little, and worker grievances accumulated by the thousands. By the mid-1970s, the very term "Lordstown" represented everything that was wrong in modern labor-management relations.

Given the general bleakness surrounding assembly line workers' lives in Lordstown, Detroit, Flint, and other automobile cities and the lack of incentives for conscientious attention to their jobs, is it any wonder that the products they turned out suffered as a consequence? There were numerous indirect but effective means of dealing with overly confrontational foremen. The hardheaded, inflexible foreman who rode his workers too hard for too long might find himself trying to explain to his superiors why a disproportionate number of units leaving his section of the line had loose bolts and missing parts. Truly alienated workers might drop bolts into car sections that were sealed up farther down the line, creating hard-to-trace rattles, which either required expensive repairs or irritated buyers for as long as they owned the car. One critic of the car culture reflected, "How ironic that in production, where scientific management techniques began, these conventional approaches now seem out of tune with the social and economic facts of the times. Production management is perhaps bringing to an end a long cycle that began with innovation and new concepts for accomplishing productivity, developed in maturity of ideas, subsequently grew into a conventional wisdom, and finally arrived at the point where we now see obsolescence."

As the American automobile industry entered an extended period of hard times in the early 1970s, numerous observers reported that Detroit increasingly resembled depressed cities behind the Iron Curtain, even Third World cities. Although some cities in the Midwest, including St. Louis, Milwaukee, and Detroit, had been in decline since the 1950s, due largely to disinvestment in basic industries, well-publicized problems in the automobile industry in Detroit attracted media attention to that city's decline. Industry critic David Halberstam noted, "Everywhere one saw signs of decay in a city that once prided itself on its grandeur. Its early citizens had envisioned Detroit on a majestic scale. The thoroughfares would reflect nothing less than Paris, handsome boulevards, radiating from the center of the city like giant spokes. Along them huge ornate buildings were constructed, some residential, some elegantly overwrought factories, monuments as much to the men who made them as to the products being manufactured." But, by the 1970s, the city built by the gasoline aristocracy was in shambles. "Now many [buildings] were empty, the windows smashed, the parking lots deserted or used as centers for late-night drug action. The great thoroughfares were now pitted with massive potholes the city was too poor to repair. . . ."

One local cynic suggested that the auto industry would only pick up when enough local citizens broke axles in the potholes. Another wrote to a local paper, "Were we bombed on the east side? Did I miss a shelling on East Seven Mile Road between VanDyke and Kelly? Those aren't potholes. They're more like shell craters." Downtown

Detroit "had become a crater, a place entered warily by workers every morning and left in the evening as quickly as possible. Unsuspecting visitors were warned against staying at hotels bearing once proud names, for reasons of security." Even efforts to reclaim the downtown's glorious past fizzled. Henry Ford II's futuristic Renaissance Center, originally touted as the cornerstone of a new downtown, stood alone; the few conventioneers who patronized its hotels felt like prisoners in a walled fortress. Visitor Herb Caen, a nationally known columnist from San Francisco, poked fun at it, stating that the "Ren Center" looked like the world's biggest cappuccino machine.

COMPETITION FROM ABROAD

In the late 1960s and early 1970s, it became painfully evident that Americans' long romance with Detroit's products was turning sour. Even formerly loyal automotive magazine editors became openly critical of the Big Three's offerings, particularly compared to foreign imports. In 1949, the United States had imported a total of two Volkswagens. In the early 1950s, Chrysler's K. T. Keller could well afford to scoff at foreign makes. However, serious foreign competition in the automobile industry became apparent soon after midcentury. Even if they were most popular in university towns, and most of their owners seemed to be college professors, by the mid-1950s, the Volkswagen "beetle" was no longer a curiosity.

The root causes of the rise of foreign competition in the domestic automobile industry are complex, but they revolve around World War II. Long before the war, Germans were renowned as automobile engineers. Hitler was highly enthusiastic about Volkswagen's early "peoples' car" models, and he had further demonstrated the Third Reich's commitment to putting more of his countrymen behind the wheel by authorizing construction of the Autobahn, one of the world's most sophisticated, impressive, restricted-access motorways in the 1930s. By contrast, the Japanese presence in worldwide automobile production was negligible until well after World War II. The overwhelming majority of Japanese either walked or rode bicycles. However, the war devastated manufacturing facilities in both of these Axis countries.

Following World War I, the victorious Allies had attempted, with disastrous results, to extract revenge from the defeated Central Powers in the form of huge monetary reparations. With the exception of the Soviet Union, which stripped East Germany of most of its remaining manufacturing facilities, they were determined to avoid repeating these mistakes following World War II. Through the Marshall Plan and other forms of direct aid, the United States embarked upon major industrial rebuilding programs in many of the countries devastated by the war. Germany and Japan not only received direct help but also gained an additional economic advantage, in that they were not permitted to build and maintain military forces or acquire weapons capable of sustaining any aggressive action against outside forces. The West committed to protecting them against Communist aggression. In simple terms, the upshot was that both Germany and Japan acquired modern, highly efficient industrial plants just when manufacturing establishments in most Allied countries were showing their age. Leaders in both countries were intent on developing modern economies, based partly on consumer goods.

In pursuing these strategies, few endeavors matched the appeal of the automobile industry. As David Halberstam revealed in his brilliant work, *The Reckoning,* foreign car producers, particularly the Japanese, assiduously courted and flattered the leading decision makers in Detroit. They visited Detroit by the dozens and asked endless questions. American auto men, basking in their images as all-knowing "big brothers" and totally oblivious to any idea that the Japanese could ever mount serious competition, basically told them almost everything they wanted to know. Through the 1950s and 1960s, the respectful, even obsequious Japanese visitors watched quietly and constantly absorbed knowledge.

Before World War II and through the first decade following the conflict, the United States was a major exporter of automobiles. High-level executives in Detroit arrogantly took for granted that they were the world's experts in automobile design and production and that they would retain that position with little effort. It went almost unnoticed that in the late 1950s the nation became a net importer of new automobiles. By 1960, the ratio was nearly four to one, as the United States imported 444,474 passenger vehicles, while exporting a mere 117,126 units. Japanese competition was not yet visible, as roughly three-fourths of the imports were from Germany. Through the 1960s and 1970s, the ratio of imported automobiles to exports would remain fairly constant, but the absolute numbers grew by leaps and bounds. In 1978, the United States imported more than 3 million foreign passenger cars, while exporting just over 700,000 units.

In 1960, Japan was not yet a force in the automobile industry. After the war, the United States had occupied Japan. Government officials, military leaders, and businessmen took pride in teaching their hosts the rudiments of democracy and capitalism. However, the label "made in Japan" still conjured up images of shabby quality and would do so until the 1960s. But as horror stories about inefficient operation, lack of safety, and poor quality control dogged one American car manufacturer after another during the 1970s, consumers flocked to foreign makers' showrooms. Swedish Volvos were renowned for durability and safety; car magazine feature writers gushed over sophisticated engineering in German makes; and Japanese brands such as Datsun and Toyota began attracting rave reviews, originally for economy and value and later for performance and design as well. In 1955, the Japanese exported exactly two passenger vehicles to the United States; by the mid-1970s, they were setting up huge sales lots along dealers' row. In 1975, sales of Japanese makes in the United States exceeded 700,000; just five years later, when Americans imported more than 3.1 million cars, Japanese brands comprised nearly two thirds of that number! Not all of those imported cars were built entirely of foreign parts by foreign workers in foreign locations. In fact, most were hybrids, partially assembled abroad, then finished in American plants by American workers. The variety of combinations of foreign and domestic contributions to imports was extremely complex. Nevertheless, by the mid-1970s, Japanese manufacturers were calling the shots, dominating the cutting edge in the automobile industry. In sharp contrast, American automobile decision makers appeared weak, reactive, and defensive in every respect. Gloomy commentators decreed that the so-called "American century" was over.

DWINDLING NATURAL RESOURCES

Of at least equal concern to thoughtful Americans pondering the nation's position as a superpower in the early 1970s was the shocking, sudden realization that the age of abundant, inexpensive energy was drawing to an end. Generations of Americans had come to expect cheap energy as virtually a birthright, an entitlement. We should examine the origins of such thinking in some depth.

For more than a century, the United States' emerging, and later dominant, industrial economy had been driven by plentiful, cheap natural resources, particularly the fuel that powered its machinery. In the middle of the nineteenth century, sturdy, experienced immigrant miners from Wales and elsewhere had extracted both anthracite and bituminous coal from the nation's plentiful deposits in the East, particularly Pennsylvania. Coal and its by-products powered the locomotives, steel mills, and much of the nation's heavy machinery from the mid-nineteenth century forward. Coal was also a prominent source of energy for heating the nation's homes. By the turn of the century, large amounts of bituminous coal were also being extracted from various rich veins in western states.

Although coal was a primary energy source for heavy machinery, it was obviously impractical for powering automobiles because it was bulky and dirty. Petroleum ultimately proved to be a far more effective source of power. Beginning in the 1860s, John D. Rockefeller and other producers had always met domestic needs, with plenty left over to export. However, a seismic shift occurred in the international energy marketplace in the 1950s and 1960s. By the early 1950s, petroleum engineers had discovered several "elephants"—enormous untapped reserves—in the Middle East. These confirmed finds dwarfed earlier estimates of petroleum reserves in the region and had profound effects on energy consumption around the world. Between 1948 and 1972, the world's crude oil production multiplied nearly fivefold, from 8.7 to 42 million barrels per day. During that same period, although U.S. production of crude oil nearly doubled from 5.5 to 9.5 million barrels per day, its share of world output plummeted from 64 to 22 percent. With Detroit factories cranking out gas-guzzlers by the millions, and more American families owning multiple vehicles, the nation's consumption of refined oil escalated rapidly. Until the mid-1950s, the nation had been a net exporter of petroleum. From the mid-1950s forward, the United States became an importer, and the volume of oil imports mounted steadily. In the wake of the Suez Canal crisis of 1956, numerous commentators voiced cold war worries about the Soviet Union's ability to interfere with deliveries of crude oil from the region; but a mere handful of astute observers raised more penetrating questions about long-term implications of the West's increasing inability to supply its own energy.

For the first seven decades of the twentieth century, Americans wallowed in the luxury of cheap fuel. Once gasoline became the primary source of power for automobiles in the 1910s, the price was usually somewhere around fifteen cents per gallon. Following World War I, prices inched slowly upward, averaging as much as twenty cents per gallon. Increases in petroleum prices over succeeding decades never came close to matching inflation. Even though consumer prices rose on an almost steady basis, automobile ownership multiplied manyfold, the demand for gasoline soared, and the flow of cheap fuel at the pumps seemed unending. As late as the spring of 1973, "price wars" at the pumps occasionally brought the price of gasoline below twenty-five cents per gallon. Across the nation, average prices in the early 1970s held steady, somewhere around three gallons for a dollar! No wonder most Americans considered cheap energy as an entitlement.

As it has been for centuries, Middle East politics remains a cauldron of seething misunderstandings, suspicion, conspiracies, and hatred. Almost any analysis of the evolution of relations between nations in that region and western powers risks oversimplification. However, from the incursions of the Romans, through the Crusades, and up to modern times, western nations had committed repeated acts that were almost guaranteed to nurture resentment among the proud people in this volatile region. As Daniel Yergin ably documented in his award-winning book, *The Prize*, over the past century, many have developed deep resentments toward western nations for having extracted seemingly one-sided arrangements for exploiting their natural resources. From their standpoint, westerners reaped far too high a percentage of the profits. Equally important, insensitive representatives of the big western petroleum companies revealed remarkable ignorance about Islamic religion, too often disrespected regional customs, and routinely treated native workers with thinly veiled contempt. In Iran, through its CIA operatives, the United States had played a major role in 1953 in propping up a highly controversial dictator, Shah Reza Pahlavi. Although the Shah was a forward-looking "modernizer" and offered generous concessions to western businessmen, beneath the surface he held his people under a ruthless dictatorship, brutally tortured his political enemies, and alienated many religious fundamentalists. Iranians seethed under his control and waited for an opportunity to overthrow him.

Perhaps most damning in the eyes of many Arabs, western powers were to blame for the creation of Israel. Even before the new nation was founded and recognized by the United Nations in 1948, most Arabs considered refugee Jews as intruders, unwelcome infidels who should be evicted at the first opportunity. In the eyes of Arab nationalists, creation of Israel was tantamount to an act of war, and they blamed the West. Although Israel's military quickly earned renown as magnificent warriors, Arab nationalists were furious at the fact that much of their arsenal was supplied by western powers, particularly the United States. In addition, the West, led conspicuously by the United States, supplied considerable economic aid to Israel. In supporting Israel, the western powers also hoped to maintain a potent bulwark against Soviet incursions into the Middle East. Unable either to annihilate the Jewish state or to extract justice from Israel, Arab leaders lashed out against western nations, who they realized were growing increasingly dependent upon their oil. Although western industrial nations were their best customers, and cutting off oil supplies hurt their own nations' economies, Arabs' desire for retaliation was becoming more intense.

Although Arab nations had considered using the oil weapon against the West during the Suez crisis of 1956, the European nations involved in the fighting were not yet sufficiently dependent on oil from the Middle East to make sanctions effective. Eleven years later, Egypt attempted to root out Israel but suffered a humiliating reversal in the so-called "Six Days War." This time, realizing the greater reliance upon their reserves by the western democracies, the major oil-exporting countries decided to test the power of their weapon. On June 6, 1967, a day after the fighting began, five of the leading oil exporters cut off shipments to countries friendly to Israel, including the United States, Great Britain, and, to a lesser extent, West Germany. However, after some initial panic and bungling, the governments of the affected countries managed to redistribute domestic reserves, or else they cobbled together deliveries of precious petroleum from non-Arab sources. Within a month of the announced Arab oil embargo, it was clear that its leaders had failed to create serious long-term supply problems for western consumers. They had cut off their primary source of income, creating few negative economic effects, except for themselves. Within two months of the Six Days War, there was an actual glut, as Arab producers flooded western markets with oil in an effort to make up for lost revenues. Although a few farsighted individuals attempted to sound warnings in the late 1960s, conventional wisdom held that cheap energy would dominate the western business environment for the foreseeable future. Although repeatedly warned of impending oil shortages, auto executives refused to listen; Detroit would confront the initial crisis in the 1970s completely unprepared.

Over the next few years, the West's good fortune regarding careless, even willfully wasteful, energy consumption finally ran out. This was particularly noticeable in the United States. Prior to 1970, producers had always been able to increase supplies whenever demand spiked upward. Domestic production of crude oil in the United States reached its all-time peak in 1970, at 11.3 million barrels per day. From that point onward, oil production in the United States consistently declined, falling increasingly short of demand. As the chairman of the Texas Railroad Commission explained in the early 1970s, "We feel this to be an historic occasion. Damned historic, and a sad one. Texas oil fields have been like a reliable old warrior that could rise to the task when needed. That old warrior can't rise anymore." Even worse, the gap between domestic supply and demand escalated sharply: between the Six Days War and 1973, net imports of oil nearly tripled from 2.2 million to 6 million barrels per day. From 1970 on, the United States had little choice but to turn to world markets to satisfy demand. Imports as a percentage of total oil consumption almost doubled during those same years, from 19 to 36 percent. In 1970, the nation paid $4 billion for imported oil. Ten years later, imports cost $90 billion!

Until the early 1970s, there certainly seemed to be little for the average consumer to worry about. Between the end of World War II and the early 1970s, through an increasingly rickety combination of subsidies, tariffs, and special tax abatements, the oil companies managed to keep the supply of gasoline high and prices low. Although gasoline prices crept upward in the mid- to late 1960s, the significance of such price moves was lost amidst a larger inflationary pattern. Moreover, worldwide supplies seemed almost infinite, and few energy experts issued any warnings of what was to come.

The age of cheap energy ended abruptly in the fall of 1973. In October, on the eve of Yom Kippur, Egypt and Syria once again invaded Israel. In the weeks leading up to the invasion, the Saudis had been pushing the Organization of Petroleum Exporting Countries (OPEC) to consider doubling the price per barrel of petroleum. Moreover, they had warned the United States against providing further military aid to Israel. After the fighting began, President Nixon defied the Arab nations and authorized a $2.2 billion weapons airlift. Just days later, OPEC announced a boycott of oil shipments to the United States and other countries aiding the Israelis.

The effects began to be felt almost immediately. Refiners, wholesalers, and retailers began rationing gasoline supplies. Long lines of drivers formed at filling stations, and consumer purchases were often limited to amounts as small as five gallons. Not surprisingly, unaccustomed as they were to any restrictions on their driving, many motorists became frustrated, irritable, and even panicky. Some became violent. There were reported shootings of impatient motorists who tried to cut into lines. Equally worrisome, the price of crude oil increased 130 percent between October and December, and prices at the pump shot upward even faster.

The OPEC embargo was not the sole cause of the nation's collective malaise during the 1970s, but it coincided with numerous political and economic problems. The chaotic events surrounding termination of the United States' engagement in the Vietnam War diminished Americans' morale, as did the sordidness of the Watergate affair and President Nixon's forced resignation. Although inflation had become an issue during the Vietnam War, and President Nixon had initiated temporary wage and price controls in the summer of 1971, annual double-digit inflation rates beginning in 1973 sapped the strength of the nation's economy for the next several years. As petroleum and foreign car imports mushroomed, so did the balance of payments. Interest rates rose, making everything from home mortgages to new venture capital far more expensive. White-collar workers saw retirement pensions, carefully accumulated over decades, quickly diminish in real value. Blue-collar workers saw hard-earned wage increases swallowed up by inflation; those unprotected by strong unions experienced actual declines in their standards of living. With aging factories and equipment and hemorrhaging energy prices, many older, inefficient "smokestack" industries found themselves unable to compete with newer, leaner foreign manufacturing establishments, and they laid off workers by the thousands. Blue-collar cities such as Pittsburgh, Detroit, Akron, and Youngstown faced unemployment levels unseen since the Great Depression. It seemed that everybody searched for scapegoats. Consumers complained that gasoline stations were hoarding gasoline. Some economists claimed that the so-called "energy crisis" was an elaborate hoax and that the oil companies were profiteering ruthlessly. Opportunistic politicians from states with small percentages of Jewish voters blamed diplomats who favored Israel. Oil companies blamed automobile manufacturers for producing gas-guzzlers. The car manufacturers defended themselves by claiming that consumers would not buy energy-efficient vehicles. Collectively, Americans instinctively shrank from the horror of facing the enormous significance of the end of cheap energy, as if wishing alone could make the nightmare go away.

Several weeks after the Yom Kippur War ended with Israel still intact, the Arab oil embargo was abruptly called off. Although gasoline supplies increased and prices eased, Americans had been shaken by the events of late 1973. There was a second major energy scare in 1978–1979, caused in part by the total collapse of this nation's relations with Iran following the death of the Shah and the dramatic rise to power of Islamic fundamentalist Ayatollah Khomeni. A psychological exclamation point to the energy crisis and this nation's inability to respond effectively was when Iranian terrorists kidnapped fifty-three people in the American embassy in late 1979 and held them captive for 444 days, until the very day President Carter left office. Nightly television images showed mobs of angry Iranian fundamentalists parading blindfolded captives through the streets of Teheran, burning American flags, or hanging effigies of Uncle Sam. A botched rescue attempt by the U.S. military resulted in a highly publicized, humiliating failure. In the words of one American historian, "Coming at the end of a decade that had witnessed America's defeat in Vietnam, the constitutional crisis of Watergate, and the OPEC oil embargo, the hostage crisis reinforced and deepened America's sense of having lost control. Humiliated, embarrassed, and seemingly powerless to do anything about it, the United States seemed, in the eyes of many of its citizens, to have become second-rate and indecisive, a helpless pawn of external forces that treated the former 'leader' of the free world with scornful contempt."

Although Iranian oil supplies were cut off temporarily, this shortage was more perceived than real. Since other OPEC countries actually boosted exports, total shipments from the Middle East declined only 4 percent. To a certain extent, the "crisis" was a by-product of greed, hoarding, and panic, as some major petroleum companies limited deliveries to retailers and opportunistically increased stockpiles, in anticipation of even higher prices later on. In the summer of 1978, consumers once again found themselves waiting in long lines at gasoline stations. Perhaps more than anything else, Americans felt enormously uneasy, even frightened, at the stark realization that they had little, if any, control over the energy situation. It seemed at the time that they were going to have to significantly tighten their belts and rein in their profligate use of energy, particularly fossil fuels. Any solutions were likely to be expensive and complicated, and their payoffs might not be evident for years.

Some Americans finally concluded that they had been passive victims of the Big Three automakers and Big Oil long enough. Although few abandoned their automobiles in favor of mass transit, bicycling, or walking to work, they temporarily questioned the future viability of reliance on big cars. In automobile showrooms, consumers finally began seriously considering economy vehicles. Although Detroit offered a few models that met consumer demands for fuel economy, many of these hastily designed and produced vehicles had major drawbacks, most noticeably poor workmanship and inadequate safety features. Buyers observed that they could get more quality and better workmanship by purchasing foreign makes, particularly Japanese cars. In 1970, three of every five automobile purchases were mid- or full-size vehicles. Ten years later, the figures were reversed, and 27 percent of the compacts had been manufactured abroad.

Presidents Nixon, Ford, and Carter all introduced policies intended to lessen the nation's dependence on foreign oil. They attacked the problem on several levels. Beginning in December 1975, more than two years after the Arab oil embargo, automakers in Detroit were required to increase average fuel efficiency significantly across their fleets every year. Most foreign makes were far more fuel efficient than American brands. Although automakers in Detroit initially squealed that they could not possibly comply with stiff requirements, they eventually performed creditably, doubling average fuel efficiency for the nation's domestic fleet from thirteen to twenty-eight miles per gallon between 1974 and 1988. In further efforts to conserve fuel, the federal government ordered states to lower highway speed limits to fifty-five miles per hour. States refusing to comply risked losing road-building subsidies from the Highway Trust Fund. The initiative generated vocal, visceral opposition, particularly in the wide open western states. Many drivers openly flaunted the highly unpopular mandate, and highway patrols in many states failed to enforce it vigorously. Far more popular, except among environmentalists, were a cornucopia of government incentives and tax breaks for the petroleum industry, encouraging exploration for new offshore oil fields, development of new finds, and relaxation of environmental regulations previously complicating the process of bringing petroleum resources to the marketplace. In the 1970s and 1980s, television viewers grew accustomed to regular reportage of environmental disasters, including huge oil spills and the decimation of vast amounts of wildlife in the nation's waterways. In an effort to persuade Americans to leave their cars in their garages at least occasionally, thereby conserving fuel, the federal government finally permitted diversion of larger amounts of Highway Trust Funds from highway building to improving mass transit. Industry leaders and politicians at several levels promoted carpooling. Freeway lanes were reserved for High Occupancy Vehicles (HOVs), and some employers offered free parking for carpoolers or subsidized monthly mass transit passes. Various federal agencies offered generous grants to scientists studying technologies devoted to alternative sources of power for automobile engines. In serious efforts to challenge the suffocating grip of hydrocarbons, high-powered and well-funded teams of engineers from universities and the private sector stepped up experiments with electric and solar-powered vehicles.

These efforts were generally praiseworthy, but none of them helped alleviate a gnawing fear among many citizens by the end of the 1970s that the so-called "American Century" was over. In foreign affairs, the country appeared to be in confused retreat, almost always reacting sluggishly to aggressive initiatives of others and constantly on the defensive. The nation was seemingly spending itself into bankruptcy; there had not been a balanced budget in years, and federal deficits were hemorrhaging out of control. Similarly, annual inflation was reaching frightening double-digit levels, and home mortgage interest rates were skyrocketing into the teens. Unemployment was also reaching sickening levels, as entire blue-collar industries were either approaching bankruptcy or cutting back production and payrolls to a fraction of earlier levels. The nation's balance of trade was growing increasingly worrisome by the month. Foreign companies flooded American markets with relatively inexpensive, high-quality goods, many of which drove competing American products off the shelves. Unfortunately, many foreign consumers either ignored or reacted negatively to overpriced, low-quality American goods. In some foreign countries where American manufacturers still attracted buyers, unfriendly governments effected policies that discriminated against American businessmen. More than any other competitor, Japan appeared to be prospering at America's expense, as its lean, efficient corporations flooded our markets with a cornucopia of cheap, well-made products, particularly automobiles and electronics. Japanese corporations reaped huge profits in exports, and many of them invested heavily in what were formerly American-owned treasures. In some locations, it seemed that the Japanese were almost literally buying America, including banks, entire businesses, and massive amounts of commercial real estate. Many doomsayers predicted that the future belonged to the hungry, aggressive nations on the Pacific Rim.

As the 1970s painfully wound down, pessimists lamented that, because it was yielding its leadership position in traditional manufacturing industries, the United States was losing its economic vitality, perhaps irretrievably. They feared that few workers were making anything tangible anymore and that the nation was being transformed into a service economy. Indeed, many of the new multimillionaires of the late 1970s produced nothing of tangible value; rather, they were experts in manipulating paper and effecting aggressive "corporate buyouts." Such elusive terms as "arbitrage," "mergers and acquisitions," and "leveraged buyouts" became the new "buzz words" in the nation's most prestigious business schools.

President Carter had the courage, if not the political acumen, to express the opinion in a national television address that Americans were experiencing a collective loss of confidence and that the country was suffering a "national malaise." Despite burning the midnight oil and discussing complicated, unattractive alternatives at seemingly endless length, government officials seemed incapable of offering effective solutions. Some Communist leaders dismissed the United States as a paper tiger: old, decrepit, losing its teeth. Its roar no longer terrified its adversaries. National policy seemed to be drifting, unfocused. Nothing seemed to be working.

In the minds of numerous social critics, the automobile, with its incessant, voracious demands for fuel, and the empty, mindless materialism associated with the entire automobile culture symbolized everything that was amiss in the United States as the 1970s petered out. Almost nobody anticipated a stunning turnaround in the nation's economy, which would begin in the 1980s. Although much of it would be driven by the so-called "information revolution," the revival of the domestic automobile industry was another key contributor; and both were just around the corner.

Chapter Eight

A REMARKABLE REVIVAL

At the end of the 1970s, the United States and its entire economy—including a severely weakened automobile industry—appeared to be in deep trouble. Beneath the drumbeat of depressing headline stories about the nation's economic malaise, however, there were signs of revival. In retrospect, some of them were quite well hidden. Although computers were useful for storing data and certain highly technical business applications, almost nobody sensed their explosive economic potential in the late 1970s. Who could have predicted how over the next twenty years the so-called Information Revolution would transform worldwide communications, generate unprecedented economic growth, and once again help transform the American economy into the world's most powerful? Many other areas contributed to the turnaround, including the automobile industry. The integration of the automobile with nearly every avenue of American consumption continued to broaden and deepen. This chapter develops these topics.

THE SOCIOLOGY OF THE CAR CULTURE CHANGES

In the 1970s, it appeared that virtually every facet of the automobile culture in the United States was being examined and, in some cases, rejected. For example, significant numbers of suburbanites, joined by some families living in outlying areas of big cities, moved back into inner cities, where they purchased inexpensive older homes in "declining" neighborhoods, then spent tens of thousands of dollars re-habilitating them. Commentators at the time labeled the phenom-enon *gentrification* and interpreted it as a fundamental rejection of suburbia, including the car culture. Numerous articles in "urban chic" magazines profiled "cutting-edge" young, affluent, rapidly upwardly mobile professional couples (nicknamed *Yuppies*), usually childless, abandoning their vehicles and either walking or bicycling to work. In fact, the gentrification phenomenon actually received far more press than numbers of participants warranted. Other commentaries noted that many suburbs were beginning to experience the same types of problems as inner cities: increasing traffic congestion, crime, drug use, and other assorted urban ills. These types of stories failed to alter significantly the flow of Americans to the suburbs. For every Yuppie family moving to the city from outlying suburbs, ten urban families enthusiastically moved out to the suburbs.

Other sociological phenomena evolving in the late 1970s and early 1980s affected the automobile culture. Birth rates continued to decline; divorce rates rose; and the size of the average household declined. Some households contained two adults, who might or might not be married; increasingly, both owned cars. Intact nuclear families, including two or three teenagers, might own anywhere from three to five automobiles. Although most teens had to make do with hand-me-down, well-used cars, Americans were buying more new cars than ever before. Between 1965 and 1985, automobile registrations in the United States almost dou-bled. As land development in most metropolitan regions continued to mushroom, homes, job sites, schools, and shopping and recreational outlets for most Americans were spread farther and farther apart. This meant that Americans typically spent increasing amounts of time away from homes and families, much of it behind the wheel.

These developments had profound effects on Americans' daily lives. Traditional sit-down family meals were no longer the norm. By the late 1990s, many citizens ate half of their meals outside of their homes. Fast food, which had basically evolved from being a curiosity or a unique and memorable experience for many Americans in the late 1940s, had become a way of life for millions of Americans a half century later. The 1980s and 1990s marked an explosive growth spurt for dozens of fast-food franchises, such as Burger King, Wendy's, Taco Bell, Pizza Hut, and Winchell's Donuts. For decades, the coffee break represented a few moments of leisure, perhaps even some quiet re-pose during a hectic workday. By the 1980s and 1990s, it almost seemed as if a large cappuccino served in a styrofoam cup and covered with a plastic lid was the new national beverage. Millions of Americans perfected the technique of sipping them, spill-free, while maneuvering their oversized vehicles through mounting traffic snarls.

CHRYSLER: EMERGING FROM THE SLUMP

As the 1970s merged into the 1980s, it was obvious that the car culture was very much alive, although the domestic automobile industry itself appeared to be gasping for its last breaths. The Big Three in Detroit essentially bottomed out in the late 1970s and early 1980s, then experienced a rebirth in the mid- to late 1980s. Their international position began improving, partly by default. "Good times" finally caught up with the Japanese automakers; in the late 1980s, they succumbed to something resembling the hubris that had afflicted their American counterparts a quarter of a century earlier. After a small taste of recovery in the early 1980s, automakers in Detroit experienced some missteps in the late 1980s, then rebounded energetically in the early 1990s.

In the late 1970s, it would be hard to imagine a more moribund operation than Chrysler Motors. By far the weakest of the Big Three, Chrysler had not originated any major changes in product design for years. Its vehicles were, for the most part, unimaginative, underpowered, and overpriced. With a few notable exceptions, management appeared listless. As red ink flowed in the mid-1970s, President Lynn Townsend had desperately trimmed corporate fat: mostly unnecessary layers of middle management. Unfortunately, top-level management cut too much; the layoffs included some talented engineers and research and development experts. Chrysler had also cut much of what little corporate muscle remained. Late in 1978, Chrysler had 100,000 unsold units gathering dust in open-air lots near its assembly plants. For years, Chrysler dealers, most of whom were losing money or operating on very thin profit margins, had played cat-and-mouse games with the home plant, delaying orders until as late in the model year as possible, and thereby angling for the deepest possible factory discounts. Board Chairman John Riccardo realized that the corporation teetered on the verge of bankruptcy and went to the White House to beg the Carter administration for a two-year exemption from meeting federal fuel efficiency requirements. He argued that retooling costs necessary for compliance would drive Chrysler into receivership.

Facing their deepest crisis in corporate history, leaders at Chrysler realized they needed a savior; the directors searched outside corporate ranks and hired Lee Iacocca, who had recently been fired by Ford. Iacocca had enjoyed a brilliant career at Ford before assuming the reins at Chrysler. Son of Italian immigrant parents in Allentown, Pennsylvania, he had worked hard for an engineering degree at Lehigh before picking up a master's degree at Princeton. Joining Ford in 1946 as a management trainee, young Iacocca promptly abandoned engineering and moved into sales, where he sensed the action was. His instincts were sound, and he quickly vaulted up the corporate ladder. By age thirty-six,

Ford Motor Company.

In the 1970s, one of the few "stars" in the moribund domestic automobile industry was Lee Iacocca, who parlayed his brainchild, the wildly successful Ford Mustang, to a brief term as company President, plus a reputation as perhaps the nation's most admired businessman.

he was vice president of the Ford Division, the company's largest marketing arm. Four years later, Iacocca masterminded development of the company's most smashing success of the mid-1960s, the Mustang. Evidence of the fact that he had entered the big time was that this achievement placed him on the covers of both *Time* and *Newsweek*.

Henry Ford II named Iacocca president of Ford in 1970, when he was just forty-six. Since "Hank the Deuce" was beginning to think about stepping down and there were no Ford family members fully qualified to assume chairmanship of the company, it appeared for a time that Iacocca would be the first non–family member to fill that cherished role. However, it was not to be. Insiders at Ford had sensed tensions between the two men for years. Although Ford respected Iacocca's talent and achievements, he never warmed up to him personally. Iacocca believed that the aristocratic, WASP Ford, educated at prep schools, then Yale, could never fully accept the son of Italian immigrants. He and Ford seldom, if ever, sat around a cocktail table at the exclusive Detroit Club, sipping bourbon and enjoying easy bonhomie, the type of environment where powerful men develop not only friendship but the intimacy conducive to harmonious working relationships. In Iacocca's mind, although promoted regularly and well compensated, he was always the outsider, the hired hand, no matter what he achieved. This was confirmed when Ford finally called him into his office on June 13, 1978, and summarily fired him! According to several sources, Ford told Iacocca to his face, "Sometimes you just don't like somebody."

Other managers at Ford were shocked and bewildered at Ford's action, but the company's loss was Chrysler's gain. For several weeks before he was offered the top job, Iacocca and Chrysler conducted an elaborate courtship. Later, Iacocca mused that, had he fully understood how bad things were at Chrysler, he probably would not have taken over the reins. It was just one month after Iacocca came on board that Riccardo made his trip to Washington to plea for federal help. According to one inside source, "President Jimmy Carter—who privately regarded automobile executives as greedy in good times and whiny in bad ones—was not sympathetic." Riccardo's lobbying for assistance also raised the suspicions of congressional critics, and they demanded that Chrysler open their books and provide thorough financial information before any type of relief could be considered. It was during this process that Chrysler executives finally realized just how chaotic and incredibly incompetent internal administration was. According to one senior executive, "We have quite detailed accounting that shows that we have lost one billion dollars in this past year." He then delivered the punch line: "The only trouble is that the systems are so bad we don't have the foggiest notion of why or where we lost the one billion."

The upshot was the so-called "Chrysler bailout," one of the most controversial incidents of congressional assistance to a threatened corporation in American history. Despite passionate criticism from foes and praise from supporters, the terms of the bailout were immensely complicated, defying simple explanation. The bottom line for the corporation was that the federal government provided $1.5 billion in guaranteed loans over the next two years that had to be repaid by 1990. Government negotiators demanded that risks be spread around. Current lenders were required to participate to the tune of an additional $400 million in new credit; and foreign lenders had to chip in $150 million. The loans were guaranteed by Chrysler's assets, estimated at a worth of $2.5 billion. Had Chrysler failed, the government could have seized the corporation's assets and sold them off, thus protecting taxpayers. In a nutshell, President Carter and the majority of congressmen concluded that they simply could not permit the nation's seventeenth largest corporation to fail.

To a certain extent, government regulation had contributed to the company's financial problems. Assisting politicians in reaching that conclusion was the full might of Chrysler's lobbyists in Washington, the powerful United Auto Workers (UAW), and the fact that Chrysler was the largest employer of African American workers in the United States. Few reflected upon the fact that Chrysler was no more regulated than other domestic producers or foreign competitors. However, if Chrysler had failed, there would also have been a strong, negative ripple effect on the nation's economy. Shutting down Chrysler would seriously hurt dozens of suppliers, and it would threaten layoffs for tens of thousands of workers. Permitting the company to fail was simply not a realistic option. At the same time, frustrated and angry critics in Congress demanded a ritualistic sacrifice, and corporate board chairman Riccardo, who had raised hackles by criticizing government regulation of the industry, fit the bill. He was removed, and Iacocca replaced him in September 1979.

The bailout permitted Chrysler to survive at about half of its former size. In the short term, there was painful bloodletting, as the company canceled money-losing projects and ruthlessly trimmed personnel. A number of observers claimed that Iacocca may have been the only executive in the nation who could have pulled off a seemingly magical turnaround at Chrysler. He was a natural and charismatic salesman with an uncanny ability to attract a dedicated team of highly capable associates; he quickly "raided" Ford and brought over some of its key leaders. He formed an effective working relationship with Doug Frazer, head of the UAW. If Chrysler failed, thousands of jobs would vanish into thin air; thus, the union chief was willing to yield major concessions at the bargaining table. By one calculation, the UAW gave up a whopping $622 million in pay and benefits to help Chrysler! Without Fraser's and the workers' cooperation, it is questionable whether the corporation could have survived.

Perhaps most important, Iacocca instinctively sensed how to present himself and his company's new products to the public. Americans loved his no-nonsense straight talk. At one point, Chrysler was indicted in St. Louis for disconnecting odometers in new cars, assigning them to company executives for personal use for weeks, even months, then bringing them back to the shop, cleaning them up, and selling them as brand new cars. As one current joke went, when a man asked his neighbor if he'd bought a new car, the neighbor replied, "I don't know. It's a Chrysler." When the odometer story broke, it could have been a public relations nightmare. Corporate lawyers urged their leader to be very careful about what he stated in public, fearing it could be used in court against them. But Iacocca ignored them. Rather than engaging in corporate double-talk and sidestepping the issue, he confronted it head on. Facing television cameras, Iacocca asked rhetorically, "Did we screw up? You bet we did. I'm damned sorry it happened, and you can bet it won't happen again. That's a promise." He admitted that his company's conduct "went beyond dumb and reached all the way out to stupid." Buyers who had been bilked would be generously compensated. Corporate lawyers were initially aghast, but Americans loved it; Iacocca's blunt admission did much to defuse public anger.

When Iacocca took over, Chrysler had little going for it except designs for a new model, the so-called K car. This new entry would cost $700 million to develop but would be a significant advance in technology in offering front-wheel drive rather than a rear-wheel power train. To their credit, Iacocca's predecessors had made the courageous commitment to K cars, even in the face of financial disaster. Some observers believed that Chrysler rushed the early models into production before the bugs were worked out, and there was merit to the claim. Others judged that the K car was underpowered, boxy, and overpriced. A basic, stripped-down K car was supposed to retail for $5,880. However, because the finance men were pushing for maximum profit per unit, the early K cars were loaded with so many options that the average vehicle listed for almost $2,000 more. Another problem was that, with inflation soaring and interest rates at all-time highs, sometimes more than 15 percent, many owners preferred to keep their old cars running rather than financing new ones. A major attraction of the K car was that, to a nation of consumers frightened at potential energy shortages, its fuel efficiency was very attractive. In many respects, the K car was far superior to anything the company had offered for years. For two decades, Chrysler had suffered from a reputation for poor quality. In one of his bravest moves, Iacocca pushed for a new 5-year, 50,000-mile warranty, which the company had tried, then discarded a decade earlier. Many of his top-level managers were opposed, fearing that recalls and repairs would further hemorrhage vital resources. But the doughty chairman insisted, and he got his way.

Iacocca's most fundamental challenge was to get the new models into production and generate anticipated revenues before creditors closed in. At times, prospects looked particularly bleak; it seemed that any good news was accompanied by setbacks. The company was trying to get into production even as it slashed personnel. On the same day plants turned out their first K cars, almost half of the company's 6,500 engineers were laid off. According to one pair of industry analysts, "for long periods in 1980 the company actually was bankrupt and existed only at the mercy of its thousands of suppliers, which it was gently and politely stiffing."

Progress at Chrysler was painfully slow, but persistence and belt-tightening eventually paid off. Between 1979 and 1983, previously unheard of efficiencies permitted the company to cut its break-even point from 2.4 million cars and trucks down to 1.1 million. Still, it took time for results to appear. In fiscal 1980, after having lost $1.1 billion the year before, Chrysler lost a staggering $1.7 billion. The next fiscal year, marking

Iacocca's first full year at the helm, brought further corporate losses of $479 million; but better days were ahead. Forced to live up to its guarantees, K-car quality began to improve. Buyers liked the fact that they got twenty-five miles to the gallon. External events also helped Chrysler. Under intense pressure from the Carter administration, the Japanese reluctantly agreed to limit automobile exports to the United States. Because they aimed most of their exports at the lower end of the American automobile market, they did not compete as vigorously against the K car, which was basically an economy vehicle. In the first fiscal quarter of 1982, thanks to the sale of its tank division, Chrysler actually showed a profit of $109 million. Legitimate profits were achieved in the second quarter, and the 1982 fiscal year returned net income of $170 million. On August 15, 1983, Iacocca, in a lavishly staged and shamelessly publicized television extravaganza, proudly repaid the balance of the federal loan guarantee, plus interest. Chrysler had indeed been reborn.

FORD: CHALLENGING FOR THE LEAD AGAIN

Although never threatened with bankruptcy like Chrysler, Ford also experienced hard times in the early 1980s, followed by a turnaround. As the decade opened, its products were undistinguished, and, in the face of brilliant, fast-moving foreign competitors, its management team appeared uninspired, almost catatonic. In response to the energy crisis, the company had redesigned the Mustang to make it more energy efficient. Unfortunately, the so-called Mustang II was essentially an underpowered compact, eliciting little enthusiasm. Reconfigured again in 1979 and outfitted with an optional five-liter V-8 engine, the car had regained some sportiness, but it was a quality-control nightmare. One evaluation claimed that it was "sadly inferior to faster, better-designed Japanese rivals such as the Toyota Celica and Mitsubishi Eclipse." Another study of the industry concluded, "Viewed strictly as a business proposition—and not as an exercise in nostalgia—the Mustang was a loser." After earning $1.17 billion in net income in 1979, Ford entered a three-year minefield of corporate losses. In 1980, Ford lost $1.1 billion, followed by a $1.7 billion deficit in 1981 and $476 million in 1982.

Like Chrysler, Ford's personnel system had far too much built-in inefficiency: too many unproductive blue-collar workers, too many projects designed by committee, and superfluous layers of middle management. But help was on the way. Under dynamic new president Donald Petersen, Ford began ruthlessly trimming fat. Between 1980 and 1984, the company closed 7 plants, fired 20,000 salaried employees, and laid off 44,000 hourly workers. The layoffs created unimaginable stress for tens of thousands of families, whose main breadwinners had to build new careers, often in cities far from Detroit. To the delight of financial analysts, management saw the bottom line only on the balance sheet. These and other economies allowed the company to reduce its break-even point by 40 percent to 2.5 million vehicles.

However, the big news at Ford was that, for the first time since introducing the original Mustang in 1964, Ford grabbed the lead among the Big Three in introducing exciting, even revolutionary, new product lines. Petersen led a rejuvenated management team that introduced *six* new product lines in twenty months, representing a total corporate commitment of $10 billion. The 1983 Thunderbird/Mercury Cougar and the 1984 Ford Tempo/Mercury Topaz, featuring advanced aerodynamic features, were radical departures from conventional design concepts. However, if a single product brought Ford back into the ranks of serious contenders for leadership in auto production and design, it was the Taurus, introduced in December 1985. Mercury offered essentially the same car, named the Sable. This aesthetically pleasing, aerodynamic, well-built sedan delighted industry critics and consumers alike. In the first ten weeks of production, Ford sold 40,000 units. The factories could not turn out enough of them, as they had by then taken orders for another 168,000 units. Without question, the Taurus was the company's most successful launch since the original Mustang, more than two decades earlier. *Motor Trend* selected it as the Car of the Year in 1986. Ford quality, once a joke, also improved dramatically. Influential industry aficionados took notice. *Consumer Reports* rated Ford products, including the wildly popular Escort/Lynx, as the most improved between 1980 and 1985. These achievements stanched Ford's red ink. Between fiscal 1982 and 1983, Ford recovered from a net loss of $658 million to net income of almost $1.9 billion. Riding the popularity of the Taurus and several other models, Ford's profits continued to mount, reaching a record $5.3 billion in 1988 before once again tailing off. For three straight years in the late 1980s, Ford exceeded General Motors in net profits. The first year of that epochal event was 1986, a triumph Ford management had not experienced since the heyday of the Model T in 1924!

GENERAL MOTORS: A SEARCH FOR IDENTITY

As the largest and most diversified of the Big Three Detroit automakers, General Motors was the least immediately threatened by external events and foreign competition. However, in some ways, GM appeared the most impervious to change. The corporate giant offered cars seemingly filling every consumer niche, and generations of Americans had developed an almost reflexive habit of buying virtually anything GM thrust into showrooms. By the late 1970s, GM had grown sluggish and sloppy. Its corporate bureaucracy was suffocating, and engineers with imaginative design concepts repeatedly saw their ideas stifled by inert management committees that seemed incapable of taking quick, decisive action. Thanks largely to John De Lorean, the Pontiac Division produced exciting designs, which drew raves from industry critics and buyers alike. Unfortunately, quality control was in shambles throughout the corporation, including Pontiac. Even at Cadillac, traditionally the top of GM's line, quality control had spiraled downward. The uninspired and underpowered Cadillacs of the late 1970s shamed their once glorious name.

However, GM was so large and had so many operating divisions and ancillary enterprises that the directors and top-level management got away with uninspired performances for years, even decades. If the corporation lost money in one area, it had recouped those losses elsewhere. In the late 1970s, years of lackluster performance finally exposed indifferent leadership; profits nosed downward, from $3.3 billion in 1977 to $2.9 billion in 1979. In 1980, GM actually lost $763 million: a pittance, particularly compared to Chrysler's and Ford's reverses the same year, but a loss nevertheless. By the late 1970s, the Big Three's stocks, including GM, were decidedly out of favor on Wall Street. It seemed that even the loyal, trusting widows holding very modest investment portfolios were finally dumping the auto company stocks that they had held for decades, through thick and thin.

Of the Big Three companies, GM's responses to mounting troubles for the domestic auto industry appeared the least impressive. For most of the 1980s, GM products inspired little genuine enthusiasm. In 1981, the company introduced a group of downsized vehicles, the J-car line, with considerable fanfare. As corporate chairman Roger B. Smith stated bravely at the time, "We decided you're not going to get a guy out of a Toyota by giving him a Toyota. You've got to give him something better than a Toyota. Our game plan is to get out ahead of the imports and stay ahead of them." Unfortunately, brave words were much easier to produce than competitive new models. During 1980, as Ford introduced its well-received Escort/Lynx line, GM worked frantically to get its own new cars into the pipeline. However, when unveiled the following year, J cars, described by one critic as "overweight, overfrilled, and overpriced," were a distinct disappointment. Smith hoped GM would do better with next year's offerings. However, insiders' initial reactions were not encouraging. The new models were described by one critic as "a peapod collection of sedans and coupes marketed simultaneously as the Chevrolet Celebrity, Pontiac J-6000, Buick Century, and Oldsmobile Ciera."

Another critic concluded that, during the 1980s, GM "stumbled from blunder to blunder" and that it "squandered billions on factories that wouldn't work while producing luxury cars that looked like economy cars, cars with engines that burst into flames, and cars afflicted with what company engineers glumly called 'morning sickness.' " Ross Perot, a rich, feisty Texan who would run for president a decade later, was a former board director, and he remained a large shareholder into the mid-1980s. Blunt, colorful, and ebullient, Perot loved both notoriety and the limelight, and he never shied away from expressing strong opinions. In Perot's view, GM's directors had spinelessly watched the company stagger and decline, without uttering even a murmur of discontent, all the while raking in their obscene salaries and bonuses. Perot called them "pet rocks," and, according to one industry critic, they became the "laughingstock of corporate America." Many knowledgeable industry observers agreed with Perot. Eventually, Perot became such a thorn in Chairman Roger Smith's and other top managers' sides that GM engineered a $700 million buyout of his shares in 1986, just to get rid of him.

Clearly, GM experienced difficulty matching Chrysler and Ford in innovativeness. However, it did initiate one significant success in 1985: the Saturn Corporation. This wholly independent entity set up its own manufacturing and assembly plant, with a totally independent dealership system. Although corporate headquarters remained in Detroit, the Saturn plant itself was in Spring Hill, Tennessee, about thirty miles south of Nashville. GM officials projected that Saturn would hire about 3,000 workers and turn out 250,000 units per year. Standard models were designed smaller and about 600 pounds lighter than the current generation of GM subcompacts. In a remarkable, tradition-defying agreement with the UAW, GM guaranteed lifetime employment for 80 percent of the new corporation's hires. All new employees would be paid an annual salary rather than hourly wages. Another Saturn innovation was particularly pleasing to buyers. The corporation established a fixed price for new cars, so customers no longer had to bargain to exhaustion, then walk out of the showroom still fearing they had been suckered into a lousy deal. For some consumers, this simple change was one of the most welcome, overdue initiatives any automobile company ever made!

Not all corporate initiatives impressed industry observers. Under Smith, GM also made a massive commitment to modernizing production, largely through innovative technology. Smith and his associates dreamed of automating as much of the design process and production as possible. In the mid-1980s, GM purchased Ross Perot's Electronic Data Systems Corporation, a computer services company, plus Hughes

Aircraft Company, for a combined total of $5.3 billion and some new stock. GM hoped, in Smith's words, to "redefine" the automobile "from a mechanical product with a few electrical subsystems to one with major electromechanical and electronic elements." Senior engineers imagined a car with lasers helping guide vehicles when visibility was poor; sensors under the hood constantly monitoring and making automatic adjustments to improve engine performance; digitized dashboards; and space-age materials that would lower body weight and increase durability. Although Smith's vision was commendable, GM's implementation was spotty, at best. There were some ludicrously inept efforts at putting automated technology into assembly lines. At the Buick plant in Flint, Michigan, a robot was supposed to install windshields but, instead, slammed them into car bodies, sending glass shards flying about. In paint rooms, paint sprayers malfunctioned, coating machinery, employees, and factory floors, as well as auto bodies. Stories of flawed assembly line experiments reaching the public through regional newspapers, magazines, and the national television networks hardly reassured potential buyers about supposedly revived GM quality.

AN AGE OF "WORLD CARS"

Still, GM and its major rivals all made important commitments to research and development. Collectively, their expenditures in this area almost tripled between 1978 and 1990, from $3.4 billion to $9.8 billion. By the late 1980s, American car men casually tossed around terms like *computer-aided design* (CAD), *computer-aided engineering* (CAE), and *computer-aided manufacturing* (CAM). Electronic scanners could trace the forms of clay models and gather precise data stored in computers in three-dimensional form. Computers could, in turn, direct pens over drawing boards to create precise engineering drawings for die making. Computerized data could also assist in evaluating stress levels to which key parts would be subjected, drag coefficients in wind tests, and many other categories of data useful in modern design.

Despite problems and occasionally embarrassing setbacks, by the end of the 1980s, U.S. automakers had caught up to and in some ways surpassed their foreign competitors in computerized modernization. However, they were just beginning to get up to speed in producing world cars, the industry's term for vehicles "designed by engineers and assembled from components made in many countries for worldwide markets." The Ford Escort/Mercury Lynx, whose component parts came from seventeen countries, was the first domestic car to fit that description. It became the best-selling car in the world. GM's J series also technically fit the description of world cars, even though they generated little enthusiasm abroad. Through the 1980s, the Japanese continued their dominant position in producing and marketing world cars. Under intense pressure from Washington, the Japanese had voluntarily placed limits on exports to the United States: initially 1.68 million units in 1981, then increased to 2.4 million four years later. Superficially, this concession sounded reassuring, but the Japanese deftly skirted it by establishing assembly plants in the United States for what were basically Japanese cars. In 1982, Honda began what nativists later labeled the *Japanization* of the country with a small, seemingly innocuous plant in Marysville, Ohio, which turned out 100 Honda Accord sedans a week. By the mid-1980s, Toyota, Mazda, Nissan, and a few smaller companies had built large plants, most of them scattered about the Midwest. Some older people found the image of large numbers of American workers taking orders from their Japanese superiors just forty years after V-J Day distinctly unnerving.

The seemingly unending chain of challenges to the Big Three automakers—including the energy crisis of the early 1970s, the endless onslaught of economical and well-crafted foreign cars, high unemployment, double-digit inflation accompanied by out-of-sight interest rates, and a recession lingering into the early 1980s—had discouraged consumers from buying American-made cars and trucks. In 1981, they purchased only 10.8 million new vehicles, including foreign brands, and that number dwindled to 10.6 million the following year. But the Big Three's hard work finally paid off, beginning in the mid-1980s. The prolonged recession in the United States had created a huge pent-up demand for new cars. President Reagan's tax cuts also helped unleash a buying spree; in 1984, Americans bought 14.5 million new vehicles, followed by an all-time record of 16.3 million two years later. For the first time in recent memory, Detroit once again waxed fat.

NEW REVERSALS IN DETROIT

Unfortunately, Detroit's respite from foreign domination appeared both slight and brief. By the late 1980s and early 1990s, the Japanese, in particular, once again had automakers in Detroit reeling. Although American design and quality were both improving, Japanese designers were doing even better. American consumers recognized superior quality; by the end of the 1980s, with direct exports to the United States and their own brands manufactured here, they controlled fully one third of our car market. That was a deeply worrisome increase from the 20 percent in 1980. Once again, each of the Big Three faced economic hard times; year-end balance sheets were positively brutal. Chrysler, which had enjoyed the most remarkable turnaround in the early 1980s, lost $795 million in 1990, then earned $723 million in 1991 before losing $2.55 billion in 1992. After earning a record $5.3 billion in 1988, Ford's profits tumbled to $860 million in 1990, followed by increasingly sickening losses of $2.25 billion in 1991, then $7.4 billion in 1992. General Motors, which in many respects made the least-successful adjustments to foreign competition and rapidly changing realities in the 1980s, was hit the hardest. After earning $4.2 billion in 1989, GM lost $2 billion in 1990, $4.45 billion in 1991, topped off by a horrific total of $23.5 billion in 1992.

The reasons behind the reversals experienced by Detroit after an aborted revival in the mid-1980s are not difficult to find. Although GM's board members might have resented their merciless roasting at the hands of Ross Perot, he was basically right: the company's brief resuscitation had evolved around largely cosmetic changes. Although Ford had made a huge impact with its Escort in the early 1980s, followed by the Taurus at mid-decade, the company abruptly lost its forward momentum in the late 1980s. A major problem was that Ford still had not learned how to develop exciting new cars without breaking the bank. For example, Mazda designed and introduced the popular Miata convertible sports car at a total cost of about $280 million, "dirt cheap by any standard." Executives at Ford were simultaneously mulling over a massive program to produce a new compact world car under a projected budget of $6 billion! In addition, Ford's upper-level management was also distracted by diversifying into defense systems and banking rather than concentrating on automobiles. Following the stunning turnaround in the early 1980s, hard times had also returned to Chrysler by the late 1980s. Iacocca, after riding a wave of immense popularity in the early 1980s, suffered a series of reverses in both his personal life and his career. By 1988, each and every pronouncement from the board chairman seemed to presage more bad news and call for more belt-tightening by workers. Iacocca was so worried about the company's future that he tried to sell the company to Fiat in 1990.

By the late 1980s and early 1990s, however, Detroit had learned some ingenious devices to shroud troubles from the general public and—even more important—investors. When sales to private customers dropped, auto men poured more and more vehicles into rental fleets. They had done this before, usually in one or two shipments a year, but now they increased the number of shipments to three or four. In 1991 alone, GM "sold" more than 800,000 cars to rental fleets, nearly one quarter of its total car sales. This practice did not truly constitute "cooking the books," on the scale of the Enron fiasco of 2001–2002, but it yielded largely short-term profits. The company ultimately wound up losing about $1,000 on every rental car it sold. By the early 1990s, the touted recovery of the nation's auto business appeared shaky.

This time, however, only a few Cassandras sang swan songs concerning overall prospects for American automakers. Without question, the situation was not nearly so dire as it had appeared in the mid-1970s. Having shifted significantly larger percentages of revenues into the critical area of research and development, the Big Three automakers were at last turning out lighter, more efficient, fundamentally sound cars. Between 1975 and 1985, the average weight of American passenger cars dropped from 3,800 to 2,700 pounds and average miles per gallon increased from 13.5 to 18.2. Pollutants released in emissions were in the process of being reduced dramatically; by 2000, the average vehicle discharged just 2 percent of the pollution of its 1970 counterpart! One enthusiast gushed, "The auto industry . . . changed more between 1983 and 1993 than it had since the days of Billy Durant, Henry Ford, Ransom Olds, and the Dodge brothers." Actually, the transformation had begun much earlier; it was simply that the fruit ripened slowly.

American producers' problems in the late 1980s were at least in part attributable to external causes. The late 1980s saw the Japanese economy at its peak. For five straight years in the late 1980s, the Japanese exported more than 6 million vehicles to world markets, roughly half to the United States and Canada. To the consternation of many, particularly in the American West, Japanese investors poured billions of yen into investments in the United States, buying up millions of acres of land and prime urban real estate.

REVERSALS IN TOKYO

Just when its economy appeared impregnable, the Japanese bubble began springing leaks in the early 1990s. Between 1988 and 1990, new-car sales in Japan showed double-digit percentage increases for three years running. The nation became incredibly prosperous, and its business leaders reaped uninterrupted praise and deferential treatment from influential international opinion makers. Photographs and paintings of leading Japanese industrialists and economic policy makers appeared on covers of prestigious business journals and magazines. Having basked in unstinted praise for years, Japanese automakers committed the mistake of believing the hype. As had their American counterparts decades earlier, some of them succumbed to hubris. They evidently believed that due to the structure, discipline, and work ethic built into their national culture, Japan was "immune from the economic swings that buffeted the rest of the world." They were wrong. In the late 1980s, the American economy entered a recession, which directly affected Japanese exports. By 1992, exports of new Japanese cars to the United States had fallen by one third. Mazda, Nissan, Mitsubishi, and Toyota dealers, who had gleefully jacked up per-unit profits by forcing American buyers to purchase expensive "add-on" packages, now learned an unpleasant new word: *discount*. In addition, Japanese car manufacturers, who earlier had enjoyed the advantages of running new, small, lean, and aggressive companies, finally experienced the downside of huge profits and rapid growth: emerging managerial conservatism and caution, generated by fear of making mistakes, and the emergence of stifling corporate bureaucracies.

However, the Japanese automakers were also hammered by international monetary factors, most importantly the rising value of the yen. In 1990 and 1991, the value of the yen compared to the dollar rose to the point where Japanese cars cost more than their American counterparts. The Big Three initially failed to capitalize on this break, as they matched the Japanese price increases. Nevertheless, American models were beginning to stand up better against Japanese competition. Although Detroit still had a way to go in matching Japanese workmanship and overall quality, by the early 1990s, the Big Three actually offered more safety features in their midsize cars than Japanese manufacturers, including antilock brakes and air bags. The Japanese began losing customers both at home and abroad. In 1991, domestic car sales in Japan dropped 4.6 percent, followed by an even more alarming drop of 8 percent in 1992. Nissan was forced to do the hitherto unthinkable; management actually closed an aging plant and laid off workers. The powerful Honda and Toyota companies cut back to single shifts in various stages, laying off thousands of workers in the process. Unfortunately for the Japanese, in 1993 alone, the yen surged another 20 percent in value, further crippling their automakers' international operations. By then, a loaded Toyota Corolla, once considered the epitome of an economy car, sold for up to $17,000 in the United States. Sales declined sharply, as many American buyers considered that sum too much to spend on a so-called economy car, no matter how well built.

The reversal of economic fortunes for many parts of Asia, particularly Japan, continued into the new millennium. During flush times, Japanese businessmen had invested billions in urban real estate in the United States. Basically, they had expanded too fast, paid highly inflated prices for land, and built far too much office space. Much of the latter remained unoccupied for months on end. They had also invested unwisely in other parts of Asia, particularly Thailand. In both automobiles and electronics, the Japanese were losing the huge edges they had enjoyed in the late 1970s and through the 1980s. Other Asian nations, including their ancient rival Korea, were catching up, even surpassing them in technological know-how and, equally important, worker productivity.

However, if many Americans secretly delighted in the abrupt collapse of the notion of Japanese "invincibility," they were far more heartened by another economic turnaround. By the beginning of 1994, in the eyes of American automakers, a stunning transformation had occurred. They had, for all intents and purposes, turned the tables on the Japanese. Since Honda built its first assembly plant in Marysville, Ohio, in 1982, followed by other firms opening additional production plants elsewhere in the United States, American car producers watched and learned. Ironically, although Detroit auto men loudly decried free trade, it helped them in the long run. Despite hard lessons and painfully bruised egos, the Japanese imparted a marvelous gift: they returned the favor from the immediate postwar years and helped teach American auto men how to build good cars—with American workers! American automobile executives were gradually learning how to nurture creative ideas from designers who were not yet at the top of managerial hierarchies. Although auto men in Detroit muffed some of their opportunities in the late 1980s, by the early 1990s, they were finally scoring some bull's-eyes.

THE SECOND AMERICAN REVIVAL AND ALTERNATIVE DRIVING MACHINES

Chrysler led the second American revival in the early 1990s. The company's stylists now dazzled the public with an unending string of new designs. Consumers drooled over the svelte and sexy lines of several new Chrysler entries, from the midsize Cirrus to the full-size models. In 1993, the company also introduced the Neon, a superb new subcompact. This well-conceived, low-priced offering "shocked the Japanese by offering dual air bags, a sophisticated multivalve engine, and other standard features for a price thousands of dollars below theirs." After suffering a $2.55 billion loss in 1992, Chrysler rebounded with record profits of $3.7 billion the following year. At Ford, a small group of engineers, who nicknamed themselves "skunks," took it upon themselves in the doldrums of 1989 to revive the Mustang yet again. They succeeded brilliantly; and, by 1993, customers were snapping them off showroom floors as fast as Ford plants could turn them out. Improvements in design of both the Taurus and Escort thoroughly rejuvenated these models; and, between 1992 and

1993, the company turned a $7.4 billion loss into a $2.5 billion profit. A year later, Ford earned a record $5.31 billion. Perhaps no American auto company needed a boost more than GM. Although the company did not introduce such spectacular successes as its primary domestic rivals, insiders engineered a palace coup and replaced a generation of tired directors wedded to the ways of the past. By the end of 1992, GM was finally headed in the right direction; after losing $23.5 billion in 1992, the company earned almost $2.5 billion the following year.

There was, however, a crucial facet of Detroit's automotive history in the last quarter of the twentieth century that we have not yet explored. In addition to conventional passenger cars, American automakers offered an amazing array of alternative vehicles to consumers, including a variety of trucks, minivans, Sport Utility Vehicles (SUVs), and numerous off-road vehicles.

At one level, this cornucopia of new vehicular products made perfect sense. From the time American consumers started buying automobiles, they demonstrated marked interest in customizing them to fit their own needs. From unique contraptions outfitted for camping in the 1910s and 1920s, to sedans modified to carry entire desperate families during the Depression, to the trailers of the World War II era, to the "hippie" (usually Volkswagon) vans of the 1960s, "alternative" vehicles appeared on American roads by the millions. The 1960s, in particular, marked the emergence of a dizzying array of one-of-a-kind shelters attached to the backs of cars and trucks. Indeed, a new slang word, *truckitecture,* was introduced into the English language.

In fact, it was trucks, not conventional passenger vehicles, that led the turnaround in the nation's vehicle business. Well into the 1960s, most American manufacturers offered only station wagons and light trucks as alternatives to the sedan, coupe, or convertible. Although they built trucks for commercial uses, as late as 1960, they turned out eight cars for every truck they manufactured. By the 1960s, however, sales of station wagons were diminishing, as many young baby boomers refused to identify with the conventional, "tied down to kids and family" image they conveyed. Except for trucks, few vehicles were suitable for off-road use. Jeeps and International Scouts were the primary off-road offerings. For the most part, these were working vehicles; they could be outfitted with snow plows, winches, rotary mowers, posthole diggers, and various hydraulic lifts.

Before the 1970s, the very name Jeep conjured up images of an incredibly rugged, versatile, basic light utility vehicle used by the U.S. Army during World War II. It had rock-hard seats, stick shift, and absolutely no amenities. However, when Jeep introduced the Super Wagoneer to American consumers in 1965, it was a wholly different vehicle, sharing little in common with its predecessor other than a degree of practicality and four-wheel drive. The new Jeep had a wealth of optional luxury features, including automatic transmission, power/tilt steering, radio, upholstery and trim packages, power brakes and windows, and even cruise control. Jeep dominated the SUV market at least for the first two decades of production, holding almost one third of the market into the 1980s. In 1978, the company introduced the luxurious Wagoneer Limited; its standard features included leather upholstery, air conditioning, and an AM/FM/CB stereo. Options included automatic transmission, power/tilt steering, power brakes and windows, and cruise control. Like most American makes, it was a big, comfortable, flashy vehicle. Anticipating a huge potential expansion of the market for such vehicles, the company introduced a shorter, narrower, and slightly lighter version called the Cherokee in 1984. Its four-door design was a key to its dominance of the SUV segment of the market, since it made the vehicle a viable alternative to the family sedan; and it helped boost Jeep sales an incredible 87 percent between 1983 and 1984.

If one includes trucks, Americans purchased more "alternative" vehicles than conventional passenger cars for the first time during the 1997 model year (although passenger cars still outnumbered other vehicles combined almost two to one in total registrations). Why were alternative vehicles so popular? Some analysts suggest that, with national prosperity, increasing disposable income, and expanding leisure time, more Americans engaged in outdoor activities and therefore "needed" vehicles capable of hauling their increasingly large and expensive recreational toys to remote locations. Others point out that millions of Americans have a do-it-yourself home improvement mentality, and they use such vehicles to haul building materials between stores and home. Although pickup trucks might do for some tasks, the increasingly popular SUV was far more versatile, suitable for in-town business and family outings. In addition, when involved in collisions, SUVs were demonstrably safer for persons inside the vehicles. Assuming that passengers used seat belts and that the unit itself did not tip over, drivers and their passengers were far less vulnerable than those in passenger sedans. Operators sat higher off the road than drivers of sedans, so their visibility was better. That the height and width of their vehicles lowered visibility for other drivers was of little concern for them.

Unfortunately, many SUV owners have been lulled into a false sense of security. Many buyers erroneously believe four-wheel drive provides far better traction when driving on ice and snow. In fact, it is easier to get them moving in icy conditions, but they require far greater distances to stop. Finally, millions of Americans have little or no practical use for SUVs, but even for those who seldom depart from concrete freeways, the vehicles apparently help them nurture self-images as rugged adventure seekers. As one industry analyst observed, "The emerging sport utility vehicle market's diverse customer base reflected these varied motivations, ranging from adventurous youths to status-conscious drivers seeking 'stylish utilitarianism.' "

By the late 1990s, although they were increasingly popular among consumers, SUVs were under withering attack from environmentalists, safety experts, and drivers of smaller vehicles. When Ford offered the nineteen-foot-long Excursion Limited SUV in 1999, many industry critics voiced outrage. One might think that its forty-four-gallon tank would permit an extended range between fill-ups, but this was not the case, because the Excursion got a measly ten miles per gallon in city driving. Standing nearly seven feet tall, the gas-guzzling monster dwarfed other vehicles. Not only did it obscure sight lines for other drivers, but it was basically a rolling fortress, threatening to demolish anything with which it came into contact. Pity the unfortunate drivers of shorter, standard-size vehicles, even smaller SUVs. As critics savaged the Excursion, even William Clay Ford, the youthful president of his family's company, admitted that the behemoth was environmentally unfriendly and he promised to curb some of its excesses in future model years. In what might be interpreted as an act of contrition, Ford Motor Company introduced the Escape in 2001, which it hyped as a subcompact SUV. Cynics might wonder if corporate executives ever considered naming it the Oxymoron.

William Ford's demurrer concerning the Excursion hardly satisfied SUV critics. In a spoof op-ed article, one author lampooned the "Godzilla SUV": "The Godzilla is big—extremely big. Excessive. Extravagant. Deadly? Of course. But not to you. It's been said that SUV owners are selfish, gluttonous, antisocial. That's exactly the customers we are looking for, and we're finding more every day. After all, somebody is going to hog the road and waste gasoline. It might as well be you." Another critic with less of a sense of humor wrote, "Perhaps the most revealing aspect of the SUV fad is the commentary on American society displayed through the car culture. Those who drive SUVs are needlessly killing those who drive economical and sensible automobiles. What [is] more disturbing is the selfishness SUV owners display to justify those deaths." Other observers expressed unrestrained anger. One wrote, "I am seriously contemplating going on a SUV smashing spree with my trusty hammer." These expressions of outrage intensified in the late 1990s; by then, SUVs had been around for twenty years, and there were more than 15 million on American roads.

Another important segment of the emerging alternative vehicle market was the minivan. Even more than the SUV, this light, functional, and inexpensive entry helped push the station wagon into retirement. It also helped save Chrysler Corporation. The company had done extremely well with the Dodge Ram, which controlled nearly half of the full-size van market in the mid-1970s. Chrysler executives attributed their success to providing passenger vehicle amenities in large vans. They guessed, correctly, that a smaller, more economical version of the Ram might appeal to younger segments of the market, who would not buy "stodgy" station wagons. Chrysler began planning the minivan in 1977. Not long afterward, the corporation began its rapid downward spiral that resulted in near bankruptcy and the federal bailout in 1979 and 1980. These events initially forced corporate strategists to concentrate scarce resources on the K car. When Chrysler President Lee Iacocca had been at Ford, he had pushed a concept similar to the minivan; according to some sources, Henry Ford II turned it down, because he didn't want to do too much "experimentation." Thus, Iacocca brought some excellent, if untested, ideas over to Chrysler, where he and several other executives revived the minivan. They believed that an inexpensive vehicle that could fit into a conventional garage, accommodate a whole family, and offer space for cargo would be a winner in the showrooms. Iacocca procured a promise of $500 million to develop the vehicle from the directors, a brave decision and huge commitment for a company facing bankruptcy.

As so often happens in the automobile business, producers seem to experience either good times or bad times, with little in between. By the time the first minivans were finally rolled off the assembly line in November 1983, Chrysler had turned the corner dramatically; the bankruptcy crisis had passed, and the corporation had paid off the government loans in full. Company executives therefore had all the more reason to bask in the glowing reception minivans received. The highly influential *Car and Driver* magazine described them as "a wonderful addition to the automotive firmament," and *Road and Track* called them "the most innovative vehicles to come out of Detroit in decades." Buyers were enthusiastic. Priced at around $10,000, they received good gas mileage, and they performed many tasks. In 1984, Chrysler minivans passed the 100,000 mark in annual sales, and they moved over the 200,000 mark in 1988. By 1995, Chrysler sold nearly 500,000 minivans and controlled about 40 percent of the market. Along with the Neon, the minivan was one of the company's most dazzling success stories.

One of the more interesting realities about the newer "alternative" motor vehicles is that the line between home and road appears to be becoming more blurry by the year. The rear section of others resembled home recreation rooms, with television sets and bars. Although these were customized vehicles, manufacturers realized that Americans were spending increasing amounts of time on the road and that they would have to accommodate the fact that many drivers were consuming numerous meals while driving. William Scott, executive designer of Oldsmobile's entry into the minivan derby, observed, "People take long trips in them. . . . People have longer and longer commutes. So just like a sailboat, a powerboat, a camper trailer, or a mobile home, we have to think of the eating that goes on." And drinking. Typically, minivan designers pay a great deal of attention to the size and location of cup and bottle holders. The Mercury Villager minivan could transport seven passengers, yet had twelve cupholders. Oldsmobile's Scott also focused on the fact that designers had to provide interior fabrics that were easy to clean, and they had to think carefully about how spills might affect expensive subassemblies. As Scott pointed out, "Spilled Cokes can get you into some very expensive warranty work." Occasional sexist commentators noted that the minivan was becoming known as "a young man's" vehicle, simply because some were literally equipped with beds behind the driver's seat. Irreverent van owners often outfitted their rigs with bumper stickers warning, "Don't laugh. Your daughter might be in here" or "If it's A-rockin' don't come A-knockin.'"

Motor vehicle manufacturers marveled at the new opportunities alternative vehicles created. Americans love variety, and alternative vehicles offered consumers many more choices. Even more important were profit margins. Minivans may have appealed in part because of economy, but the same could not be said for SUVs. By the 2002 model year, buyers could spend as much as $60,000 for fully loaded Mercedes or BMW SUVs. Although a handful of luxury sedans reached or even surpassed that price range, a typical well-equipped family sedan might cost $30,000. Simply put, for a long time, manufacturers enjoyed far larger markups on SUVs, so they pushed them hard. During the boom times of the late 1990s, with gasoline prices remaining steady at just over a dollar a gallon, buyers responded enthusiastically. In the fall of 2001, Freightliner introduced a truly grotesque SUV entry, the Unimog. This monstrosity weighs 12,500 pounds, stretches out fully 20 feet, and stands nearly 10 feet tall! At a base price of $84,000, the parent company, Chrysler-Daimler, will undoubtedly enjoy added riches if it catches on. Fortunately, sightings of Unimogs have been exceedingly rare—so far.

In 1999 and 2000, with an economy running full tilt, SUV manufacturers raked in rewards. The units generated huge profits, as much as $15,000 for a $40,000 unit. They were not about to cut back on production. When gasoline prices spiked upward and the economy experienced a downturn in 2001, industry critics felt a small degree of satisfaction driving by dealer lots jammed with unsold SUVs. Newspaper advertisements offered deep discounts, up to $12,000. However, unless gasoline prices reach $3 or more per gallon and remain there, Americans will probably maintain their affair with these cumbersome gas-guzzlers.

As noted, in 1997, for the first time in history, sales of trucks exceeded those of cars, capturing just over 51 percent of the domestic market, with 6.2 million units sold. American manufacturers dominated the domestic minivan and SUV market. In 1997, Detroit sold just 66.3 percent of new passenger cars to American consumers, but 93 percent of all trucks. Ford sold 695,926 F Series trucks, followed by the Ford Explorer at 444,817 and Chevrolet's C/K Pickup. By then, Jeep's Grand Cherokee had fallen to fifth place. Ford's Econoline Van claimed the final spot in the top ten. Trucks were even more vital in maintaining the United States' competitive position in the worldwide marketplace for motor vehicles. In 1997, the nation produced just over one-fifth of the world's output of 39.4 million cars. However, with 7.9 million trucks and buses, the United States turned out just over half of the world's total output of 15.7 million units.

Another highly visible alternative driving machine is the recreational vehicle (RV). Before discussing this phenomenon, some background appears in order. Historically, there have been wide varieties of accommodations on wheels for mobile families, and some clear distinctions should be made. When looking closely at a family on the road, even the casual observer can usually tell whether they are moving out of necessity or by choice. The initial images of American families on the move might focus on the desperately poor "Okies" and residents of other nearby states who fled the Dust Bowl during the 1930s in cruelly overloaded jalopies, often in hopes of finding rumored jobs in California. John Steinbeck memorialized their plight in his 1939 classic novel, *The Grapes of Wrath*. Another persistent theme is Americans' longtime use of trailers, which create negative images in the minds of some. Many observers associate trailer parks with "white trash," pairing them with images of rootlessness, poverty, and family dysfunction. To be sure, some Americans have little choice but to live in trailers, but others prefer this lifestyle. By the 1970s, if not sooner, a new word had entered the American vocabulary: *snowbirds*. This refers to the tens of thousands of families, often retired couples on pensions, who migrate seasonally between permanent homes, usually in the Northeast or Midwest, and semipermanent trailer and RV hookup sites in balmy Florida or the Southwest. When making seasonal moves from one location to the other, they often haul huge trailers behind SUVs or heavy-duty pickup trucks.

The earliest trailers were homemade; but, by World War I, entrepreneurs sensing a large potential market started producing lightweight camping units that could be pulled behind a family sedan. By the 1940s, thousands of distinctive Airstream trailers—attractive, aluminum-sided, bullet-shaped units capable of housing several people in reasonable comfort for extended periods—appeared on American roads. Eventually, manufacturers graduated to homes on wheels that no longer had to be pulled behind trucks. This was the RV. Although the interiors of most were very compact, they often provided many of the comforts of permanent homes: kitchens featuring all the necessary cooking and refrigerating facilities, television sets, music centers, private bedrooms, and showers with hot and cold running water. By the end of the twentieth century, some units were luxurious, and a well-heeled buyer could plunk down $100,000 for a loaded model.

Recreational vehicle sales did not escalate at the same rate as those of trucks, but they have enjoyed a generally upward climb over the past quarter century. There is a wide variety of RVs, including several types of travel trailers, and an equally wide choice of motor homes. The former included conventional, fifth wheel, folding camping trailers, and truck campers. Motor homes included type A conventional, type B campers, type C chopped vans, and multiuse van-conversions. The RV industry was definitely big business, and affluent consumers could either buy units equipped with everything they wanted or pay to have a basic type of RV customized to fit their tastes. In 1975, Americans bought 339,600 RVs of all kinds. By 1994, sales had climbed by more than 50 percent to 518,800. Suggesting its status as essentially a luxury item, sales of RVs tended to follow economic trends closely: brisk during boom times, sluggish during recessions.

A REMARKABLE TRANSFORMATION

By 2002, the car culture in the United States had experienced a remarkable transformation from what it had been at the end of World War II. In 1945, there were just over 45 million motor vehicles worldwide, and Americans owned three fourths of them. By 2000, the figure approached 800 million, of which Americans still owned nearly 30 percent. Significantly, the car journey of 2000 was far more "homogenized" than it had been fifty-five years earlier. Roadside business had become a huge factor in the nation's economy, and roadside franchises in Oregon were virtually identical to those in Florida. Nowhere was homogeneity more evident to travelers than during extended trips on the interstates. The visual landscape from behind the wheel was basically the same in eastern Virginia as in southern Illinois. As one approached exit ramps, huge, unsightly billboards advised drivers just where to locate the nearest Burger King, Taco Bell, or "all-you-can-eat" breakfast bar at Shoney's. Tired travelers could find a Comfort Inn in Rhode Island or Texas.

In all likelihood, if they think about it at all, most Americans would equate with "progress" the availability of standardized, tasty, and sanitary (if usually fat-laden and highly unhealthy!) food and the security of knowing that one can almost always reserve the same antiseptic room at the Holiday Inn 700 miles farther down the road. One seldom encounters detours on the interstates; a few miles of single-lane driving where resurfacing is taking place might delay drivers just a few minutes. Most travelers also welcome the virtual disappearance of chance or unpleasant surprises; a rare mechanical breakdown even in a relatively remote area becomes little more than a temporary inconvenience to travelers equipped with a AAA membership card and a cellular phone. Drivers simply call for help; they don't have to figure out anything for themselves.

A few purists lament the loss of a sense of adventure, spontaneity, even serendipity, experienced by travelers of half a century or more ago. Before the interstates, even the national highways usually plowed straight through cities, but they also passed through charming small towns, where dusty tourists might have discovered a fabulous one-of-a-kind local ice cream stand. They might have passed by a local park and seen a spirited game of baseball; if they weren't in a hurry, they could decide to stretch their legs and perhaps watch a few innings before meandering on down the road. Sure, picking a motel was occasionally an adventure; during tourist season, if they hadn't made reservations, a family might have had to stop a bit earlier than planned, denying Dad a chance to "make more time" as he had planned. After rooms were rented, uninvited "critters" occasionally made unwelcome visits to the bathroom sink or shower. But effective parents could use time in a strange town to stimulate curiosity in their children. Since there were no television videos, parents might have taken the children for a walk along a river bank to discover sights and smells they didn't encounter at home. Since there were no homogenized "happy meals" at McDonald's, they might (with considerable finesse and persuasion) have induced a reluctant child to try a new kind of food. Travel by automobile today might be both faster and safer, but it is also a lot more predictable. And without question, it simply is not nearly as much fun.

Chapter Nine

THE FUTURE OF THE AUTOMOBILE

About the time of the first energy crisis in the early 1970s, a number of anti-automobile social critics stridently proclaimed that the automobile was an aging and outmoded dinosaur and that the industry producing them was on its last legs. John Jerome opined that the industry was "beginning to die" in the 1960s. Some critics fantasized about their disappearance, at least from city streets, by the mid-1990s. Others claimed, with considerable justification, that along with junk food and television, the automobile was a key factor in turning the typical American consumer into a jelly-bellied couch potato.

At the turn of the twenty-first century, it was patently clear that although comments about Americans' declining levels of fitness were sadly on target, predictions about the imminent demise of the automobile industry were spectacularly wrong. When the first of those forecasts were made in the early 1970s, there were about 110 million motor vehicles on America's roads; today, the number has doubled. With the automobile industry setting new all-time annual production and sales records approaching 17 million cars and trucks in 2000, the domestic automobile industry had never appeared stronger. To be sure, it is difficult today to tell a domestic from a foreign car, but consumers have never enjoyed a more dazzling array of choices than they do now. Sedans, convertibles, compacts, subcompacts, vans, minivans, sport utility vehicles (SUVs), and a seemingly endless array of trucks and off-road vehicles tempt consumers. At the beginning of the new century, millions of Americans were indulging their most extreme automotive fantasies. Many buyers thought nothing about spending as much for a car or SUV as they had thirty years earlier for their homes.

Although the statement might be made for most institutions in any given historical moment, it appears that the American automobile industry is at a crossroads. This chapter considers the future relationship between individual consumers, mass transit, and the automobile. In so doing, we need to examine the motor vehicle's recent past. We also examine the latest thinking about future designs for automobiles. Many experts predict that the "driving experience" will be completely transformed in the early twenty-first century, that the human factor will be largely eliminated. Will there be private transportation in twenty or fifty years? If so, what will it be like, and how will it be integrated into public transportation? High-tech optimists predict a virtual utopia in ease and convenience of personal mobility. Are their projections achievable, and, if so, are their thoughts about how such systems might be funded realistic?

THE FUTURE OF MASS TRANSIT

As we have seen, the relationship between advocates of mass transit and defenders of the automobile has been tense, when not downright hostile, for the past century—ever since cars began appearing on the streets of the nation's cities in large numbers. Over the past century, extremists favoring one side have brazenly predicted the total demise of the competing means of mobility. Although their relationship remains uneasy, it now appears evident that both forms will continue to exist into the foreseeable future.

Thirty years ago, public transportation appeared to be in deep trouble. Mass transit was almost never quick and convenient. Many people associated it with aging, smelly, dilapidated buses, which were not only slow but seldom ran on schedule. Future prospects appeared dismal. In contrast to the automobile, petroleum, and road construction industries, which successfully lobbied for huge amounts of federal assistance, public transit had few politically powerful friends at any level. Few mass transit systems could even meet operating expenses, let alone fund capital equipment needs through fare box revenues alone. They required large public subsidies, which were not popular with most voters. Thus, most systems were languishing, just struggling to hang on. At least a handful of experts, not all of them mere shills for the automobile industry, argued that any public service that catered to "just one percent" of Americans and sapped so much money in subsidies was irrelevant. According to some conservative public policy analysts, inefficient, and noncompetitive, mass transit systems should simply be allowed to die.

Defenders of mass transit excoriated such Darwinian views, which they perceived not only as cold-blooded dismissal of the needs of the poor and many disabled Americans but also as incredibly shortsighted public policy lunacy. In a recent article, mass transit expert William C. Vantuono attacked the "one percent" argument, claiming that evidence revealed that when and where viable mass transit was available, significant percentages of urban commuters left their cars at home, including middle, and even upper-income Americans. Although personal preference played a part, many commuters used automobiles because they had no realistic alternative. Equally important, advocates of mass transit pointed to what would happen if mass transit disappeared. Not only would those not owning cars be totally stranded but, Vantuono claimed, "The hard fact is that if transit suddenly ceased operating in any large American city, commuting would become almost impossible."

The energy crisis of the 1970s, real or imagined, precipitated a mild turnaround in public attitudes toward mass transit. Despite increases in gas prices and occasional shortages, most Americans still used their automobiles for most trips. A few began commuting to and from work by mass transit, and almost everyone acknowledged the need to maintain public transportation, even if they personally used it only in emergencies. The key point is that, from the early 1970s forward, a political climate far more friendly to the needs of mass transit gradually evolved. In 1973, for the first time, Congress broke precedent and diverted some of the hitherto inviolable Highway Trust Fund billions for construction of mass transit systems. The newly created (1965) Department of Transportation provided increasing amounts of funding for building modern new "state-of-the-art" transit systems in several cities and refurbishing older ones. Between 1980 and 1984, the federal government invested $15 billion in urban mass transit and another $8.2 billion in railroads, versus $36.5 billion in highways. Mass transit had not yet reached parity with automobiles in the minds of most influential decision makers, but it was once again a serious public policy issue.

Part of the reason for politicians' newfound willingness to fund mass transit may be that the vision of highway solutions to Americans' desires for unlimited mobility had turned sour. The Interstate Highway System is now nearly a half century old; for decades, it has been pounded by monster trucks carrying huge loads. Even twenty years ago, large sections of it were falling apart and were in urgent need of repair. In part because they wanted to provide the most road for the least expenditures, interstate highway engineers originally built the roads to last approximately twenty years. In Europe, by contrast, highways are built to last roughly twice as long. One must also remember that in constructing the Interstates, the lowest bidder got the job; thus, quality was not the most important consideration. Interstate decision makers assumed that, once the highways were built, states would take over maintenance and repair. The end result was that, by the late 1970s, financing repairs for thousands of miles of crumbling roads and unsafe bridges had become an increasingly worrisome financial burden, and few politicians had the courage to address the problem directly. Most continue to dodge these issues today.

Even before the energy crisis, construction of the initial stages of the Washington Metro and San Francisco's Bay Area Rapid Transit (BART) subway systems signaled the beginning of a turnaround in politicians' attitudes toward public transit. The 1980s and 1990s marked beginnings of new mass transit systems, particularly light rail, in approximately two dozen other American cities. In 1991, Congress enacted the $155 billion Intermodal Surface Transportation Efficiency Act. This landmark legislation profoundly affected highway trust funds formerly under the tight control of the highway lobby. Money would be distributed directly to the states, which could, at least in theory, divert up to 50 percent of the funds for mass transit rather than repairing highways or building new ones. This made it much harder for the highway lobby to hog the funds, because it would have to coordinate campaigns in fifty states. As one of the bill's key supporters, U.S. Senator Daniel Patrick Moynihan (D–NY) put it, "We've poured enough concrete." Even Los Angeles, considered by most experts on urbanization to be the ultimate automobile city, began building what promises to be an enormously expensive subway system. In addition to extensions of present systems, many more plans for new light rail systems were on the drawing board at the opening of the new century.

Thus, mass transit, if not thriving, is very much alive in the early twenty-first century. In fact, available evidence reveals that after bottoming out in the early 1970s, there has been a slow, steady rise in numbers of Americans using mass transit. Because of the number of riders who either transfer or use multiple forms of mass transit moving from one place to another, it is impossible to count accurately the number of persons relying solely on mass transit. However, the American Public Transportation Association (APTA) estimated in 2000 that approximately 13 million Americans used mass transit each workday, with the number halving on Saturdays, then halving again on Sundays. The Department of Transportation reported that Americans took 7.98 billion trips on urban transit in 1997, up slightly from 7.84 billion trips in 1987. Considering daily trips in cities, most of which were commutes to and from work, in 1995, 90 percent were by motor vehicle, 3.6 percent were on some form of transit, while 6.5 percent were either by foot or bicycle. Adding in use of mass transit in smaller cities and towns, APTA President William W. Millar estimated that in 1999 Americans took more than 9 billion trips on public transportation, "the highest ridership in nearly four decades" and a 4.5 percent increase over 1998. Millar pointed out that motor vehicle travel grew by only 2 percent over the same period, which suggested that, given free and available choices, public transportation competed very effectively with the automobile.

THE NIGHTMARE COMMUTE

Public transit spokesmen are also banking heavily on the undeniable fact that urban commuting by automobile is becoming increasingly stressful, time-consuming, and unpleasant every year. The horror stories of life behind the wheel are all too familiar. There is no fast lane any more, at least not on the nation's urban freeways. The very notion of rush hour is absurdly outdated; urban freeways become jammed at almost any hour between 7 A.M. and 7 P.M. and sometimes deep into the evening hours. Bad weather alone can turn freeways into parking lots, in some cases even raging rivers. The most minor accident stalls traffic for miles, partly because gawkers slow down in passing, presumably hoping for glimpses of human gore.

Willfully dangerous driving by far too many Americans is clearly exacerbating urban commuting by automobile. During those rare occasions when freeway traffic is flowing smoothly, courteous drivers obeying speed limits risk being run off the road by those determined to make up for time lost in the traffic jam a mile back. Cruising surface streets is no less stressful, as selfish drivers routinely run red lights; many considerate, sensible vehicle operators consciously pass through intersections as yellow lights are turning red, simply out of fear of being rear-ended by dangerously aggressive drivers closely tailgating them. Experienced pedestrians obeying walk signals learn to keep a constant lookout for defiant and careless drivers. Frustrated and immature drivers, stalled in irritating traffic jams, increasingly succumb to road rage, cussing each other out, cutting each other off, and even resorting to violence. Driver shootings over traffic disputes seldom make headlines any more; they have become routine, and newspaper accounts often appear in short columns in the back pages.

THE RESHAPING OF URBAN SPACE

Will this madness get any worse? Have the limits of human tolerance finally been reached? Beginning in the 1960s, numerous sophisticated urban geographers, regional planners, and public policy analysts, along with a few developers, insisted that the only viable solution to unchecked urban sprawl and the so-called tyranny of the automobile was dense settlement in various forms of cluster housing and hundreds of billions of dollars invested in mass transit nationwide. They called for nothing less than a fundamental reordering of national priorities and wholesale reshaping of urban space. Housing developers built experimental pilot projects, which featured open space, limited automobile access, and several types of cluster housing. Reston, Virginia, was the best known. Editors of cerebral, liberal magazines sent their star reporters to sample life in these enclaves; several gushed that they had seen the future and that it worked.

Sierra Club spokesmen often lament the seemingly insatiable appetites of suburban developers who, in their minds, are gobbling up real estate and blighting regional landscapes across the nation. Inevitably, the next guy's development is, in your eyes, suburban blight. Hundreds of thousands of hopeful but inherently naïve new home buyers move into far-flung suburban homes offering magnificent views of pristine landscapes, only to find that within a year or two, their views have been ruined by yet another huge development even farther from urban cores. To some alarmists, it almost seems that the entire wilderness has been developed. They have attracted a large number of followers, in part because much of the open space that is disappearing is immediately adjacent to big cities.

Defenders of the automobile and suburban sprawl sometimes exacerbate tensions by mocking the concerns of environmentalists. In a recent column in *Car and Driver,* Brock Yates labeled then Vice President Al Gore a "pedantic dope" and an "environmental Savonarola" because of his vocal opposition to further sprawl. Yates complained that Gore's central theme was that "the demon car has fractionalized and dispersed populations across the landscape while defiling billions of acres of pristine land. He whines that unregulated growth has consumed millions of acres that otherwise might be the habitat of bunnies and Bambis and butterflies. Like many of his pronouncements, this is hysterical nonsense." However divisive and inflammatory Yates's rhetoric, it contained some truth; even the Sierra Club reports that new housing starts cover an additional .002 percent of the nation's land each year. At that rate, if left unchecked until 2050, projected suburban development would cover an additional one percent of the nation's land. However, Yates ignored a crucial consideration, one that deeply affected increasing public concern over sprawl. The very land that was getting covered over by voracious developers was the most visible to large numbers of people. Yates figuratively twisted the knife in claiming that if the

© Bettman/Corbis

By the end of the twentieth century, suburbs housed a majority of all Americans, but critics lamented the monotony of sprawl and lack of human warmth in a landscape almost totally shaped by the demands of the automobile.

"Gorenolas" prevailed, "government bureaucrats will tell people where to live, i.e., in cozy high-rise developments reachable only by mass transit."

Although millions of Americans enjoy the convenience of living in dense housing configurations, including apartments, condominiums, town homes, patio homes, duplexes, row homes, and various other hybrids, the detached single-family home with a front yard and a slightly more private backyard remains the preferred living arrangement for the majority. Barring catastrophic shortages in energy and water, gasoline prices exceeding five dollars a gallon, and subsequent government decrees mandating massive commitments by developers to build cluster housing, it is difficult to imagine a combination of political, economic, and social forces strong enough to restructure significantly the national landscape. Despite expanding federal support for public transportation, nine tenths of all urban trips are still taken by automobile. Although they disagree on particulars, most experts concede that individual transportation and suburban development will dominate living arrangements for the foreseeable future.

NEW SOURCES OF POWER?

How will the automobiles of the future be powered? Ever since gasoline-driven internal combustion engines took over the marketplace before World War I, critics who deplored their unpleasant side effects have hoped for and repeatedly predicted their imminent demise. An obvious, more recent incentive is to eliminate or reduce dependence on oil from the politically unstable Middle East. Finally, beginning thirty years ago, a number of industry analysts peered into their crystal balls, examined scientific data, and predicted when the world's petroleum reserves would run out. Some believed that, given exponentially soaring worldwide demands for petroleum, reserves could be exhausted as early as 2025 or 2030. It was not a matter of if the internal combustion engine could or would be replaced but simply when and how.

At the dawn of the new millennium, automotive engineers searched diligently for alternatives. A few thousand experimental local service vehicles were powered by propane or electrical batteries. Researchers today are also putting a great deal of effort into developing fuel cells, which would react hydrogen with air to produce electricity, and which would not only power the vehicles but be pollution-free. Futurist Amory Loving of the Rocky Mountain Institute predicts such vehicles in widespread use by 2020, powered by engines "so efficient that SUVs get 100 mpg, family sedans twice that." There are, however, huge obstacles to developing hydrogen fuel cells. Even with today's scientific expertise and technological know-how, it is still extremely difficult and expensive to harness hydrogen. Technological optimists even talk of converting garbage and biomass into hydrogen, but the potential benefits of such solutions appear to be decades away.

More immediately promising are "parallel hybrid" cars, which are already being produced and are available on a few showroom floors. These cars combine gasoline and electric power drivetrains. Internal computers monitor when electric power sources are more efficient and when the gasoline-powered drivetrain will take over. When quick acceleration is required, both drivetrains can be engaged for short bursts. Historically, one problem with vehicles powered solely with electricity was that they had very limited range because their batteries had to be recharged frequently; thus, they could not be used for long trips. However, the hybrids have solved that problem. When it is below quarter charge, the battery can be recharged while the vehicle is being powered by the gasoline drivetrain. In addition, during the braking process, the vehicle uses "regeneration" to recapture energy that would be wasted in the braking process to help recharge the electric battery. Thus, the only fuel purchased is gasoline. When stuck in slow, stop-and-go city and freeway traffic, the hybrids are far more economical and environmentally friendly, insofar as they operate solely on electricity. In the 2000 model year, Honda introduced the first hybrid, a two-door coupe called the *Insight*, priced at around $20,000. Capable of delivering unheard of fuel efficiency at sixty miles per gallon in city and seventy-one on the open highway, the Insight is the most energy-efficient car on the market so far. Honda produced about 8,000 Insights in 2000; approximately 4,000 were sold in the United States. Toyota followed a few months after Honda with its somewhat larger, four-door Prius. Toyota's entry is almost six inches shorter than the Corolla model, but four inches higher. In all likelihood, the hybrids are an intermediate range response to the challenge of finding viable alternatives to the internal combustion engine. Early consumer response has been lukewarm. The drawbacks are that they are expensive, cramped, underpowered, and definitely not sexy. There was an upward surge in energy prices in 2000 followed by a slump in 2001. Unless gasoline prices remain high and the public becomes totally convinced that energy shortages will be chronic, the hybrids may be largely curiosities.

Automotive developments in other countries may also provide glimpses into the future. The so-called *Smart Car*, originally built by Swiss watchmaker Swatch and later acquired by Daimler–Chrysler, is reminiscent of the Isetta. This tiny offering also features extremely light materials and, because of its miserly consumption of gas, is gaining some popularity in Europe. Another promising project, dubbed the *China Car*, introduced by Daimler-Chrysler in 1997, features prototypes built with structural thermoplastic bodies, which may potentially eliminate steel subframes.

With all of these alternative automotive concepts, major hurdles remain. Some industry forecasters suggest that predictions of the internal combustion engine's demise are extremely premature. Oil men, in particular, insist that it will dominate markets for decades. Their reasoning is simple. Many industries connected directly or otherwise to the internal combustion engine employ millions of people around the globe. These powerful interests command immense political power. Their numerous sophisticated lobbyists argue that it would be extremely foolish for politicians and decision makers to countenance rapid conversion away from internal combustion engines to those using some alternative form of energy. Were petroleum to lose its primary position or even become significantly less important as an energy source, the world economy could experience a catastrophe, at least in the short term.

These powerful petroleum interests have honed their arguments and strengthened political alliances over decades. Oil men even claim that, contrary to popular conception, the United States is not dependent on foreign oil; we buy it simply because it is cheaper than domestic oil. They also discount the long-term viability of the OPEC efforts to limit production and maintain artificially high prices, pointing out that, historically, cartels have never proven effective over time. Furthermore, in a worst-case scenario, even if the United States is forced to rely on domestic sources, it will be a minor inconvenience because oil extraction is far more efficient today than it was in the early 1970s, when the first energy crisis occurred. In 1973, nobody had heard of horizontal drilling; today, it's old news. Petroleum engineers have discovered ways of extracting far more raw petroleum from existing wells far more efficiently. Back then, it cost oil companies an average of $22 per barrel to find new sources in the United States; in 2000, it cost $4 per barrel. Although gasoline prices are undeniably high in Europe, Japan, and a few other portions of the globe, oil men point out that, despite occasional shortages and upward spikes in prices, when compared to other commodities, petroleum remains a tremendous bargain over the long term. Although they acknowledge that older internal combustion engines were inefficient polluters, many oil men act genuinely puzzled that some despise their product. As one observer noted, "among the cultural elite, [petroleum] ranks below the Saturday-night special and the Ebola virus as a pox on civilization."

Automobiles used to be among the worst air polluters, but they have gotten much better. Both oil men and auto producers point with pride to significant and undeniable gains in efficiency and the enormous advances in lowering emissions in the past two decades. According to one industry spokesman, "the gasoline-powered internal combustion engine is so efficient, so clean, and so inexpensive to manufacture that it will be impossible to replace with any alternative that fails to perform better in all respects." Some technological optimists contend that recent gains in internal combustion engine efficiency have simply scratched the surface, that even greater advances will be made in the next decade, and that it will continue to dominate the automobile market for the next half century.

Clearly, the future is highly unsettled, but it appears that, for the first time in eighty years, the internal combustion engine at least has some potentially viable competitors. And more choices for consumers almost invariably stimulate further technological gains and greater efficiency. Considering automobile engines, we are almost certainly gazing into an exciting new frontier.

HOMES ON WHEELS

How about interiors of twenty-first-century vehicles? Computers are quickly and profoundly changing American lifestyles in offices, the home, and on the road; these changes will become even more dramatic in the years ahead. One of the ironies of the modern age is that differences between "home" and "road" are narrowing. Automobile manufacturers are keenly aware that, with the continued development of suburbs and decentralization of most cities, driving commutes are becoming longer. Since Americans are spending increasing amounts of time on the road, automakers are consciously making cars, trucks, minivans, and SUVs as officelike and homelike as possible. Laptop computers can be plugged into cigarette lighters, and cellular phones allow drivers to conduct business while stuck in traffic.

As for homelike amenities, cup holders in minivans are simply the tip of the iceberg. CD players are old hat. In 2000, several minivan manufacturers, led by Oldsmobile, made rear-seat entertainment centers, including flip-down LCD color monitors, optional packages. In the "olden days," parents determined to keep the kids from squabbling on a long, hot, boring drive tried to entertain them by thinking up word games or getting them to look for vehicles with out-of-state license plates. Preliminary sales reports suggest that today's parents taking long-distance trips love the fact that the kids can watch television or rental movies. When not watching videos, riders may enjoy static-free radio through Satellite Digital Audio-Radio (SDAR). No longer will riders become irritated when transmission signals from good local stations begin to fade out, then are lost. Driving from Los Angeles to New York, they will be able to pick up their favorite DJs in Los Angeles, or Vin Scully, the voice of the Dodgers, even when they are on the Ohio Turnpike. Formerly, the kids might plead for heavy metal, while Dad wanted to listen to the ballgame. Not to worry, as CD players with portable headsets seem to have resolved that problem. In the future, the need for sustained family communication may be all but eliminated, as each member can become insulated in his or her solitary technological cocoon.

More and more driver functions are becoming computerized, even automated. Onboard GPS navigation systems, which offer turn-by-turn voice directions between virtually any two points on the map, are becoming standard equipment in luxury cars. The technology was initially marred by the fact that families traveling long distances had to exchange disks when they moved from one zone to another. Honda recently introduced the next generation of navigation tools in the DVD system, which requires but a single disk. The operator can drive from an address in Seattle to one on Long Island without changing disks. In the future, it may become difficult for even the most bull-headed driver to get lost.

Although the automobile of 2000 was already loaded with crea-ture comforts, future offerings will be even more luxurious. Car seats are in the midst of huge changes. An hour's driving can leave riders hot and sticky or with stiff joints and muscles. New models feature climate-control seats, which have their own integrated heating and cooling elements. Both Cadillac and Mercedes-Benz already offer seats with massaging backrests. The "Active Comfort Seat" offered by BMW "brings orthopedic massage to the lower cushion, which, when acti-vated, alternately raises and lowers the cushion's left and right halves by about a half-inch each in subtle, one-minute cycles." Future seats will be designed that, when activated, will massage the upper and lower back regions. Can we be far from a seat capable of adding the shoulders and back of the neck?

SAFER AT ANY SPEED

Even more important, the motor vehicles of the future will be much safer to operate. The "all-new 2000 Cadillac DeVille" was equipped with a safety feature called Night Vision, an innovative thermal imaging sys-tem that relies upon the same infrared technology that the military uses. It extends a view of the road three times farther than low beams, allow-ing the driver to pick up people, animals, and any other heat-producing objects that might not be visible through conventional headlights for critical additional seconds. This feature may well become indispensable in allowing older drivers to remain safely on the road. Future air bag sys-tems will be smarter. Mercedes-Benz already offers a "Baby Smart" sys-tem that automatically deactivates the passenger side front air bag when a child seat is installed. Can we be far from a computerized passenger safety system that "measures" each passenger's height and weight and automatically adjusts air bag pressure and deployment?

Future cars will certainly be equipped with numerous warning features to help drivers avoid foolish mistakes. Cruise control systems will contain sensors that automatically set distances behind other ve-hicles on the road. When any unexpected situation instructs vehicles to swerve suddenly, much of the jolt will be removed by sophisticated active suspension systems designed to counteract all types of body lean, so that cars stay as flat as possible in all driving situations. Even luxury sedans may possess much of the tight cornering control of a sports car. Parallel parking creates primal fear in many drivers. It should be far easier early in this century, thanks to new packages like Mercedes-Benz's Parktronic system, which uses radar to measure how close the vehicle's rear bumper is to other objects and signals the driver with both video and audio alerts. Similar packages may well be standard equipment on most vehicles by 2010.

Late in the twentieth century, many drivers became accustomed to using cellular phones with digital dial features. This practice concerned safety experts because operators have to look away from the road while placing calls. A few states have passed laws outlawing the practice of using cell phones while driving. Use of cell phones while moving also infuriates many other drivers, some of whom sport bumper stickers that read "Hang up and drive." By the early twenty-first century, such concerns may be put to rest, as digitally operated cell phones in vehicles will become obsolete, or at least unnecessary. Although automotive engineers have encountered innumerable bugs in developing voice-recognition technology, complicated, no doubt, by thick accents and competing highway and street sounds, the advent of the "talking car" appears imminent. Drivers (and passengers) will soon be able to activate telephones by voice command. In July 2000, buyers of 2001 Cadillac Seville and DeVille models were able to receive e-mail messages, plus Internet information, stock quotes, sports scores, and weather information, without taking their eyes off the road, thanks to a voice-activated interface and text-to-voice software that "reads" information to passengers through a voice-synthesis system. This package currently costs about $2,000, but the price should drop as technology improves and more automobile companies offer the system.

The automobile engine of 2000 was a thousand times more complicated and sophisticated than that powering Henry Ford's Model T of eighty years ago. Although Ford's cars were deservedly renowned for durability, breakdowns, flat tires, and getting stuck in mud holes were still everyday experiences for drivers. Automobile owners were far less vulnerable if they possessed some mechanical know-how and considerable muscle. The engines were simple enough that persons with average mechanical skills could usually figure out malfunctions. Equally important, when one lifted the hood to work on a balky engine, there was sufficient space to maneuver; problems could often be fixed quickly with a wrench and perhaps a screw driver. Today's cars possess many sophisticated parts, which are packed closely under the hood; even if drivers know what to do, they might be helpless to do much about it without highly specialized tools. Breakdowns on the road used to be daily experiences. Now, they happen rarely. Most drivers who get stuck today reach for their cell phones and their AAA cards and call for roadside assistance. In the future, all they will have to do is push a button. Mercedes-Benz's "Tele Aid" system automatically connects the operator to a twenty-four-hour center that can even track the caller's location. This system will also save lives in case of serious accidents and when cars are stalled due to extreme weather conditions.

VISIONS OF THE FUTURE

Thus far, we have considered probable changes in the driving experience during the next few years, but what will become of the automobile culture in the more distant future? Since the beginning of the information revolution, prognosticators have suggested that the need to commute from home to work is becoming technologically obsolete. Some question why Congress should spend hundreds of billions of dollars modernizing the Interstate Highway System or expensive mass transit systems when the most critical future mobility is clearly along the information superhighway! With ever more sophisticated computers and near universal access to the Internet, telecommuting possesses enormous potential for lessening traffic congestion. By working at home, white-collar workers may be able either to eliminate journeys to work entirely or to at least stagger their office hours, along with the times when they are on the road. Urban planners and decision makers have debated the potential of telecommuting for years. As early as 1985, a study by the Southern California Association of Governments estimated that if just 12 percent of all workers stayed off the freeways, congestion would be reduced 32 percent. The chief benefit of staggered hours would be to spread freeway use somewhat more evenly over the day and evening, perhaps even deep into the night. Yet, no simple solutions to congestion exist. Some experts estimated that certain factors associated with telecommuting could actually increase auto use; for example, some workers at home might succumb to "cabin fever" and take short joy rides.

Various studies have suggested, however, that aggressive promotion of telecommuting may be a more powerful (and far less expensive) strategy for relieving congestion than building more freeway lanes, designating some lanes for exclusive high occupancy vehicle (HOV) use, or installing cameras to record license plates and automatically assessing modest tolls for drivers using freeways during peak commuting hours. Some question whether we actually need to spend tax dollars expanding our massive concrete highway system. Perhaps freeways will eventually become obsolete or at least less important in promoting commercial intercourse. Private interests are pouring hundreds of billions of dollars into expanding fiberoptic networks. In effect, regional telephone companies, cable operators, and computer and software companies are all financing the electronic superhighway. For better or worse, by the early twenty-first century, "high-tech" companies had achieved the same position that heavy industry, including automobile manufacturers, had enjoyed until the late twentieth century: they were truly the bellwether forces in the American economy. One commentator has intimated that the Internet may challenge the relevance of the automobile, pointing out that the Internet, like the automobile a century earlier, "arrived . . . like a whirlwind."

However, decisionmakers would be wise to heed the warning of transportation expert Stephen B. Goddard in 1994: "The dizzying pace the information revolution is taking also calls to mind the late 1950s, when the highwaymen's rush to build the interstates overwhelmed those calling for a moratorium on construction so that America could plan more carefully how to integrate the superhighways into the nation's life." The information superhighway has its inherent limitations. At the very least, today's concrete highways should experience a long life transporting vast amounts of commercial products . . . along with millions of travelers.

If one accepts the idea that technology will continue to evolve almost exponentially, will there even be a driving experience 100 years from now? If so, what will it be like? A few technological optimists envision eliminating ground-level congestion through widespread use of flying cars, which can be maneuvered either through the air or on the ground, as circumstances dictate. Such visions have existed since the days of Jules Verne, and imaginative designs of auto-aircraft regularly appeared in such magazines as *Popular Science* and *Scientific American* in the years immediately following World War II. During the war, Stanley Hiller, a California inventor, advanced plans for a device he called a "Hiller Copter," an extremely simple, self-operated individual craft, whose controls could be mastered in a matter of minutes. Noted industrial magnate Henry J. Kaiser was so taken with the idea that he negotiated the rights to mass produce the device if it ever became practical. Likewise, even "responsible" and respectable mass circulation magazines, including the *Saturday Evening Post* and the *New Yorker,* circulated stories and cartoons featuring futuristic, self-driven "aircraft."

In hindsight, it seems incredible that writers, designers, and even cartoonists assumed that individual operators could be trusted to operate such devices safely and responsibly. They were evidently conditioned by Depression and World War II era social norms, which stressed conformity and repression of antisocial behavior, since they voiced no concern whatsoever about the danger or sheer mischief that might ensue in the event that individual Americans gained access to virtually any air space they desired and at all hours of the day or night.

Yet the dream of flying cars continues to be a "Holy Grail" for a few inventors even today. Paul Moller, a driven aeronautical engineer, has been experimenting with such devices since the 1960s. Moller established an experimental laboratory in Davis, California, where he has been testing such devices for nearly four decades. He has developed a four-seated, fiberglass prototype, the so-called M-400, which he believes will eventually be capable of replacing automobiles on trips longer than 100 miles. Moller imagines a range of 900 miles, with a cruising speed of up to 350 mph. At the moment, he envisions powering them with eight Wankel-type rotary engines. It will supposedly be capable of vertical takeoff and landing, using technology similar to that of Boeing's V-22 Osprey helicopter.

Given the latter's miserable safety record, this particular choice may be ill-advised. Technological, financial, and legal hurdles extend far out onto the horizon, and prospects of success appear slim. For example, even if such devices proved practical to manufacture and they fell within the price range of significant numbers of consumers, the devices would almost certainly disturb neighborhood peace and quiet and at the very least invade residents' privacy. How would safety be monitored? The inventor claims that the M-400s would be equipped with parachutes that would automatically deploy if the craft encountered mechanical difficulties while airborne. In answer to the objection that the devices would be dangerous in the hands of irresponsible operators, Moller claims that they would not really be in control of the craft; instead, they would essentially be passengers, guided by sophisticated computerized software. Although his concept is clearly a long shot, Moller has generated a cadre of supporters willing to pay $5,000 for positions on the waiting list to buy them, if and when they are ever produced. Moller's most dedicated followers wear colorful M-400 T-shirts and display "My next car will be a Skycar" license plate holders.

Predictably, the end of the millennium marked considerable speculation in automotive magazines about the long-term future of the motor vehicle. Various editors polled automobile company executives, engineers, academics, city planners, politicians, and a variety of semi-experts about what they envisioned for the future. Equally predictably, there was a wide range of thoughts, but there was surprising consensus concerning several issues. Virtually all agreed that some form of individualized, personal transportation would dominate physical mobility into the foreseeable future. The editors of *Automotive Engineering* opined, "Personal transportation will still be the choice of those who can afford it." However, they continued, "Ownership of personal vehicles may disappear and daily or hourly rental of vehicles will be common." They suggested that usage fees could be billed monthly and that they would vary depending on the number of vehicle rides ordered, the length of journeys, and the times of day in which vehicles were used. They predicted that the cost of automobile transportation will comprise a much smaller portion of a typical family's income than it does today. Significantly, they also envision a bright future for mass transit. Due to crowding and congestion, only mass transit vehicles capable of carrying ten or more persons should be allowed in the most densely settled sections. Parking lots and streets bearing automobiles may disappear from downtown areas. Passengers could be deposited on the peripheries of urban cores, then whisked to final destinations with the assistance of moving sidewalks.

Long-distance travel, whether by automobile or some other device, may be quite a bit different. Several European countries have initiated successful high-speed trains between major cities. The French government first opened its *Trains a Grande Vitesse* (TGV) between Paris and Lyons in 1981, built to operate at speeds up to 168 miles per hour. In fact, TGV engineers have actually tested trains, with passengers aboard, reaching top speeds over 300 miles per hour. Among the many attractions of high-speed train travel is that trains run from one urban core to another. This eliminates annoying, time-consuming side trips from downtown areas to airports, and vice versa, which often wipe out the speed advantages enjoyed by airlines. In all likelihood, city-to-city distance travelers of the future will enjoy more viable options, particularly for short- and intermediate-length trips.

Some forecasters envision monorails that would allow for high-speed automobile travel. One imaginative designer, obviously with far too much time on his hands, posted the following "solution" on the Internet. "When a cat is dropped, it ALWAYS lands on its feet, and when toast is dropped, it ALWAYS lands with its buttered side facing down. Therefore, I propose to strap buttered toast to the back of a cat. When dropped, the two will hover, spinning inches above the ground, probably into eternity. A 'buttered cat array' could replace pneumatic tires on cars and trucks, and 'giant buttered cat arrays' could easily allow a high speed monorail linking Chicago and New York."

Since animal-loving organizations such as PETA and SPCA would undoubtedly establish insurmountable barriers to this initiative, we need to look elsewhere. Some serious engineers propose long-distance, underground tunnels. "Drivers" would program final destinations into dashboard computers. Vehicles then would enter limited-access "highways," where they would be elevated slightly above the roadbed with some sort of magnetic levitation device. Thus, there would be no contact of tires on roadbeds and virtually no chance of mechanical breakdown. Assuming future automobiles are adequately equipped as business offices or entertainment centers, passengers on long-distance trips may well be able to ignore the monotony of the ride itself. Virtual reality games, even virtual scenery, could also relieve passengers of extended boredom.

Since vehicles moving in large numbers close to each other would be electronically controlled, in theory, at least, there would never be any accidents, since no two vehicles would be allowed to get dangerously close to each other. Once they exited from high-density traffic corridors, "drivers" could lower the vehicle onto its wheels and take over manual control. Even here, however, computers might well be programmed to reassert control should any operator attempt to maneuver a vehicle in a "deviant" manner.

Regarding bulk commercial shipments, some futurists envision the end of the trucking industry as we know it. Automobiles may no longer have to contend with trucks. Most heavy shipments would be handled by a separate rail system, then transported to final destinations by some form of hovercraft. Other scenarios suggest that, assuming the likelihood of high-speed long-distance travel, trucks could still use the underground tunnels, but only during certain hours of the night. Some thinkers looking perhaps a century out into the future envision underground tunnels filled with helium, a gas with an atmosphere more than seven times lighter than oxygen. In such conditions, drag would be reduced by a factor of seven, permitting much higher speeds of travel. Exits from tunnels would lead through air locks into open air. In rare underground emergencies, oxygen masks would automatically deploy, just as they do in today's commercial airplanes. However, futurists envisioning this type of scenario have not yet fully considered whether passengers traveling long distances underground would feel sufficiently secure from possible terrorist attacks or massive, catastrophic breakdowns in the system. Only time will tell whether the horrific terrorist attack against New York City's World Trade Center and the Pentagon on September 11, 2001, will exert long-term effects on planning for such futuristic, high-tech solutions.

When considering automobility and social control, some forecasters predict that as the world's population increases and more people want to enjoy personal mobility, humans will have little choice but to endure increasingly large doses of Big Brotherism. Freedom on the open road may well become an anachronism; even the practice of driving may be greatly curtailed. These issues may arouse intense opposition, particularly in the United States. Even in the short run, will Americans be comfortable with electronic monitors on toll roads, recording their movements and providing automatic billing information? Will we tolerate hidden public authorities knowing where we are at any given moment? Will Americans accept congestion pricing, whereby computers automatically assess tolls from drivers using roadways during high-volume driving hours? Some public policy analysts urge charging gas-guzzling, heavy cars premiums, but will Americans willingly pay a horsepower penalty? Others propose levying road use taxes in addition to license fees and gasoline taxes. For example, drivers would be assessed annual fees according to odometer readings; those doing the most driving would pay more. In the early twenty-first century, however, most such scenarios face enormous political obstacles; there appears to be a vicious, potentially dangerous backlash against the perceived assault on personal freedom and privacy, whether by commercial interests or government agencies.

Many experts contend that, within the next few decades, most persons moving from place to place will essentially be passive vehicle occupants, delivered to destinations electronically. The concept has been around for decades. In the 1970s, some transportation experts were excited about personal rapid transit (PRT) systems, wherein commuters might be able to summon pod-shaped cars holding a half dozen or so riders, who then would choose destinations from a menu. What few of the proposals addressed in any depth was how multiple-destination routes would be determined. Would first occupants receive initial drop-offs, perhaps to out-of-the-way locations, forcing vehicles to double back and deliver later boarders to spread-out destinations, or would computers automatically figure out the most efficient sequence for distributing all passengers? Experimental PRT systems were set up in several locations, but they soon disappeared. Automated people movers (APMs) holding several dozen passengers have been set up in numerous airports, large universities, and amusement parks with considerable success. A major difference between conventional mass transit and the APM is that the latter travels shorter distances and requires far fewer employees to operate.

As for automobiles, some experts predict that only one or two big companies will manufacture them and they might lose much, if not all, of their individuality. For starters, some futurists predict cars will look very much alike. The use of thermoplastic, adjustable frames might allow vehicles to be quickly modified to accommodate the required number of passengers. While the front and rear and powerplant will remain the same, extensions could be added or subtracted. According to this scenario, automobiles would vary primarily in length. Yet one hitherto important social variable has received insufficient attention. *If* future cars are used just for transportation, they will lose their role as extensions of people's personalities and financial and social status. They may well be boxy and completely utilitarian rather than stylish. Assuming they are made of plastic component materials, they could be far lighter than today's behemoths, perhaps less than 1,000 pounds for a full-size passenger vehicle. One scenario envisions them as being able to be parked standing upright, on their noses, so to speak. Such a storage system would dramatically reduce space needed for parking facilities.

Any government attempting to put such a system into place would sooner or later have to impose a compulsory removal of older vehicles. Authorities would also have to implement it gradually, over a period of as many as twenty years to phase out older, noncompliant vehicles. This process could be messy and extremely complicated. If future vehicles are largely guided by computers, how would Americans deal with the final loss of freedom behind the wheel? One scenario envisions permitting nostalgia buffs to operate selected older vehicles in theme parks. In the short run, perhaps individuals diagnosed with vestiges of that formerly common affliction of road rage, or self-indulgent thrill-seekers with money to burn, could be allowed to buy old wrecks and bash into each other in demolition derbies!

As one ponders numerous high-tech scenarios, most of which disagree with each other only on details of precisely how scientists and engineers will conquer future traffic challenges, the contemporary observer might be startled by the persistence of deeply ingrained technological optimism. The confident tones of many of today's scientists, engineers, and traffic planners closely resemble those of Jules Verne and other technological optimists of a century ago. In addition, there is a certain Orwellian tone to most projections. Almost all futurists envision the inevitable curtailment of individual choices and freedom on the road. Although some futurists briefly, and often indirectly, address messy and potentially complicating issues, including public angst, opposition to, and even sabotage against rigidly controlled personal mobility, almost all of them begin their presentations from an eerie sort of immaculate conception, with Big Brother's systems already magically in place. Few, if any, futurists paint believable pictures, even in the most general terms, of how political decision makers will implement, let alone finance, such massive public works projects.

Slick high-tech solutions to today's massive traffic problems may be possible, but are they realistic? They face enormous challenges. Perhaps the most formidable is that they will require unprecedented levels of political consensus, nearly universal public acceptance. It is difficult to imagine such a scenario unfolding in the United States. Americans may feel even more protective of their right to own and drive their individual automobiles when and where they want than they do about their right to keep firearms. Therefore, developing a workable consensus imposing far more tightly regulated traffic systems will test the sagacity and persuasive abilities of the wisest and most capable leaders.

There is also the inertia factor. Some political entity would basically have to coordinate development of such a system. This would inevitably affect the functions of many of today's entrenched bureaucracies, from the local to the national level. By nature, bureaucrats resist change. Significantly reforming the Civil Service system has defied the attempts of one presidential administration after another. State, regional, and local-level reformers have enjoyed only marginal and often short-term success in streamlining lower level bureaucracies. The challenge of eliminating inefficient, politically entrenched entities involved in some way with transportation, from the local to the national level, and developing a workable, efficient political entity regulating the entire system could well defeat even those leaders with the wisdom of Solomon and the patience of Job.

Instituting massive overhauls of today's transportation systems would also entail huge economic readjustments. Products created by hundreds of corporations employing millions of workers would become obsolete. Technological optimists contend that the same scenario was evident a century ago, when blacksmith shops and carriage companies were threatened, then ultimately put out of business by the automobile. Some companies would die, but new ones would emerge. However, today's political environment is far more complicated than that of a century ago. Many industries that would be threatened by a massive overhaul of today's transportation system appear far better organized, and they are represented by powerful and sophisticated lobbyists in Washington. Even if leading manufacturers connected to the automobile industry are persuaded that vast new opportunities lie ahead in the transportation industry and that they have a major stake in it, and perhaps most importantly, coordinating economic readjustments will be a difficult task.

Finally, and perhaps most importantly, none of the futurists have effectively addressed the issue of costs. It is one thing to present scenarios of transportation systems that are possible. But working out the grubby details of potential costs, who would pay for them, and how, are difficult, if not impossible. How many trillions of dollars would an underground interstate transportation system, virtually immune from large-scale computer breakdowns and adequately safeguarded against any and all potential future terrorist attacks, cost? Perhaps many futurists avoid such work because budget forecasting is so palpably difficult, and it makes boring reading. How many billions would it cost to retrain workers rendered obsolete by changing technologies? What would be the environmental impact of building tunnels hundreds of miles long, and how much would it cost to implement environmental safeguards in building them?

In conclusion, virtually every aspect of future transportation is open to question, and the outcomes are highly uncertain. We must be wary of those who offer simple answers and poorly thought out solutions. In all likelihood, the automobile or some sort of individualized transportation will be with us for decades, if not centuries. However, one truth appears certain. Given the rapidly expanding world population pressures and the enormous environmental challenges accompanying this growth, the automobile will have to accommodate to humankind's requirements rather than, as has been the case all too often in recent decades, the other way around.

INDEX